ADULT EDUCATION TEACHERS

Designing Critical Literacy Practices

ADULT EDUCATION TEACHERS

Designing Critical Literacy Practices

Rebecca Rogers

Mary Ann Kramer

Lawrence Erlbaum Associates
Taylor & Francis Group

New York   London

Lawrence Erlbaum Associates
Taylor & Francis Group
270 Madison Avenue
New York, NY 10016

Lawrence Erlbaum Associates
Taylor & Francis Group
2 Park Square
Milton Park, Abingdon
Oxon OX14 4RN

Printed in the United States of America on acid-free paper
10 9 8 7 6 5 4 3 2 1

International Standard Book Number-13: 978-0-8058-6243-0 (Softcover) 978-0-8058-6242-3 (Hardcover)

Library of Congress Cataloging-in-Publication Data

Rogers, Rebecca.
    Adult education teachers : developing critical literacy education / Rebecca Rogers and Mary Ann Kramer.
        p. cm.
    Includes bibliographical references and index.
    ISBN-13: 978-0-8058-6243-0 (alk. paper)
    1. Adult education teachers--United States. 2. Reading (Adult education)--United States. 3. Literacy--United States. I. Kramer, Mary Ann. II. Title.

LC5219.R574 2008
374.11--dc22   2007018003

Visit the Taylor & Francis Web site at
http://www.taylorandfrancis.com

To Michael Mancini and Lawrence Chapman

Contents

Foreword

Culturally relevant pedagogy asks that both teachers and students engage in acts of questioning what Ladson-Billings (1994) calls the "structural inequality, the racism, and the injustice that exist in our society" (p. 128). In this book, the authors extend the discussion begun by Ladson-Billings and focus on contexts for literacy instruction, examining the implementation of culturally responsive pedagogy in a variety of literacy contexts and the ideologies which inform instruction. The text also documents the relevance of pedagogy that responds to learners' needs while challenging inequities and drawing on cultural understandings of learner and teacher identities.

In 2005, I was asked to be the discussant for a symposium focused on culturally responsive pedagogy in adult education at the National Reading Conference. Rebecca Rogers and Mary Ann Kramer shared a part of the research presented in this book during this symposium. During the session, I pointed out the many ways in which the issues of culture and diversity had permeated the lessons, formal and informal, that adult literacy teachers were involved in creating. I chose to make an example of the kind of culturally relevant teaching that I had to do at a university where I integrated all of the classes that I taught. Being Black, female, immigrant, Caribbean, interested in multimodal forms of literacy, and decidedly feminist in my analytical approach to text put me in the minority in my classrooms. My job, then, as a teacher interested in reaching the preservice teachers, was to learn what these descendants of Russian, Polish, Dutch, German, Mexican, and, very seldom, African roots considered their "culture." Further, I set about the job of making use of those valuable pieces of information to take them to other vistas of information that they would find useful as teachers among diverse students. It is this intentional and deliberate crossing of borders that we read about from the exemplary adult literacy teachers in this book.

The review of research tracing the conceptual development of what has come to be known as culturally responsive pedagogy aims at addressing the needs of diverse students. The journey begins with

Brice Heath's (1983) ethnography, an initial recognition of cultural-specific reading and writing behaviors of students who come from diverse backgrounds, and continues with the creation of a "holistic system of practices" (Murrell, 2002, p. 15) designed specifically for culturally diverse students. The results of this historical study call for more explicit teaching of the "culture of power" (Delpit, 1995) and culturally reflective teaching (Ladson-Billings, 1994). It may be that a pedagogical model focused on a difference-centered reflexive pedagogy, as we see from the teachers in this book, may well serve adult literacy teachers in their classrooms. This may be useful to teachers if we believe that all learners, regardless of race, ethnicity, gender, or class, bring issues of identity that are interconnected to the language, habits of mind, and ways in which they approach formal education.

In an effort to answer the research question "What are the instructional beliefs and practices of exemplary adult education teachers?" Rogers and Kramer build on and share the knowledge and practices of exemplary adult education teachers. Using Collins's (2000) framework of "visionary pragmatism," they outline a theory of effective adult education teaching that begins with the lived realities of the adult education classroom and also keeps an eye on a social world that is concerned with the issues related to justice. The study also documents the classroom practices of the teachers in order to unpack possible points of synergy and tension between the teachers' interviews and their classroom practices. The analysis of the interviews with adult literacy teachers and classroom observations indicates that the adult education teachers in the study engage with literacy practices in real and socially meaningful ways (e.g., Clark, Brown, 2000), use innovative literacy practices which include culturally relevant and critical andragogy (e.g., Mitchell, 1998; St. Clair & Sandlin, 2004), and attach learning to critical social purposes that accelerate their students' progress toward passing the General Educational Development (GED) test and becoming active and engaged citizens.

Across the still frames presented by these diverse classrooms, there are similar colors, characters, sets, and dialogue. As in a movie, we come to take the environment for granted. In every case, teachers are struggling to find ways to be successful with their students. In some frames of the movie, it seems that the teachers do not look like the students in their charge, or they don't think or have "ways with words" like their students (Brice Heath, 1983). In an effort to find a way to the students' literacy ability and make it blossom in the traditional settings described, the teachers reach into their bag of tools and use culturally responsive pedagogy. In other words, the age-old wisdom of teaching as an art is invoked: take them from the known to the new.

In every classroom we are taken into in this book, we find the issue of naming ourselves, that is, class, race, sex, and social position, an important aspect of finding the ground as teachers, and an important part of the teacher's philosophy. This process is relevant to understanding the complexity of the site in which we find ourselves working to lead students upward in their formal education. The more we can identify the matrix of identities that we represent, that is, white, Jewish, middle class, female, educated, daughter, or new teacher, the better we are able to identify, and then work with, the complexities that our students and colleagues represent. In such an environment of acceptance, or rigorous self-analysis, the tensions that we face as we cross the boundaries of school/university, teacher/student, classroom/community, and learners/leaders take on different meanings and serve to support the effort to embrace complexity and work within its constraints and gifts.

The question raised in this book, among others, is "How do we act in the name of social justice and a culturally responsive framework given the context within which we must live and work?" I am left wondering if we must put our teacher agendas in front of the students' ambitions to fly below the radar of political involvement and just get by. Do we allow the university, school, or community to dictate the ideals and values that frame our work as people who acknowledge the validity of a culturally relevant philosophy? In this quandary, fraught with opportunities to learn and grow and come into new knowledge, I am reminded that the teacher is also a learner who values a practice of questioning, critiquing, and embracing the new as she grows in wisdom.

The *emergent framework* that Rogers and Kramer present in this book provides a complex road map for the teacher-researcher who is constantly adjusting herself to the demands of cultural relevance and academic achievement within the classroom of adult students, and the community within which she teaches. Understanding that the students do not represent a monolithic culture, but a mosaic of values, beliefs, and life experiences, the teachers in this book stretch themselves intellectually, socially, and philosophically in order to find ways of bringing the students into the literacy club.

They use the processes of examining relevant literature, class discussions, political activism, and, ultimately, the winning of the GED diploma as their capstone literacy achievement with their students.

The adult literacy teacher, like the beginning teacher, moves toward a better understanding of the day-to-day experiences of the students and the context within which they enact their lives. The goal, as with every literacy teacher, is to know better the students' ways with words and to bring that knowledge into the service of taking the students to another level of reading and writing where they can become successful in the literate world.

At the end of this book, I am forced to ask myself about the students who the teachers are working to serve. How do they experience the teachers' efforts to learn their ways through culture and literary expression? Do they believe that the teachers are authentic workers in the name of social justice or culturally relevant pedagogy, or just the means to the end that is called a GED or an advance to another literacy class within the formal education structure? These are valid questions if we are truly working to be servants of the community that the students represent. It is an invitation to my colleagues who read this book to start gathering student responses to their culturally relevant teaching and put it to use in their lesson planning, teaching, and community work.

How does our being specific to the population that we are serving in the name of social justice help the students who we work with in our classrooms? Can we be too narrow in our focus and thereby leave out the rest of the world and all it offers in the way of difference and newness? Do the knowledge of and use of such culturally specific practices hamper the entry of the students into the vast world of knowledge that is at their fingertips at an ever increasing speed through the Internet and other technological innovations?

I feel that Delpit (1995), Ladson-Billings (1994), and Brice Heath (1983) remind us to "love the one you're with" or "dance with the one who brung you," as they say in Trinidad. If cultural forms represent our deepest level of learning and being in the world, then it would seem foolhardy to leave those lessons behind and embark on learning in the ways that other cultures have established. As one African proverb reminds us, you can't dance in someone else's dress. It is important for us to know that others have similar ways with words as we do, just as it is important for us to know that everyone has a mother and father. But it is not necessary for us to go around saying, "My father is bigger than your father," in an effort to prove that we have some worth in the eyes of others who we know and value. Each of us has important knowledge about who we are in the context of the life we live. Once that is established in our own minds, we can go on and do the bridge building and crossing that take us back and forth to the other side of our lives. Promoting the philosophy that supports our students' interest in the places where other people's children and parents can teach us their ways and beliefs as a means of sharing seems the central purpose of our work in classrooms devoted to justice.

This book allows us to listen to and consider what others think about the importance of cultural relevance and the ways in which we play a part as cultural transmitters in all our roles as teachers. The participants and researchers remind us that teachers have a culture as a professional group. We cannot overlook our biases and expectations of students within the formal educational frameworks that we occupy. Our way with words, our actions in the name of social justice, and our choices under the rubric of culturally relevant pedagogy all represent a way of being that we have adopted so that we might be successful in our lives. We live by our professional and personal creed, and need to admit that we have such a rubric of values that organizes our life in and outside the classroom. The way of the teacher is the path that we have decided to negotiate in order to experience fulfillment as part of our community.

If we are to engage in the work of finding out the beliefs, goals, and values of the students who we work with, and hopefully on behalf of, we must stop to ponder the kind of preparation that will ready us for the journey among the unconverted. What kind of thinking, working, reflecting, and practicing will create the space within us to reach our highest potential among our students? Do we need to become co-learners, fellow journeymen and -women, collaborators, conspirators, or workers on the "underground railroad" to intellectual liberation? Where do men come down on these issues that affect their classroom? These are not questions with easy answers. We are faced, once again, with the issues of context and content. Where will we find ourselves, with whom will we be working, and for what purposes, as we build bridges to and between our students? And that, I believe, is the essence of the discussion in hand.

Can we serve well and not become servile? Can we be ourselves even as we learn to be available to those who have different values and ambitions than our own? Are we ready to answer the call when our students are a different race, creed, language group, or national origin? Let us see what the twenty-first century offers us as we experience the ways in which culturally relevant pedagogy begs us to adjust our lens to the global village that has become a fact of life in and outside our classrooms.

Joanne K. Dowdy
Kent State University

Preface

The field of adult literacy education, much like the field of K–12 literacy education, is characterized by diverse and oftentimes competing conceptual paradigms (Demetrion, 2005). Adult literacy education programs tend to get labeled as either critical or noncritical (Degener, 1999). In this book, we shift the focus from the *program* to the *teacher* and argue that labeling programs, practices, or teachers as either participatory or functional, or as critical or noncritical, is not useful in terms of developing and sustaining meaningful literacy education. Rather, a more fine-grained understanding of the complexity of instructional designs in adult literacy education is in order. Situated within New Literacy Studies, this book describes the literacy beliefs and practices of adult education teachers who were nominated as exemplary teachers by the communities in which they teach.

To draw on what Ladson-Billings (1994) has referred to as the "wisdom of practice" of experienced and respected teachers, we designed a survey and nomination form to solicit nominations of exemplary teachers. We used what Foster (1997) has referred to as the process of "community nomination," where we asked members of the adult education community to nominate exemplary teachers. This nomination form was distributed to adult education and literacy sites in the metro St. Louis area. We conducted in-depth interviews with nine of the nominated adult education teachers and followed up with observations in their classrooms. In this book, we draw on the tacit theories of the adult education teachers and provide thick descriptions to describe how they design responsive literacy education.

The teachers taught in a wide range of programs and consequently worked with a wide range of students. Some of the teachers taught adult education and literacy students and General Educational Development (GED) students, others taught in family literacy programs, English for Speakers of Other Languages (ESOL) programs, workplace literacy programs, or homeless shelters. All of these teachers, whether they had been teaching for two years or twenty years, were successful at accelerating their students within a critical framework. The teachers had a variety of background experiences before finding their way into adult education.

We demonstrate how all of the teachers were teaching for literacy acceleration within a critically responsive framework. The teachers are flexible as they move in and out of critical and accelerative literacy practices. We refer to this movement between critical and accelerative literacy practices as an "emergent framework" for adult literacy education. On a continuum between critical and noncritical, and functional and participatory, the teachers in this study design literacy education that enables their students to progress toward traditional measures of achievement and are also preparing them to be responsible citizens, change agents, and participants in democracies.

We realize that, oftentimes, adult education teachers are not encouraged to make their voices heard. Indeed, they are often marginalized in the field of education and, in real time, in districts and communities. Our intention in conducting this study and writing this book has been to create a space where the voices of nine adult educators could be heard and used for the development of future teacher development initiatives.

In essence, we dedicate this book to those educators who have made significant contributions in the lives of their students and in society. We hope you find the energy and hopefulness that we have found in adult literacy education in the pages of this book.

STRUCTURE AND ORGANIZATION OF THE BOOK

Chapter 1 introduces the context of the book and the adult literacy teachers. We situate the study within the New Literacy Studies and argue that as the teachers interact with their students, the local contexts, and the materials, they engage in a process of designing and redesigning responsive literacy education.

Chapter 2 outlines the contemporary landscape of adult literacy education. The teachers in this study outlined an approach to teach reading and writing within the context of a critical framework. We refer to this approach as an "emergent framework" for adult literacy education. Their approaches were not defined by participatory or traditional approaches to literacy education, or by critical or noncritical approaches. Rather, in the flexible and highly creative manner that is characteristic of exemplary teachers, these teachers drew from a range of strategies and techniques that were on a continuum between traditional and participatory, critical and noncritical. The emergent framework might be characterized by imagining a constantly shifting continuum, one that includes both accelerative and critical-participatory literacy practices that shift depending on the context and the student.

Chapter 3 takes us into the context and description of the teachers in this book. We provide the historical backdrop of the struggle for equitable education in St. Louis. We see the St. Louis context as a window and a mirror into learning more about the literacy practices of adult education teachers across the nation. While St. Louis has a specific history and context, many of the characteristics of the exemplary teachers can be used as a springboard for inquiring into and learning more about the literacy practices of educators across the life span.

In chapters 4–15, we represent case studies of each of the nine teachers. These chapters are broken into three parts with three case studies in each part. The cases presented in each of the chapters provide a "thick description" of the teachers' background experiences, their classrooms, their literacy instruction, and their goals for creating a more just society. We have tried to stay as close to the teachers' voices as possible. You will see that each of the teachers' stories represents a range of perspectives from the exemplary adult education teachers. We have organized the cases into three parts, organized by contrasting cases. We ask that the reader keep in mind the emergent framework of critical and accelerative literacy practices as they read each of the chapters. We need to emphasize that we do not wish to highlight any hierarchies in this organization. Rather, the point should be made clear throughout this book that while some of the teachers were more "traditional" in their approaches to literacy education, all teachers were exemplary in contributing to social justice in more complicated ways than are acknowledged in the field. In each of the chapters, you will hear the teachers attending to the dual goals of literacy acceleration and social justice.

We have grouped the cases into three parts, with a cross-case analysis chapter included at the end of each part. Part 1 includes the cases of Carolyn Fuller, Sara Bramer, and Vivian Jett. Their cross-case analysis chapter focuses on the theme of "Designing Relevant and Engaging Instruction." Part 2 includes the cases of Dorothy Walker, Holiday Simmons, and Janet Omurtag. This part's cross-case analysis chapter focuses on the themes of "Recognizing and Valuing Multiple Literacies." Part 3 includes the cases of Angy

Folkes, Sister Martha Jaegers, and Sarajane Campbell. The cross-case chapter for these three teachers focuses on "The Struggle for Critical Literacy."

We have chosen contrasting rather than similar cases to put in each part, which invite the reader into the book in a participatory manner. As mentioned above, a cross-case analysis of the cases presented in each part follows the set of three chapters. In this analysis, we reflect on similarities, differences, and important themes related to adult literacy education that are brought out in each of their cases.

In each cross-case chapter, we included a part called "Rethinking Practice" which invites the reader to try out some of the concepts and practices introduced in the preceding chapters. We also include additional resources and readings for people who are interested in the issues explored.

In the final chapter (chapter 16), we pull together the threads of the book and offer future directions for professional development in adult literacy education. Throughout, we illustrate how the teachers in this book are resolving the tensions between sometimes competing instructional frameworks and how they have developed practices that are more expansive than the current philosophical and practical foundations in adult literacy education.

We have placed our research design and methodology as an appendix to the book. In appendix 1 we explain our process, which included using what Foster (1997), as discussed above, has referred to as the process of "community nomination," where we asked members of the adult education community to nominate exemplary teachers. We discuss the specifics of our data collection and analysis process, processes guided by critical and feminist frameworks. Patricia Collins's (1998) concept of "visionary pragmatism" has made a great deal of sense to us in our research methodology. Visionary pragmatism links "caring, theoretical vision with informed, practical struggle" (Collins, 1998, p. 188). As with other feminist research, visionary pragmatism starts with the interests of the participants and seeks to build understandings in reciprocal, dialogic ways.

Acknowledgments

We would like to extend our gratitude to the adult education teachers who participated in this research. Through interviews and classroom observations, we grew to understand the complexity of their teaching practices and the struggles and joys they faced in their classrooms. When we extended an invitation to the teachers to read and revise their chapters, they did not hesitate. Their continued ideas for revision made each of their chapters stronger. Their commitment to professional development and to education is a source of inspiration for us. At the heart of all of this work are the adult education students who continually inspire and challenge us to rethink our practices. A special thank you to Bob Weng and Sarah Beaman-Jones for supporting this research and for providing us with feedback on a draft of the book manuscript. We would also like to thank Del Doss-Hemsley for granting us an interview with her on the history of adult literacy education in St. Louis.

There are many people who have contributed to making this a better book. We would especially like to thank our editor, Naomi Silverman, for her commitment to pushing the edges in educational research. Thank you also to Erica Kica and Joy Tatsuko at Lawrence Erlbaum Associates for their support throughout this project. Participants in the Literacy for Social Justice Teacher Research Group (LSJTRG) and the Acting for a Better Community (ABC's) forums provided us with ongoing intellectual stimulation that only teacher-activists can. Participants at several conferences have heard and given feedback to earlier forms of the research presented in this book. Thank you also to the following people for their feedback or assistance at various points in the project: Cheryl Dozier, Florence Williams, Jessica McLean, Sarah Hobson, and Melissa Mosley. We would particularly like to thank Steven Brookfield and Carolyn Colvin for their supportive and challenging reviews of the book. Their comments and suggestions made the book stronger. A special thank you to Joanne Kilgour Dowdy for writing the foreword. Most importantly, we are grateful to Michael Mancini and Larry

Chapman, as well as to our families and communities for their support and encouragement of all of our work.

Part 1

Framework and Contexts

1

Exemplary Adult
Literacy Educators

Holiday, an African American adult education teacher, copied the lyrics from the song "Stand by Me" and distributed the text to the adult education students in her classroom. She asked them to listen to the song first, without reading the words. The students listened, many of them singing along and swaying in their seats. She played the song again and asked her students to follow along with the words in their packet. The students followed with their pencils. They continued to sing along and dance in their seats. Line by line, Holiday and her students went through the song and talked about what the lyrics meant. The cultural knowledge they bring with them served as an entry point for their literacy learning.

Holiday: What's someone's favorite line?
Student: "Just swallow your pride..."
Holiday: That's one of my favorite ones, too. What does that line mean to you?
Student: It means to go forward in life.

As the student talked, Holiday recorded her words on the board: "go forward in life." Holiday asked another student what the phrase "swallow your pride" means. Drawing on real-life experience, the student responded, "When food stamps came out that was embarrassing for some people.... We had to swallow our pride and go on up in there." Sitting in a chair, with her legs crossed, facing the student, Holiday carefully listened to her student's experiences. She immediately stated, "That's a great example."

She continued to make connections with her students' lives, encouraging them to do the same, as they gave examples of their favorite lines and what the lines meant to them. Holiday shared her favorite line in the song with the class: "My favorite line is 'I'll share your load if you just call....' I like that one because you know whatever your problem is, if you are really a true friend, a true friend will be there. (Field notes, November 2003)

Holiday* is one of the nine adult education teachers in this book accelerating her students' literacy development within a critical framework. In this vignette, Holiday captures the complexity of adult literacy education. Drawing on materials that are relevant in her students' lives, encouraging dialogue, and making connections between the students' in-school and out-of-school lives are but a few of the threads we see in the tapestry of Holiday's teaching. Holiday is an African American poet and a social worker, and brings many experiences with social activism into her adult education classroom. On any given day, you could walk into Holiday's classroom and see a student-centered curriculum in action, one that is problem based and reflects her students' local literacies and lives.

Adult education has deep historical roots and has always been situated between the dialectic of oppression and activism. While there is some debate about the official origins of the movement, most scholars associate the beginning of the adult education movement with the founding of national organizations of adult education between the years of 1924 and 1961. However, as early as the colonial period, adult education was seen in town meetings and legislatures, teaching the tools of liberty and government. The movement in the United States can be traced to powerful educator-activists such as Booker T. Washington, Septima Clark, Myles Horton, Joanne Robinson, Aimee Horton, Harriet Jacobs, Cora Stewart Wilson, Frank Labauch, Ruth Colvin, Sequoyah, bell hooks, John Berry Meachum, and Susan Baker King Taylor, among others. Despite this rich and complex history, we still know very little about adult education teachers or their instructional practices (Degener, 2001; Smith, 2006). This is a particular concern given that in the contemporary context of the United States, high school dropout rates average 25 percent

---

* The teachers have given us permission to use their real names in the book.

and in urban high schools reach 60 to 70 percent (Fine, 1991). A disproportionate amount of these students are African American, many of whom have difficulty reading and writing (Bickel & Papagiannis, 1988; Perry, Steele, & Hilliard, 2003).

The National Adult Literacy Survey (NALS) reports that 43 percent of American adults have a limited ability to perform a variety of real-world literacy tasks (National Center for Education Statistics, n.d.).* Many of these adults have dropped out or, as Fine (1991) notes, have been "pushed out" of high school programs yet find their way back into adult education programs (Fine, 1991; Weis, Farrar, & Petrie, 1989). Smith (2006), in a chapter in the *Review of Adult Learning and Literacy* (vol. 6), asks the following question: what does the Adult Basic Education (ABE) teacher workforce look like now? Smith (2006) suggests that more research is needed to understand the characteristics of adult education teachers. Our book is a response to this call.

Our focus in this book is on exemplary adult education teachers and how they teach literacy. There are many different types of adult education teachers. Some work full-time, and others work part-time. Some teachers work in industry and are employed by adult education institutions. Others work for school-based programs or teach in informal education programs in industry. Despite the widely cited relationship between teacher preparation and student achievement (e.g., Darling-Hammond, 2000), caring professionals with little formal training in educational theory and practice comprise the overwhelming population of adult educators. There seems to be little disagreement about the need for qualified and knowledgeable adult education teachers. There is, however, debate over what constitutes quality, preparedness, and effectiveness (e.g., Brookfield, 2005; Galbraith & Gilley, 1985; Sabatini, Ginsburg, & Russell, 2002; Shanahan, Meehan, & Mogge, 1994; Smith, 2006).

People are often attracted to teaching in adult education because it offers flexible work hours and relative freedom in designing instructional practices, and because they are committed to educational outcomes. Those who choose adult education as a vocation

---

* According to results from the 2003 National Assessment of Adult Literacy (NAAL), "between 1992 and 2003, there were no statistically significant changes in average prose and document literacy for the total population ages 16 and older, while average quantitative literacy increased" (National Center for Education Statistics, "Literacy in Everyday Life" report, pp. iv).

do so because they are interested in challenging social issues such as poverty, poor health and limited access to health care, environmental pollution, discrimination and racism, sexism, and classism (Baptiste, 2001). However, there are few incentives to retain and promote qualified and effective teachers such as competitive starting salaries, benefits, or tenure. Teacher preparation (whether in the form of state or college certification; background experiences in K–12 teaching; working with adults in businesses, industry, organizing; or the like), teacher retention, and ongoing professional development are important issues that impact teachers' effectiveness and overall satisfaction with their jobs.

Most adult education teachers work part-time, without benefits and job security. Smith, Hofer, and Gillespie (2001) conducted a study with ninety-five adult literacy teachers on the quality of their working conditions. They found that of the ninety-five teachers in their study, 65 percent stated there was no teachers' room where they could meet with colleagues. Twenty-three percent received no paid professional development time, and 32 percent received only one to twelve hours per year of paid professional development time. Of the ninety-five teachers, 65 percent had not participated in a study circle in the past year, and 79 percent had not participated in practitioner research in the past year. Smith (2006) argues for the importance of full-time, well-supported, and long-term employment which includes access to high-quality professional development. What is remarkable is that despite the lack of education credentials, the lack of professional development, and the lack of resources given to this hardworking group of educators, adult educators historically have managed to make significant social change (e.g., Clark & Brown, 1990; Nelms, 1997; Moore, 1973; Purcell-Gates & Waterman, 2000).

Given this context, we wanted to know more about the adult education teachers who have been identified as highly successful in the major Midwestern urban area of St. Louis. The intent of our inquiry was to document the beliefs and practices of highly effective Adult Education and Literacy/General Educational Development (AEL/GED) teachers. To draw on what Ladson-Billings (1994) has referred to as the "wisdom of practice" of experienced and respected teachers, we designed a survey and nomination form to solicit nominations of exemplary teachers. We used what Shulman (1987) has referred to as the process of "community nomination," through which we asked members of the adult education community to nominate exemplary teachers. This nomination form was distributed to adult education and literacy sites in the metro St. Louis area. We conducted in-depth, semistructured interviews with nine of the nominated adult education teachers and followed up with observations in their classrooms and focus group discussions. For a complete description of the research design and methodology, see appendix 1. We draw on the tacit theories of the adult education teachers and provide case studies based on thick descriptions of their beliefs and practices about literacy education.

Specifically, the research questions that guided our inquiry were as follows: what instructional beliefs and practices, specific to literacy instruction, do exemplary adult education teachers hold? How do adult education teachers understand literacy learning and development? What can the "wisdom of practice" garnered from adult education teachers tell us about teacher preparation and professional development?

THE NEW LITERACY STUDIES AND ADULT LITERACY EDUCATORS

Several decades of research demonstrate the many ways in which adults interact with literacies in multiple domains of practice—including families and communities (e.g., Barton & Hamilton, 2000; Rogers, 2003; Taylor, 1983), school (e.g., Horsman, 2000; Luttrell, 1997; Purcell-Gates & Waterman, 2000), and work contexts (e.g., Goldstein, 1997; Gowen-Greenwood, 1992; Henning, 1998; Hull, 1993, 1997). Such studies have broadened the field's understanding of the complexity of language and literacy practices and the ways in which learning occurs within communities of practices.

The New Literacy Studies (NLS) offers a framework for capturing the theoretical tenets of much of this work in adult literacy education. NLS grew out of a set of focused discussions with the New London Group in New London, Connecticut (Cope & Kalantzis, 2000b; New London Group, 1996). Recognizing the intersections of the local and global and the changing nature of the work world, the thrust of the NLS movement is away from decontextualized literacies to recognizing the historical, situated, local-global nature of literacy practices. NLS argues for understanding literacy practices not as static, isolated endeavors but as deeply situated in specific contexts, purposes, and identities that are evoked when people interact with literacies. NLS includes studies conducted across the life span—including adult education. Indeed, quite a few studies under the umbrella of NLS have focused on adult and family literacies (e.g., Barton & Hamilton, 1998; Hawisher & Selfe, 2000; Jones, 2000; Pitt, 2000; Rogers, 2003; Stein & Slonimsky, 2006). Combined with the studies previously mentioned, we arrive at a broadened framework to conceptualize literacies. Such a framework includes the following assumptions (e.g., Barton & Hamilton, 2000; New London Group, 1996):

- Literacies are situated, historical, and political, and are carried out for social purposes.
- Different spheres of social life (e.g., family, work, spiritual practices, and school) include different literacy practices.
- Literacy practices change to meet new social demands.
- People carry histories of participation with literacy practices with them into different domains of social practice.
- Literacies (and associated identities) are acquired through informal learning and participation in communities of practice.
- Literacy practices are simultaneously local and global in their orientation.

The NLS movement marks a departure from viewing literacy as an autonomous, neutral practice to a set of practices that are inherently ideological social practices that evoke particular types of identities. How, then, does this broadened understanding of literacy impact the teaching and learning of literacy? Educational researchers have taken up this very question—primarily in K–12 education to research the ways in which teachers can structure multiliterate classrooms (e.g., Kist, 2005; Lankshear & Knobel, 2003; Pahl & Rowsell, 2005, 2006; Richards & McKenna, 2003). There have been few, if any, examples of adult literacy teachers engaging with New Literacy Studies. This is unfortunate, because adult literacy teachers are uniquely positioned to contribute to the theoretical and practical development of New Literacy Studies, because their students readily bring a diversity of literacies with them into the classroom; they are at the nexus of a new work world; and their curriculum allows more flexibility to design literacy practices that build on multiple literacies.

Like all other professionals, adult education teachers have tacit knowledge about teaching and learning that they draw on in their classrooms. Tacit knowledge is often referred to as "intuition," "common sense," or "practice wisdom." Tacit knowledge is a meaningful and important source of information that informs practitioners' actions and decisions (Schon, 1983). While tacit knowledge may be difficult for teachers to talk about, it can be ascertained through talking with teachers and viewing their practice "in action." Our role as researchers was to make sense out of how they theorize (in talk and practice) about their beliefs and practices and make such implicit theories about literacy teaching and learning explicit, using their narratives to do so.

Scholars in the New Literacy Studies suggest teachers may be seen as *designers* of learning processes and environments, which includes orchestrating practices and continually redesigning based on responses to curricular designs (Cope & Kalantzis, 2000a; Kress, 2000). Adult education teachers design learning environments based on their professional knowledge, which includes knowledge of content areas, learning processes, and the cultural and linguistic dynamics of the classroom. Teachers use resources or "cultural tools" that are available to them and their learners to design and ultimately redesign learning spaces (Gee, 1999/2005). There are many different available designs or cultural tools that comprise a learning environment, such as texts (both oral and written), relationships, cultural routines, language patterns, and social structures that enable and constrain certain instructional possibilities (Bowers & Flinders, 1990). Obvious interactional patterns in classrooms include observable behaviors such as turn taking, the use of space to arrange the classroom, the physical proximity of the teachers and the students, the use of materials, and the tempo of the dialogue between adults in the classroom. Less observable are the implicit cultural patterns that structure verbal and nonverbal modes of communication as well as the histories of participation that adults have with texts, topics, teachers, tests, and schools. Teachers call on explicit and implicit interactional patterns as they design learning environments. Teachers interpret the ongoing interactions in their classroom that include verbal and nonverbal cues such as the use of space (proxemics), body language (kinesics), and voice tone and intonation (prosody). Based on their assessment of the complexity of these interactions, adult education teachers design and redesign learning spaces.

Related to our belief that adult education teachers are constantly designing best practices is our understanding of the role of teachers as public intellectuals (Gramsci, 1971; hooks, 1994). Public intellectuals are those people in society who traverse boundaries of teaching and activism and do so in a way that connects theory and practice and contributes to positive social change. In the sense that adult education teachers often have their attention dually focused on individual students accelerating toward passing the GED test and on the social structures and practices that perpetuate injustice and illiteracy as one symptom in society of such injustice, we consider all adult education teachers to be working toward justice. While not all of the teachers directly link their practice to the larger political terrain, we argue that all of their practices are, indeed, rooted in wider political contexts. Gramsci (1971) referred to public intellectuals as "organic intellectuals" and believed that their job was "to organize human masses and create the terrain on which [people] move, acquire consciousness of their position, struggle, etc." (p. 377). Similarly, West (1982) stated that adult educators "combine theory and action, and relate popular culture and religion to structural social change" (p. 121).

PARTICIPANTS: ADULT EDUCATION TEACHERS

The teachers in this study were diverse in terms of race, age, experiences in the workforce, and experiences in adult education. They taught in a wide range of programs and consequently worked with a wide range of students. Some of the teachers taught adult literacy students and GED students. Others taught only GED-level students. Others taught in family literacy programs, English for Speakers of Other Languages (ESOL) programs, workplace literacy programs, or homeless shelters. Some of the programs were housed in K–12 schools. Others were located in community agencies.

As diverse as the number of programs are, the types of students that the teachers worked with are equally diverse. While almost all of the AEL/GED students were African American, there was a wide range of diversity within the population of African American students. Some of the students were in homeless shelters, others had recently dropped out of high school, and still others had been living and working in the community for several decades before returning to school. What all of the students have in common is their belief in education as a means of upward mobility in society and their desire to get their GED (Dowdy, 2003).

Table 1.1 includes information for each of the teachers. Each of the teachers included in this book is listed with descriptive information about her background as a teacher, her programs, and her students. We include the teachers' race/ethnicity, the number of years they have been teaching, and their background educational and work experiences. In terms of their adult education programs,

Table 1.1 Description of Teachers

Teacher	Race/Ethnicity	Program Information	Program Description	Number of Students	Student Demographics	Educational Background and Number of Years Teaching
Sara Bramer	European American	Even Start Head Start; urban school district adjacent to city; Monday–Friday 9:00 a.m.–2 p.m.	Family literacy with an ESOL component	15 daily on average	70% African American, 30% European American, 90% female, and predominantly below the poverty line	Human environmental planning with minor in family studies (BA); 10 years as an AEL teacher
Sarajane Campbell	European American	Urban League Community Outreach, Southside Women's Center, and Salvation Army; inner-city sites; twice weekly at each site, 3 hours per day	Community- and shelter-based programs	13 daily on average	Urban League: 99% African American, 50% male, and 50% female; Southside Women's Center: 60% European American, 40% African American, 85% female, and 99% below the poverty line; Salvation Army: 100% female, 60% African American, and 40% European American; shelter residents	Elementary education (BA); reading (MS); 6 years as an elementary teacher, 25 years as an AEL teacher
Angy Folkes	European American	International Institute; South Side inner-city site; Monday–Friday a.m. and p.m. classes daily	ESOL—Refugee Resettlement Program that provides English instruction to refugees and immigrants	125 daily on average (multiple classes)	100% multinational immigrants and refugees: 50% male and 50% female	American studies (BA), TESOL (MA); worked in a factory; 5 years as an ESOL teacher

(continued)

Table 1.1 (continued)   Description of Teachers

Teacher	Race/Ethnicity	Program Information	Program Description	Number of Students	Student Demographics	Educational Background and Number of Years Teaching
Carolyn Fuller	African American	Prince Hall; North Side inner-city comprehensive services site; Monday–Friday 8:00 a.m.–4:00 p.m.	Community center	15–20 daily on average	99% African American, 50% female, 50% male, and mixed economically: the majority are below the poverty line	Political science (MS); parole officer, grant writer, FBI employee; 5 years as an AEL teacher
Sister Martha Jaegers	European American	YMCA Literacy Council, and Missouri Board of Probation and Parole Day Program; near Southside inner-city site, Monday–Friday 8:00 a.m.–12:00 p.m.; central inner-city site, Tuesday, Wednesday, and Thursday, 1:00–3:30 p.m.	Community based, with AEL and ESOL; rehabilitation program for adult probationers and parolees experiencing difficulty on probation or parole supervision	15–20 daily on average	YMCA: 33% African American, 33% multinational immigrants and refugees, 33% European American, and mixed economically; Board of Probation and Parole: 99% male and 85% African American; on parole; the majority are below the poverty line	Education (MS); taught K–12 (nearly all grades) for 20 years since 1958; member of a Catholic religious order; 19 years as an AEL teacher
Vivian Jett	African American	Redevelopment Opportunities for Women (ROW); near downtown inner-city site; Monday 9:00 a.m.–4:30 p.m., Tuesday–Thursday 12:30–4:30 p.m.	Family literacy	12–15 daily on average	100% female, 80% African American, and 20% European American; shelter residents	Employment training; 11 years as an AEL teacher

Janet Omurtag	European American	Southside Catholic Services; near Southside inner-city service site; Monday and Thursday 9:00 a.m.–12:00 p.m.	ESOL	10–15 daily on average	99% female, 99% Latina, and mixed economically: the majority are below the poverty line	Teaching (BA); 5 years working in a Turkish hospital; 10 years as a high school teacher (English and speech classes); 5 years as an ESOL teacher
Holiday Simmons	African American	Adult Learning Center; central inner-city site—administrative offices; Monday–Friday 8:00 a.m.–3:00 p.m.	Adult Education and Literacy	25 daily on average	99% African American, 60% female, 40% male, and mixed economically: the majority are below poverty line	African American studies, women's studies, and environmental science (BA), social work (MA); 3 years as an AEL teacher
Dorothy Walker	African American	Family Literacy Program at Clark Elementary School; central-west inner-city school; Tuesday, Wednesday, and Thursday 8:00 a.m.–1:00 p.m.	Family literacy	7 daily on average	99% African American, 65% female, and 35% male; economically below the poverty line	Education (BA, 1940s); worked in post office and map making; K–12 teacher (3rd, 4th, and 8th grades); after retiring, 10 years as an AEL teacher

Note: The description of student demographics is based on averages from each site.

we included information about student demographics and the average number of students in the program on a daily basis.

PROFESSIONAL BACKGROUNDS OF THE ADULT EDUCATION TEACHERS

Four of the nine teachers in this study did not have any experience with teaching or any formal education related to education or teaching. The five teachers who did have experience teaching before becoming adult education teachers taught in K–12 settings. Four of the teachers taught in middle school or secondary school. One of the teachers was certified as an elementary education teacher and a reading specialist. None of the teachers in this study had a degree in adult education, but all were certified in Adult Education and Literacy through a series of workshops in adult education practice to be certified by the state prior to teaching in the AEL classroom.

Most of the teachers, even if they were K–12 classroom teachers before coming to adult education, did not have plans to become adult education teachers. Many of them "fell into" adult education. One of the teachers stated, "I never knew adult education existed before a year and a half ago." Another teacher stated, "I started working with adolescents about six years ago and I stayed in the field and started teaching adult basic education." There were three primary reasons why these teachers found their way to adult education: there was a job opening, their background experiences fit with the population and/or program where there was an opening, or they wanted a part-time job once they retired. Sara Bramer was looking for a job after she got her bachelor's degree in human environmental planning with a minor in family studies, and found an opening for an adult education teacher. She thought her background experiences might match the job description and applied. Sara stated,

I had not really planned on being a teacher per se. I had gone home to my hometown and looked for a job. Even Start had an opening for a teacher and since I had family studies in my background, I thought I would understand children as well as adults.

Similarly, another teacher was in between jobs and had previously worked in a prison as a parole officer. She was asked to teach in a prison literacy program because of her experience with corrections.

Other teachers expressed a limited set of options for women in the workforce when they started teaching. One of the participants explained, "Teaching is just what we [women] did." Sister Martha stated, "I wasn't sure that I wanted to be a teacher, but I loved school." Another one of our participants (Dorothy) could not become an elementary teacher when she graduated from college (before the civil rights movement) because teachers were not allowed to marry or have children. Consequently, she took a job as a mapmaker and found her way back into K–12 education. Several of the teachers in the study wanted to stay in education and work part-time after they retired from K–12 teaching. Sarajane was the teacher in the study who held a graduate degree in reading. She taught elementary school (first graders), took a leave of absence when she had her own children, and then returned to school to get a master's degree in reading and started teaching in an adult education classroom.

All of these teachers, whether they had been teaching for two years or twenty years, whether African American or European American, had very clear ideas about teaching literacy education. Below we offer a brief introduction to each of the teachers that will be expanded upon in chapters 4–15.

Holiday Simmons, who as mentioned previously is an African American poet and a social worker, brings many experiences with social activism into the adult education classroom. Holiday taught for two years at an adult learning center in the context of a critical literacy lab as well as in a comprehensive classroom where she teaches both literacy students and GED students. Before her work as an adult education teacher, she was an ESOL coordinator and a full-time student in a graduate-level social welfare program. Her undergraduate degree is in women's studies, African American studies, and environmental science. She comes from a family of educators and cites her family—particularly the female influences in her life, her mother and grandmother—as her primary influence in learning how to teach. Her philosophy of education is rooted in justice and following the lead of the learner, concepts she learned from bell hooks, Paulo Freire, and her mother and grandmother.

Carolyn Fuller is an African American woman in her late thirties and the primary teacher in an adult education classroom. Carolyn does not have a history of participation with teacher education, nor is she a certified K–12 teacher. Her previous careers were working as a probation officer and working for the FBI. She has a BA in criminal justice and an MS in political science. She participates in the

Literacy for Social Justice Teacher Research Group (LSJTRG) and teaches English and composition at the local community college.

Angela (Angy) Folkes had taught ESOL at the International Institute for five years. A European American woman in her late thirties, Angy worked for many years on the floor of a machine shop. She holds a master's degree in Teaching English as a Second Language (TESOL) and a bachelor's degree in American studies. Activism—both in her personal life and in her teaching—was a strong thread through Angy's case. As she said, "For me it is an innate sense to fight for social justice, so you do that on the job every day."

Sara Bramer is a European American woman in her mid-thirties who grew up in rural Missouri. Her degree is in human environmental planning with a minor in family studies (bachelor's degree). She worked as the Even Start coordinator before working as an adult education teacher. She has been teaching in adult education for ten years. She teaches in a family literacy program where most of her students are reading between a ninth- and tenth-grade reading level. She described her role as an adult education teacher: "my piece is to help adults increase their literacy level so they can hopefully reduce or stop the dropout rate of younger children and to increase the literacy levels at home so children are more successful in school."

Sarajane Campbell, a European American teacher, was formally educated to become a teacher and has a master's degree in reading. Sarajane has worked at many different sites and with many different students. She has consciously chosen to work with students who are women. She worked at the Southside Women's Center and the Salvation Army Women's Shelter. She also worked at a family literacy program in a suburb of St. Louis. Sarajane currently teaches an adult education class located at the Urban League. Sarajane has an undergraduate degree in elementary education and taught elementary education for six years, and then she went back and got a master's degree in reading. She has been working in adult education since 1980.

Sister Martha Jaegers was a K–12 teacher for twenty years, starting in 1958. She taught in almost every grade in the K–12 system. She has been an adult education teacher for nineteen years. A member of a Catholic religious order and a European American woman, Sister Martha has a master's degree in education and taught first in a junior high school in the math department, but also taught social studies and science. Her entry into adult education was through volunteering as a tutor. Like Janet, Sarajane, and Dorothy, she was educated professionally to become a teacher. However, she became a teacher because that was a viable option for women in the 1950s. As an adult education teacher, she works at two sites—the YMCA Literacy Council and the Missouri Board of Probation and Parole. She uses a range of approaches in her literacy teaching. She is very socially active in her own life in terms of the peace movement and the women's movement.

Janet Omurtag is a European American woman and ESOL teacher who worked at various adult education sites—including the South Side Catholic Center, Oak Hill Family Literacy, and a hotel teaching workplace literacy. After college, Janet went to Turkey and prepared materials in a hospital in Turkey for five years. When she returned to the United States, she taught part-time in an ESOL classroom in a college setting. She then took a job in a high school in the public school setting and taught English and speech classes there for ten years. After retiring from high school teaching, Janet went back into adult education as an ESOL teacher.

Vivian Jett is an African American woman in her sixties and has been an adult education teacher since 1994. She teaches in the community where she lives. Her background is in employment training. She currently is teaching at Redevelopment Opportunities for Women, a resource center for women in shelters or transitional housing. She primarily works with literacy students but does have some students who are closer to getting their GED. The program is part of a family literacy program that has four components: adult education, early childhood education, parenting classes, and Parent and Child Together Time (PACT).

Dorothy Walker is an African American woman who was certified as a teacher from a historically black teaching college in the 1940s. Dorothy taught many grades across the life span. After she retired, she taught adult literacy education with St. Louis Public Schools for another ten years. In her teaching, she draws on her deep familiarity with St. Louis communities and her years of experience as a K–12 educator.

RESEARCHERS/TEACHERS

Like the teachers in this book, we are also adult education teachers. Presently, Rebecca Rogers teaches at the university level, where she teaches courses on literacy instruction and assessment, critical literacy, and discourse analysis. She has taught literacy in an elementary school and also in an adult education center. Her research and teaching focus on literacy development across the life span. Her entry into adult education was through a grassroots literacy program in upstate New York, where she volunteered to teach an adult reading and writing course. She went through the tutor training, and her first tutoring placement was a group situation in an inpatient mental health program located in a hospital. After years of working as a volunteer literacy tutor and earning her bachelor's in English, she worked as the program coordinator for the same grassroots literacy organization. Here, she organized tutor trainings, matched adult learners with tutors, developed and implemented family literacy programs, and worked on recruitment and retention of volunteer tutors. At the same time, she worked on a master's degree in English and connected to the work of Paulo Freire and his revolutionary ideas about participatory literacy education and social revolutions. Inspired by his theories and methodologies, she applied for a job as an adult education teacher at an adult learning center. She had been working as a tutor in the classroom, and when the classroom teacher left, she applied for the job. Here she tried out participatory methods such as language experience stories and group learning projects. It was in this classroom that she met June Treader, an African American woman who would become a participant in her book that focuses on the intergenerational nature of literacy learning (Rogers, 2003). As she worked on her PhD, Rogers became certified as a K–12 reading specialist and also worked in an elementary school as a reading specialist. Inspired by the many connections she saw between adult and children's literacy development, she continues to inquire into such connections today. She is the cofounder, with Mary Ann Kramer, of the LSJTRG.

Not unlike several of the other teachers in this study, Mary Ann Kramer comes to adult education via alternate routes. She credits the diverse people and communities that she has been privileged to live and work with as profoundly impacting her life and perspectives. She integrates lessons learned from these relationships and experiences with values based in feminism and liberation theology into her work in adult education. Mary Ann's degree emphasis is in women's studies, and her previous work includes community organizing, carpentry, teaching assistance in various classroom settings, and ten years as the director of a women's resource center. While tutoring at the center in an adult education class, she witnessed the risks women took to pursue their education. Recognizing education as a powerful means of socialization (for better or worse), Mary Ann sought a position in adult education with the local district. She was initially hired to teach 16–21 year olds in a job readiness program and later assumed her current position as literacy coordinator. This role affords her the opportunity to collaborate with others to advance literacy and social justice concerns through the development of multiple resources and programs.

Drawing on in-depth interviews and classroom observations, we present case studies of each of these teachers as they speak about teaching for literacy acceleration within a critical framework (e.g., Dozier, Johnston, & Rogers, 2005; Johnston, 2004; Rogers, 2007). The "wisdom of practice" from the exemplary adult education teachers suggested that a critical education without the strategies and knowledge to access the dominant codes of power of a literate society is not enough for adult learners. Thus, the twin pillars of setting up the contexts in which students accelerate as readers and writers at the same time they are learning to critique and change power structures are needed. Indeed, all of the teachers represented in this book attended to the dual goals of accelerating their students toward traditionally defined academic goals (increasing literacy levels and obtaining their GED) and, at the same time, teaching within a culturally responsive, social justice framework. Their case studies demonstrate the ways in which adult literacy education is contributing to social change in more complicated ways than is currently acknowledged.

The adult education teachers in St. Louis serve as a window and a mirror for other literacy teachers and researchers to inquire into and reflect on the complexities of critical literacy education. As a window, their practices can provide valuable insight for teachers and researchers who work in different contexts—rural or suburban educational programs, and K–12 educators working in a wide range of contexts who are consciously trying to teach for literacy acceleration within a critically responsive framework. As a mirror, the cases presented in this book can provide affirmation and extend the practices of those educators and researchers working in similar contexts.

2

Literacy Acceleration within Critical Frameworks
An Emergent Framework

ADULT LITERACY EDUCATION

There has been much debate over the teaching of literacy with adults (Alamprese, 2001; Kruidenier, 2002b; Stahl, 1999; Venezky, Oney, Sabatini, & Richa, 1998; Weiner, 2005/2006). Indeed, the field of adult education is characterized by diverse and oftentimes competing conceptual paradigms (Demetrion, 2005). Adult education programs, in theory, often espouse a model of literacy instruction that is based on relevant and authentic reading materials from the adults' lives (Auerbach, 1996; Degener, 2001; Freire & Macedo, 1987; Greenwood Gowen, 1992; Purcell-Gates, 2002; Purcell-Gates & Waterman, 2000; Stein, 2000; Sticht, 1989, 1997). These researchers believe that adults should learn to read with material that has direct transference to their daily lives with integrated instruction on problem-solving skills at the word level (Mikulecky, 2000; Mikulecky & Lloyd, 1997; Purcell-Gates & Waterman). Further, this approach includes a critical analysis of social structures and aims at raising critical consciousness of both the teacher and the student, which ultimately leads to social action. Demetrion (2005) refers to this approach as a "participatory approach" to literacy education. It is also often referred to as "critical literacy," a set of frameworks we discuss below.

Another paradigm of literacy education is what Demetrion (2005) refers to as a "functional approach." The release of *Research-Based Principles for Adult Basic Education Reading Instruction* (Kruidenier, 2002b) is one such example of a functional approach to literacy education. The report argues that adult literacy education should be informed by research that is "reliable and replicable" and emphasizes five components of the reading process: phonemic awareness, phonics, fluency, vocabulary, and comprehension. There is little doubt in anyone's mind—researcher or educator—that each of these components is important in the reading process. What *is* questionable is the extent to which any one of these subcomponents of the reading process is emphasized at the expense of meaningful, relevant, and purposeful reading and writing. Indeed, the recommendations of Kruidenier's (2002b) *Research-Based Principles for Adult Basic Education Reading Instruction* have not gone without critique. Weiner (2005/2006) illustrates the way in which the Partnership for Reading (PFR) uncritically accepts the National Reading Panel's (NRP) recommendations for adult literacy research and practice. Critiques have been written about the NRP's report, the report on which the PFR bases its recommendations for literacy research and instruction (Allington, 2002, 2004; Coles, 2000). Mainly, the research base drawn on was flawed, excluded many studies, and disregarded models of adult literacy campaigns and initiatives that have proven effective. The argument for promoting and disseminating the report in adult literacy education seems to be based on the perception of a lack of alternatives, rather than on the best recommendations for adult learners. Kruidenier, an advocate of using the NRP results in adult literacy education, put it this way: "a convincing argument can be made for the use of K–12 results with adults when no research based practices exist at the adult level" (2002b, p. 11). Indeed, more research needs to be conducted on adult literacy education. However, to argue that there are "no research based practices" is irresponsible to the many studies that have been conducted in this area, for example, those conducted under the National Center for the Study of Adult Learning and Literacy (NCSALL).

Research has demonstrated that, in practice, most adult education classrooms rely on literacy instruction that might be characterized as taking a functional approach. This literacy instruction is often decontextualized and comes from a scripted program or from commercially prepared workbooks, rather than from the adults' lives (Purcell-Gates, Degener, & Jacobson, 2001; Young et al., 1994). In these programs, literacy development progresses in a sequential manner and is closely measured and monitored through traditional assessments. Further, some reading researchers in adult education believe that adults need sequential skills to fill in gaps in what they have missed in becoming literate (Gottesman, Bennett,

Nathan, & Kelly, 1996; Greenberg, Ehri, & Perin, 1997). These approaches often overrely on phonics instruction at the expense of other strategies, are decontextualized, and do not respond to adults' life experiences. Campbell (2001) discusses the difference between participatory and functional approaches as the difference between "bottom-up" and "top-down" approaches.

Bottom-up refers to a process where students are participants in setting the agenda of their learning experience; they are active subjects of their learning. Top-down, on the other hand, refers to a process where students are passive recipients of a predefined agenda; they are objects of learning. (p. 60)

What is left out of both paradigms of literacy education (functional and critical) is attention to strategic reading, problem solving, and the creation of a self-extending system. Such elements of literacy education are essential to literacy development, regardless of the paradigm.

Conceptualizations and implications of adult literacy education policies and programs are incomplete without the voices of adult education teachers. The teachers in this inquiry suggest that classifying approaches to literacy education as either participatory *or* functional is too simplistic a representation to characterize the complexity of literacy teaching in adult education. In a direct response to Demetrion's (2005) call for a "third way" in adult literacy education, the adult education teachers in this book outline a set of approaches to teaching reading and writing contextualized within critical frameworks. On two constantly shifting continua that intersect to form an emergent framework (described below), the teachers are both accelerating their students toward traditional measures of achievement and preparing them to be responsible citizens, change agents, and participants in a democratic society. In the following sections, we use the thread that emerged from the teachers' interviews and classroom practices, teaching for literacy acceleration within a critical framework, to build an argument for this "third way" in literacy education. First, drawing on literature in literacy education, we review what we mean by teaching for acceleration. Second, we review critical-participatory approaches to literacy education. Finally, we suggest, following the teachers' practices, a combination of these approaches is in the best interest of the students whom adult literacy education is intended to serve.

TEACHING FOR LITERACY ACCELERATION

Teaching for literacy acceleration is primarily intended to help the slowest developing students (e.g., elementary, high school, or adult education students), through focused reading and writing instruction, to accelerate as readers and writers (e.g., Dozier, Johnston, & Rogers, 2005). Clay (1993) writes that acceleration is "achieved as the [learner] takes over the learning process and works independently discovering new things for himself inside and outside the lesson" (p. 9). Teaching for acceleration is particularly important for adult education students and teachers because often adult education students have had difficulty with reading at some point in their educational experiences. Often they were tested and placed in remedial reading or special education classes. We know that while these classes offer individualized instruction, they often over-rely on a phonics in their approach to teaching literacy. Consequently, the very students who need the most reading and writing in context often receive the least (Allington, 1977).

An understanding of the reading process is in order to understand teaching for literacy acceleration. When fluent readers are reading, they are efficiently using three cueing systems (that represent linguistic systems)—semantics, syntax, and grapho-phonics. "Semantics" refers to word meanings, "syntax" refers to the grammar of a sentence, and "grapho-phonics" refers to the relationship between letters and sounds (or, put simply, the actual words on the page). When learners have difficulty with reading, some part of the cueing system has broken down. Learners are either overrelying on grapho-phonic cues at the expense of meaning (e.g., when a reader substitutes nonsense words such as "tirlish" for "tarnish") or when a reader "calls" words but does not understand what she is reading, or is overrelying on meaning cues at the expense of grapho-phonic cues (e.g., when a reader substitutes the word "home" for "house"). In this example, the words mean the same thing, so the reader is relying on the meaning-cueing system but the words do not look alike—thus the reader is not attending closely to the grapho-phonic cues of the word.

Noticing and naming (Johnston, 2004) the cueing systems that are being used, overused, or not used are especially important with learners who are emergent to transitional readers. In these stages, readers are developing a repertoire of problem-solving strategies to use when they encounter unknown words. As learners move into the self-extending stage of reading—the stage that is often equated with reading beyond a fifth or sixth grade level in adult education—less attention is given to the problem solving of unknown words, and more attention is given to fluency, comprehension, and stamina as a reader.

Regardless of whether the adult is reading at a first or an eighth grade reading level, we think of teaching for literacy acceleration. This approach focuses on developing flexible, strategic reading and writing in the student's zone of proximal development. The zone of proximal development (ZPD) is a person's "actual developmental level as determined by independent problem solving and his or her level of potential development as determined through problem solving [with guidance]" (Vygotsky, 1978). The instructional zone is the difference between what a learner can do independently and what she can do with support. Instructional-level texts are those that a learner can read with an accuracy rate between 90 and 95 percent, which means that a learner is engaging in problem solving to figure out unknown words and concepts but the problem solving is not interrupting fluency and comprehension. Each student may have multiple ZPD's in her literacy development. For example, students will have an instructional zone in reading nonfiction texts that are relevant to their lives and another instructional zone for reading nonfiction texts that are not relevant to their lives.

The teacher's role within an accelerative literacy curriculum is to know her students as readers, the range of texts that might fall within their instructional zone (e.g., newspapers, workbooks, literature, and magazines), and how she can support her student as a reader in these texts. In other words, there is a complex interaction between the reader, the text, and the teacher. Other than workbooks that are often leveled by grade, materials that adult education teachers may use in their classroom (especially those that are most relevant and meaningful to their students) do not arrive preleveled. This means that the teacher needs to know various characteristics of texts that will either support or hinder the reading process for a particular student. There are many different ways of leveling texts, but we like the approach developed by Fountas and Pinnell (2001) which includes a gradient of texts from the simplest texts (with a word on each page to correspond to a picture) to complicated literary texts with highly metaphorical language and well-developed characters.

Referring to reading levels and books or texts using grade levels can often be unproductive for adult learners. For instance, telling a forty-year-old adult with a lifetime of real-world experiences that he is reading at a third grade level can have devastating personal impacts and cause him to not come back to the classroom. Referring to the characteristics of texts that will provide support and challenge for him as a reader, however, can help him to see his strengths as well as the areas in which he needs to work. Texts that have predictable language structures, familiar content and themes, a few characters, and short chapters may support this adult. Once a teacher becomes familiar with the various characteristics of texts, including the formatting of the print, density of the vocabulary, range of themes and topics, character development, illustrations and graphics, number of lines per page, genre, and so on, she can find a good match between the adult reader and the text rather than relying on prefabricated workbooks alone.

The teacher then crafts a book introduction that will debug the difficulties in the text for the reader and make the text more readable. The book introduction could introduce tricky vocabulary or language patterns, or introduce a problem-solving strategy that will be helpful in reading the text (Clay, 1991). Indeed, one of the important roles of the adult education and literacy teachers is to bring texts—from books to newspapers—into an instructional zone for their students. In order to do this, teachers need to know their students and the texts and what is needed to support their reading of the text. Teachers may decide they need to introduce background information because the student is unfamiliar with the content in the book. Or, they may need to introduce specialized vocabulary or a word part that occurs frequently throughout the book.

Assessing the adults' oral reading as they read this text can help teachers to determine if the text is too easy, just right, or too hard (Johnston, 1997). Teachers can use one of the many available methods for recording oral reading in which errors (miscues) and self-corrections are recorded. By analyzing the adult's patterns of reading behaviors, including the logic of errors that are made, teachers can design strategy instruction and a plan for continual progress. Once teachers have determined their students' approximate instructional reading levels, they can then find texts that fall within their instructional range to ensure they are reading-manageable material (Allington, 2007).

Within any given adult education classroom, there will be a range of reading levels—ranging from emergent readers to readers who are proficient reading a wide range of materials at higher levels.

Adult literacy educators assess reading levels using a combination of formal and informal assessments (e.g., the Test of Adult Basic Education [TABE], the Comprehensive Adult Student Assessment System [CASAS], Running Records, and Informal Reading Inventories) and then design instructional contexts that will continually accelerate the reader through increasingly difficult texts. Teachers may use small, flexibly arranged groups as opportunities to provide support and guidance to readers as they encounter increasingly more challenging texts. Within these guided reading groups, teachers can introduce new books; teach mini-lessons on problem solving, comprehension, language structures, or fluency; and then support the adults as they read, either aloud or silently (Fountas & Pinnell, 2001; Massengill, 2003). Following the reading, the adults in the group will discuss the themes in the book.

Book clubs are another literacy structure that can be used within an accelerative literacy curriculum. Book clubs include less teacher support than guided reading, and the emphasis is on talking about literature that has been jointly experienced—through reading, listening to the literature on tape, or read-alouds. Specifically, learning occurs in a book club as students read, write, and discuss texts within the shared norms of a community of practice (McMahon & Raphael, 1997; Rogers & Fuller, 2007). There are four different components of book clubs: reading, writing in response to literature, discussion, and community share.

Every adult in the adult education classroom, regardless of reading level, can participate in guided reading and book clubs. Each literacy structure can fulfill the goals and aims of teaching for literacy acceleration. Johnston (2002) describes three guideposts that are integral to teaching for acceleration: (1) the development of an executive system or a self-extending system, (2) emphasis on teaching context-based strategies from the outset, and (3) the importance of responsive teaching (p. 637).

SELF-EXTENDING SYSTEM

When students independently problem solve in a new context, they are generating a self-extending system, a system that is self-generative. In teaching for acceleration, the teacher's goal is to help readers learn to move continuously through texts, reading for meaning and attending as needed to higher level details (e.g., interpretive comprehension) as well as lower level details (e.g., decoding and spelling).

The goal of literacy instruction within an accelerative approach is the development of a self-extending system (Clay, 1993). Clay describes how teaching for acceleration leads to a self-extending system:

The teacher will foster and support acceleration as she moves the [learner] quickly through the program, making superb decisions and wasting no unnecessary time, but the teacher cannot produce or induce it [acceleration]. The teacher cannot decide that the time has come and she will accelerate the rate of progress. It is the learner who accelerates because some things which no longer need his attention are done more easily, freeing him to attend to new things. When this happens at an ever-increasing rate acceleration of learning is occurring. (p. 9)

The self-extending system is facilitated in teaching sessions through prompts, particularly cross-checking prompts such as "Does that make sense?" "Does that sound right?" and "Does that look right?" The goal of using such cross-checking prompts is to integrate key cueing systems in language (grapho-phonic, semantic, and syntactic) in a fluent manner. Readers learn to use their previously developed knowledge as they problem solve while reading in a variety of different texts, increasing in the level of difficulty. As Johnston (2002) writes, "The idea is to help [the students] theorize productively about the organization of print" (p. 642). This approach varies from other approaches because teachers clearly focus on teaching context-based strategies rather than word- or sound-level strategies. This assumes that fluent readers are orchestrating three cueing systems simultaneously and effectively. Strategy instruction, within an accelerative framework, is aimed at generalization, that is, students will be able to generalize their problem solving from one context to another. Accelerative approaches assume that phonemic awareness and word identification are acquired as learners interact with reading and writing (rather than before learners interact with texts) and have opportunities for self-corrections, cross-checking, and feedback within purposeful literate contexts.

CONTEXT-BASED STRATEGIES

Self-corrections and other forms of self-monitoring such as making inferences and predictions are evidence of comprehension and engaged reading, important aspects of literacy acceleration. Major aspects of motivation for reading consist of curiosity, involvement, and preference for challenge. Evidence of reading to learn about the world, becoming absorbed in the text, and reading complex material predicts students' reading frequency and reading comprehension (Guthrie, Wigfield, Metsala, & Cox, 1999; Padak & Bardine, 2004). Further, engagement with a text, whether it is based in situational or personal interests, creates a self-extending system where readers will desire further inquiry and reading in this area (Guthrie & Wigfield, 1998). Hickey (1997) proposes a model of understanding engagement as "motivation in context," which focuses on "the relationships, social supports, opportunities, and emergent interactions that empower individuals to seek new challenges within that scaffolded environment" (p. 409). Swanson (1989) argues that it is impossible to understand motivation outside of human relations. Engaged reading is not purely a cognitive activity but an emotional one as readers enter the text world and empathize with characters (Lewis, 2001). Engaged reading also can lead to a more active engagement and participation in the social world, traditionally the goals of sociopolitical frameworks rather than accelerative frameworks.

RESPONSIVE TEACHING

In responsive teaching, teachers are guided by a map of possibilities for how to not only set up the conditions for learners to accelerate but also watch the learner closely and follow the learner's lead, or as Lyons, Pinnell, and DeFord (1993) state, follow "the [learner's] way to the teacher's goals" (p. 286). Teachers set up the contexts in which students learn to problem solve with support and, gradually, independently (Dozier & Rutten, 2006). For example, when a student asks the teacher what an unknown word is, the teacher turns the question back to the learner and asks what she can use to figure the word out, providing support when necessary. Bowers and Flinders (1990) describe responsive teaching as a complex set of interactions where teachers have knowledge of content areas, learning processes, and the cultural and linguistic dynamics of the classroom.

While teaching for acceleration is aimed toward those learners who need to be accelerated in their reading and writing, critical literacy is necessary for the same learners because they are likely to be the learners who are the most oppressed by literate and social structures (Ellsworth, 1989; Perry, Steele, & Hilliard, 2003; Richardson, 2003; Rogers, 2003). Thus, an approach that places teaching for literacy acceleration within critical frameworks is in order. In the next section, we review critical or emancipatory approaches to literacy education.

CRITICAL FRAMEWORKS

We use the construct of "critical frameworks" to refer to the myriad of ways in which educators develop critical literacy. We emphasize a set of frameworks, rather than an approach or a technique, because "critical" frameworks focus on power and unequal relationships. There is no one critical framework or set of methods or approaches that characterizes a critical teacher. A critical framework includes an analysis and critique of systems of oppression (e.g., race, class, gender, sexual orientation, and ableism), but it also includes tools for social change and action.

Critical frameworks start from the assumption that adult literacy education is defined by the struggle over power and knowledge (Brookfield, 2005; Cervero & Wilson, 1999; Mays, 1994). In the sense that power and knowledge are never neutral but are defined by those who have access to resources, critical adult education practices seek to redistribute power-knowledge relationships. This redistribution means recognizing, challenging, and rebuilding relationships that are fundamentally built out of the fabric of oppression. To do this, we need multiple frameworks to notice and name oppression. Thus, we recognize the multiplicity of critical perspectives—from antiracism to class-based instruction, culturally relevant instruction, multicultural education, and feminist teaching—and our stance is that they all add to the struggle for human liberation. Underlying each of these frameworks is a set of values that conflicts with the values of dominant institutions. For example, underlying culturally relevant instruction is the purpose of recognizing the values and perspectives, the ways of knowing, of people who have historically been silenced. When such values become part of the curriculum, they often conflict with the values of the institutions themselves. Structuring a curriculum where the stories of people of color are elicited and heard, without interruption and critique, conflicts with the Eurocentric norms and values of dominant institutions. Similarly, structuring a classroom that is community centered rather than centered on the individual runs counter to the dominant values of individualism and competition that comprise this society. Thus, engaging in instructional practices from any of these perspectives, we would argue, is engaging in a form of resistance and struggle, a struggle that opens space for traditionally marginalized voices and, at the same time, restructures the institutions themselves. Any one of these frameworks (or a combination of them) added to social action is a form of social justice. Thus, the action component of practice is essential in the movement toward social justice.

When critical frameworks guide literacy education, they are referred to as "critical literacy" or "participatory literacy education." Critical literacy has deep roots in the struggle of historically marginalized people to become educated in the United States (e.g., Clark & Brown, 1990; Freire, 1970; Horton, 1989; Spring, 1994/2007). Literacy has always been political and involved in social struggles for freedom and justice (e.g., Monaghan, 1991; Moore, Monaghan, & Hartman, 1997; Weber, 1993). Richardson (2003) writes, "The first Black American texts (enslavement narratives) were political acts. Students need to know that they are heirs in this tradition of struggle" (p. 117). Critical literacies arise from literacy practices that are already taking place in the community as people interact with literacy to accomplish important social tasks. Critical literacy, in theory and in practice, seeks to critique problematic textual and social practices and, at the same time, construct productive and agentic narratives for all students.

Critical literacy takes many shapes and forms. The focus of critical literacy that is taken up in the United States, Australia, Canada, and Europe is grounded in Systemic Functional Linguistics (SFL). SFL is a theory of language that emphasizes the relationship between language form and language function as well as the choices people make as language users (Halliday, 1978). SFL assumes that the form of language is always connected to particular social practices, including textual, interpersonal, and societal functions. Liberal genre theorists have taken up these issues in Australia and elsewhere (e.g., Cope & Kalantzis, 2000a; Martin, 1991). Critical genre theorists argue that certain language forms (and functions) are privileged over others (e.g., language varieties, and written language over spoken language). Thus, the goal of critical literacy instruction is to provide students access to dominant genres (Cope & Kalantzis; Janks, 2002). In the sense that the form and functions of language are patterned together in ways that privilege some groups of people over others, language practices are never neutral (Christie, 2003; Luke & Freebody, 1997, 1999).

Another approach to critical literacy is a multiple literacies approach that stems out of the ethnographies of communication in the early 1980s (Barton & Hamilton, 1998; Brice Heath, 1983) and, more recently, the New Literacy Studies (Cope & Kalantzis, 2000a; Gee, 2001; New London Group, 1996). This work illustrates the many different ways of using texts in families and communities in an effort to accomplish social goals. This model foregrounds the need for teachers to recognize and respect the cultural and linguistic resources that learners bring with them into the classroom. Teachers use these resources to transform, or redesign, the curriculum. This model also assumes that texts—both spoken and written—are never neutral; rather, texts are shaped by and shape social practices and social structures (Street, 1985). Talk and texts have material consequences that privilege certain groups of people at the expense of others (Collins & Blot, 2003; Fairclough, 2003; Gee, 1996).

A third, common approach to critical literacy is what might be referred to as a "social justice approach." This approach is commonly credited to Paulo Freire, the revolutionary Brazilian adult educator and sociologist who popularized the notions of generative themes, language experience, and dialogic education for adults. Many successful literacy campaigns in the United States (e.g., the Citizenship Schools and the Freedom Schools) and worldwide (e.g., Cuba's "Great Campaign" circa 1960, the Nicaraguan Literacy Crusade circa 1980, and the Venezuelan literacy campaign circa 2003) have used these principles. In these campaigns, the effectiveness of the programs was not assessed by traditional literacy assessments (e.g., Tests of Adult Basic Education or the General Educational Development test [GED]) but whether the program had accomplished its social goal, that is, liberation.

We know what critical literacy instruction sounds like in theory, and there are a limited number of portraits of teachers practicing critical literacy (see Auerbach, 1989, 1992b; Campbell & Burnaby, 2001; Purcell-Gates, 1995; Purcell-Gates & Waterman, 2000; Shor, 1996; Shor & Freire, 1987; St. Clair & Sandlin, 2004). Further, there have been steady calls for critical literacy instruction in adult education (Brookfield, 2005; Degener, 2001; Demetrion, 2005; Heaney, 1992; St. Clair & Sandlin). However, such calls are increasingly silenced by federal reform efforts that promote a narrow, functional view of literacy and education. Indeed, critical theory is increasingly marginalized in the current educational reform movement. Degener (2001) complicates the call for critical instruction in adult education, arguing for a more complicated portrait of what counts as critical education. Degener writes:

Critical theorists are elegant and prolific in their criticisms of traditional, noncritical adult education programs. Unfortunately, their criticisms have resulted in an "us versus them" mentality that often puts noncritical programs on the defensive rather than open to the idea of change.... Dividing adult education programs into two categories is too simplistic and does not adequately represent the field. In reality, some programs may be noncritical but may also have the potential to evolve—that is, they may be making program changes that reflect a shift towards critical pedagogy. (p. 29)

We emphasize the teachers, rather than the programs, as the site of critical literacy instruction. Further, as discussed in the preceding section, critical instruction without literacy acceleration, especially for students who have not acquired basic or full "literacy skills," will not do in terms of justice. Both are needed. Degener (2001) continues, "Rather than labeling programs as either critical or noncritical, it may be more useful and beneficial to the field to think about adult education programs as falling somewhere on a constantly shifting continuum between noncritical and critical" (p. 2). We like this notion of a continuum of critical to noncritical frameworks and have chosen to talk about this in terms of "emergent critical frameworks" that the teachers develop as they theorize about their practices.

These emergent frameworks are important for adult literacy education because critical theory has been unable to move from critique to substantial vision. Indeed, as Gore (1993) points out, critical pedagogy is often a fractured "pedagogical project" which includes a social and political vision but does not attend to the details of linking practice with a larger social and political vision that could activate solidarity. In this book, we demonstrate, through the voices of the adult education teachers, multiple entry points into a vision of possibility.

TEACHING FOR LITERACY ACCELERATION WITHIN CRITICAL FRAMEWORKS

Accelerative approaches to literacy instruction have tended to focus on the cognitive and linguistic aspects of learning, giving less attention to the participatory and critical aspects of becoming literate. Given the increasingly strict requirements of state and federal standards, those charged with the teaching of adults are less inclined to teach literacy skills and strategies that promote active, critical analysis within the context of small-group instruction and are more apt to teach the mechanics of passing the test and subskill components of literacy.

Critical educators, on the other hand, have taken up issues of power and agency in the process of becoming literate but have not attended to the cognitive and strategic dimensions of becoming literate that their accelerative counterparts focus on. Seminars or workshops on critical literacy, for example, are not likely to address the technicalities of learning to read including problem solving of unknown words and increasing comprehension. While they emphasize how power-knowledge relationships can be critiqued and transformed, they often start with the assumption that people are already readers and writers. Critical literacy theorists and practitioners have had little to say about accelerating students with reading and writing (for exceptions in the K–12 literature, see Bomer & Bomer, 2003; Heffernan & Lewison, 2003; Lensmire, 2000; Luke & Freebody, 1997, 1999; Vasquez, 2003). There are also models of adult literacy programs that have attended to the details of becoming literate while, at the same time, they have contextualized literacy within a framework of social transformation. Three adult literacy campaigns—in Nicaragua, the United States, and Venezuela—illustrate this model of adult literacy education.

Prior to the 1979 Sandinista revolution, there was almost no education in the rural areas of Nicaragua (where illiteracy rates were 75–90 percent); some children received schooling through the early primary grades but nothing more (Hirshon & Butler, 1983). In the cities there were private schools for the wealthy and a few public schools. Many of the educational materials came from outside the country and presented a false history and reality which had little to do with Nicaragua. Nicaraguan culture, poetry, and literature were taught in ways that supported the values of the ruling class. The economic and political elite wanted and needed an obedient, uneducated working mass of people who could not read or write and were thus less likely to organize and protest. The government in Nicaragua believed that the system under the Somoza reign was unjust. After the revolution in 1979, a mass literacy campaign was planned. The Sandinistas hoped that the ability to read and write and understand Nicaraguan society would cause the mass of the population to work for progress through teaching others, continuing their own self-growth, volunteering to harvest crops, and focusing on democracy building at the community level.

In the Sandinista literacy campaign, the people were taught to read the word and their world. That is, they learned to read and write the words that they were hearing and using every day in the new society—words like "agrarian reform," "democracy," and "freedom." The content and language of the campaign's workbooks introduced the people to the development program of the society. The teachers in this campaign were not educators formally schooled in the Freirean method or in political philosophy, but were 60,000 youths and 30,000 adults of varying backgrounds trained in two weeks for a five-month campaign (Hirshon & Butler, 1983). They taught in all areas of the nation. They would work during the day, teach at night, and live with local families. The organizational support for the campaign came from citizen groups, workers' associations, and public institutions. The trained volunteers canvassed the people to see who was illiterate, did fundraising, and arranged for accommodations and supplies. This was a national project, and some 400,000 people mastered elementary reading and writing skills through their study of history and revolution. Their aim was to go beyond literacy to bring about change in the attitudes of the literates so they could fundamentally change society. The democratic essence of this campaign is that the people taught themselves to think, criticize, and participate in the economic and political decisions of their daily lives. On the campaign, Fernando Cardenal (1980) stated:

Literacy is fundamental to achieving progress and it is essential to the building of a democratic society where people can participate consciously and critically in national decision making. You learn to read and write so you can identify the reality in which you live, so that you can become a protagonist of history rather than a spectator. (cited in Hirshon & Butler, 1983, p. 5)

In the United States, Myles Horton established a popular education school called the Highlander School in 1932. Highlander used the method of popular education to teach adults how to actively plan for social change through education. Small community-based groups came to Highlander to learn to organize in their communities for better working conditions, civil rights, and international rights (Horton, 1989). Horton and the people involved in the Highlander School were responsible for leading educational workshops where people learned to see that the answers to their community problems resided within the people in the community. Highlander played a critical role in the labor rights movement and the civil rights movement. Their educational philosophy was governed by beliefs in democracy and that people could make decisions for themselves. Aimee Isgrig Horton, a kindred popular education spirit, met and married Myles

Horton in the early 1960s. At Highlander, she served various roles such as fundraiser, report writer, and observer of workshops. Aimee Horton wrote the history of Highlander called *The Highlander Folk School: A History of Its Major Programs, 1932–1961* (Carlson Press, 1989). Later, Aimee Horton and Tom Heaney founded the Lindeman Center in Chicago, a center dedicated to nurturing grassroots educational initiatives aimed at helping local communities identify and solve their own problems.

Septima Clark, one of the leading figures in adult literacy education and the civil rights movements, attended Highlander and learned about the importance of adult education in order for adults to take and pass the voter registration test (Clark & Brown, 1990). Septima Clark and Myles Horton started the Citizenship Schools, which were primarily aimed at helping African Americans learn to read so they could pass the literacy tests required to become eligible voters in the South. The schools played a critical role in building a base for the civil rights movement by helping those African Americans who were among the 2.5 million functionally illiterate people in eight southern states participate in politics. The Citizenship Schools were designed to teach adults to help educate themselves. In a five-day course, they learned to use words that came from people's experiences as the basis for a generative dialogue. Teachers at the Citizenship Schools would elicit words like "citizen," "democracy," and "constitution" from the people. They would talk about the meaning of these words, and then they would write a sentence that summarized their discussion. All adults would write this sentence, and then add another sentence based on their own experiences. In this way, they were learning to read and write using their own experiences as the basis of the curriculum. Highlander transferred the Citizenship Schools to the Southern Christian Leadership Conference (SCLC). The schools resulted in the training of more than 800 people in methods that were used to stimulate voter registration throughout the Deep South.

Heaney (1992) makes the point that unlike current adult literacy initiatives that focus on reading education in terms of narrowly defined skills and strategies, Highlander provided not only literacy classes but also classes where the people learned to protest, register to vote, and demand their rights. Horton (1989) said, "They learned that you couldn't read and write yourself into freedom. You had to fight for that and you had to do it as part of a group, not as an individual" (p. 104).

More recently, Venezuela's adult literacy campaign was initiated. Venezuela, under the leadership of democratically elected Hugo Chavez, has undergone a massive redistribution of budgets away from foreign debt and corporations and into education, health care, and social welfare (Ellner & Hellinger, 2003; Gott, 2005). In the midst of a literacy campaign aimed to educate the millions of people who did not have access to education under former regimes, over 1.4 million formerly illiterate Venezuelans adults have learned to read. Article 103 of Venezuela's new constitution proclaims that "every person has the *right* to a full, high-quality, ongoing education under conditions and circumstances of equality." The "missions," include adult literacy classes, high school equivalency classes and technical classes. They serve adults who were denied the right to attend school. Presently, over 1 million undereducated adults are working to complete the sixth grade, and 800,000 are studying at the high school level. The teachers use materials from the adults' lives, books prepared for the campaign that stress liberation and freedom, and the constitution. The constitution, approved in 1999, was written and adopted in a democratic and participatory manner which leaves little wonder about why this document has become a countrywide icon—a symbol of participation, democracy, and solidarity.

Each literacy campaign—in Nicaragua, in the Citizenship Schools in the United States, and in Venezuela—was motivated and mobilized by a politically responsive literacy project. The purpose of reading and writing was freedom—freedom to participate in society in active and meaningful ways and to help further the community and its people toward justice and economic well-being. Each campaign also illustrates that a politically empowering education without the strategies and knowledge to access the dominant codes of power of a literate society would not have been successful. The literacy instruction was based in problem solving, vocabulary development, and a problem-posing/problem-solving model of education. From these campaigns, we learn the necessity of the twin pillars of literacy acceleration and critical frameworks. Adults accelerate as readers and writers at the same time they are learning to critique and change power structures. We are also reminded that we know too little about the adult literacy education teachers—the unsung heroes—who made these literacy campaigns possible.

OVERVIEW OF FINDINGS: AN EMERGENT FRAMEWORK

The teachers in this book described a set of frameworks for teaching reading and writing within the context of critical frameworks. We refer to these frameworks as the "third way" for adult literacy education. Their approaches were not defined by emancipatory or traditional approaches to literacy education, or by critical or non-critical approaches. Rather, in the flexible and highly creative manner that is characteristic of exemplary teachers, these teachers drew from a range of strategies and techniques, strategies that were on a continuum between traditional and emancipatory, critical and non-critical. The "third way" might be characterized by imagining two constantly shifting continua which intersect—similar to a compass with four points. One continuum represents literacy practices. The other continuum represents critical frameworks.

LITERACY CONTINUUM

At one end of the literacy continuum are practices that might be considered accelerative and emancipatory. Emancipatory and accelerative literacy practices include relevant materials that are student chosen, are historically situated, and encourage dialogue and critical reflection. Within this framework, the teacher provides explicit instruction around reading and writing skills. This end of the literacy continuum includes integration of critical literacy and also contains the important structural elements of a reading lesson (e.g., book introduction, appropriately leveled materials, reading of the text, and rereading of and responses to the text). Teachers who taught within this framework utilized flexible grouping of reading groups and had multiple purposes and forms for reading in the classroom (e.g., silent reading, partner reading, round-robin reading, and read-alouds). Literacy instruction at this end of the continuum included elements of acceleration (e.g., self-extending system, strategy instruction, flexible grouping, and self-monitoring). In general, teachers, rather than materials, are understood to carry professional knowledge in this approach.

Toward the middle of this continuum would be a combination of emancipatory and traditional approaches to literacy education. The teacher may have some relevant materials and some materials that do not apply to the students' lives at all. The materials are generally a combination of teacher- and student-chosen ones. There may be pockets of dialogue and critical reflection in the classroom, but the structure of the class does not turn on dialogue. Teachers toward the middle of the literacy continuum may include a few aspects of critical literacy but do so sporadically rather than consistently. Similarly, in terms of literacy instruction there may be evidence of some aspects of the reading lesson (e.g., book introduction, reading and rereading of the text, and responding), but it is not done on a consistent basis. Work tends to be done on an individual basis in a middle classroom. When group work does appear, the groups are generally static rather than flexible. There may be evidence of a few forms of accelerative teaching (e.g., teaching for strategies or self-monitoring), but it is not done in a consistent manner.

On the other end of the literacy continuum is what might be considered the "traditional" approach to literacy education. In this approach, teachers rely mainly on workbooks and other prepackaged or scripted materials rather than student-focused materials. The work in the classroom is generally individual. Group work is rarely evident in the classroom. Critical literacy is rare but may occur in isolated incidents. Dialogue may exist, but it is not connected to the curriculum. The teachers in the traditional approach are still active and working with students one-on-one, but the individual student mediates her reading individually without strategic support. Strategy instruction in this approach emphasizes mainly phonics and literal interpretation of texts. The teachers who teach from this approach tend to strictly adhere to grade levels as they are determined by the TABE. Learning in this framework is sequential, and the tasks are based on discrete skills rather than on a holistic view of the material. By and large, the emphasis is on the materials rather than the teacher.

CRITICAL FRAMEWORKS

Another, intersecting continuum in this emergent framework consists of critical frameworks. At one end of this continuum are educators who explicitly see education as value laden and ideological—and because education works to the advantage of some and not others, they think the goal of education should be to change these inherently unjust structures. Often the teachers at this end of the continuum are very socially active in their own lives and encourage social activism from their students—both in and out of the classroom. They do not see a separation between their lives as teachers and their lives as activists. Rather, they are teacher-activists. These teachers bring multiple critical frameworks with them into the classroom and interrogate multiple forms of social injustice (e.g., racism, classism, sexism, and ableism). They deliberately introduce material that focuses on critical social issues and seek out multiple perspectives, understandings, and critiques of these materials. As teachers, they are deliberately self-conscious and reflexive on their roles as teachers and reveal their positionalities to their students. They promote dialogue and reflection and invite all students' voices into the classroom.

Toward the middle of this continuum are educators who also see education as value laden and ideological but do not necessarily see their role as an educator to change society. They believe that education can be used as a tool for reforming society. These teachers may be socially active in their own lives, but there is a separation between their activism and their teaching. While they would not discourage their students from being activists, they do not actively integrate actions into their classroom teaching. They may, however, recognize their students as leaders and activists in the community—thus seeing the entire person and not just a student. Oftentimes, teachers located at this point in the continuum might follow their students' lead when a social problem comes up that they want to solve but do not deliberately introduce a problem-based education. The teachers may bring multiple critical frameworks (e.g., feminist, antiracist, multicultural, and culturally relevant) into the classroom, but they appear less consistently. They emphasize student experience, voice, and building relationships in the classroom. In terms of their role as a teacher, sometimes they are conscious of their role. They may promote dialogue, but it is not a staple of their teaching.

At the other end of the critical frameworks continuum are teachers who see education as value "free" or "noncritical." These teachers see the goal and purpose of adult literacy education as promoting change through academics and obtainment of the GED diploma. They may discuss making connections with students' lives and using cultural materials to engage their students, but their purpose here is to help them succeed with traditional academics. These teachers are also concerned with bringing in students' voices, experiences, and relationships in the classroom. They are minimally socially active in their own lives. They readily discourage the merging of the roles of teacher and activist because they do not see it as the role of the teacher to promote social change. There may be moments of critique, but they occur in isolation and are not connected to any kind of an integrated whole. Teachers at this point in the continuum can be learner centered, however, with the purpose of advancing students toward the obtainment of the GED or other identified literacy goals.

Both continua—literacy education and critical frameworks—intersect in the middle of each continuum. Surrounding the two continua are four fields (A, B, C, and D) which represent the points of intersection between the two continua. See figure 2.1 for a visual of this heuristic. It is important to stress that there are an infinite number of positions and places that a teacher may teach from within this framework. We will describe each of the fields in this framework.

Field A: accelerative/critical. This field represents the intersection of the accelerative and critical parts of the continua. When teachers are located in this field, they would be teaching for literacy acceleration within a critical framework. They may be either high or low in each of these dimensions.

Field B: traditional/critical. This field represents the intersection of the traditional literacy teaching and the critical parts of the continua. When teachers are located in this field, they would be traditional in their approaches to literacy education and would also be critical in their approach to teaching and learning. They may be high or low in each of these dimensions.

Field C: traditional/noncritical. This field represents the intersection of the traditional literacy teaching and the noncritical parts of the continua. When teachers are located in this field, they would be traditional in their approaches to literacy education and would be noncritical in the frameworks in their classroom. They may be either high or low in each of these dimensions.

Field D: accelerative/noncritical. This field represents the intersection of the accelerative and noncritical parts of the continua. When teachers are located in this field, they would be teaching for literacy acceleration (either extensively or minimally) but would be noncritical in their framework (either extensively noncritical or minimally noncritical).

The teachers in this book, much like exemplary adult educators across the nation, did not fall into one field or another with regard to literacy instruction or critical frameworks. Rather, they move in and out of instruction that might be characterized as on continua from emancipatory to traditional literacy instruction and from critical to noncritical practices. For example, some teachers tended to be more traditional in their literacy instruction but incorporated feminist and social justice practices into their classroom. Other teachers completely integrated teaching literacy within a critical social justice framework. Still others seemed to teach for acceleration within a critical framework part of the time, and at other times they relied on traditional materials. Because of the complexity of positions that the teachers could occupy in terms of their approaches to literacy education and critical frameworks, we rely on the "emergent framework" we described to illustrate how they teach for literacy acceleration within a critical framework. Such a view provides multiple entry points for professional development and practice.

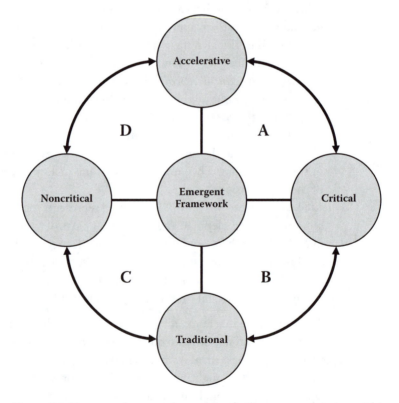

Figure 2.1 Emergent framework: teaching for literacy acceleration within a critical framework

3

Context
Adult Literacy Education in
St. Louis: Window and Mirror

THE STORY OF ADULT EDUCATION IN ST. LOUIS

St. Louis has been described as having a Southern segregation leg-acy with a Northern political geography of separate city and county (Heaney & Uchitelle, 2004; Stuart-Wells & Crain, 1999). The city has been characterized as maintaining the status quo with regard to inequities along education, housing, and employment lines despite progressive reform attempts such as school desegregation (Morris, 2001; Stuart-Wells & Crain, 1999). The history of race and public education in St. Louis is interwoven with the history of residential segregation. Cited as the nation's fourth most segregated city, St. Louis has been described by Portz, Stein, and Jones (1999) as hav-ing a "legacy of systemic racism" (p. 108). St. Louisans make close links between a school and social class, beliefs, and values. The St. Louis public school district has a tumultuous history of strug-gling to meet the educational needs of students who live in the city (Ayres-Salamon, 2006; Heaney & Uchitelle; Portz et al.). Missouri is forty-third in the country in terms of per pupil funding. The most economically disadvantaged schools exist in the city of St. Louis.

There is a long history of the struggle for educational rights for African Americans (adults and children) in St. Louis, Missouri. African American students were systematically denied access to free public schools. Despite the fact that education for them was not only prohibited but also punishable, many people of color and white allies sought to provide educational opportunities for African Americans. James Milton Turner, born a slave in Missouri in 1840, later bought his freedom. He was appointed assistant superinten-dent of schools and was responsible for establishing the Freedom

Schools in Missouri. Turner became known across the state of Missouri as an advocate for education and for the right of black men to vote. Turner was also heavily involved in establishing the Lincoln Institute in Jefferson City, Missouri, the first school to offer higher education to blacks in Missouri (Kremer, 1991). John Meachum, an African American reverend and activist, with the support of James Milton Turner, started the Freedom Schools to provide free education to African American children.

Born into slavery on May 3, 1789, John Meachum eventually earned enough money to buy his freedom and later the freedom of over twenty other slaves, including his wife. Once free, he attended the First Baptist Church of St. Louis, where Reverend John Mason Peck taught him to read and write (Moore, 1973). At age thirty-six, Meachum became the reverend for the First African Baptist Church of St. Louis when it opened in 1825. As a reverend, Meachum used his pulpit and connections to encourage black adults to band together to bring about changes for their children, including education and a good moral upbringing. He further encouraged families to create "union bands" to bring a bit of money together and use the sum for a school fund so the youngest generation could receive a good education. Meachum clearly saw the importance of educating adults as well as children.

Meachum took the creation of schooling for blacks into his own hands. He established Candle Tallow School, which taught black St. Louisans, free and enslaved, to read and write. In 1847, the state of Missouri passed a law that prohibited teaching blacks to read and write. Despite the law, John Meachum kept Candle Tallow School running under the guise of technical training in sewing, which was then an acceptable trade to teach to blacks. When police raided Candle Tallow and arrested the teacher, Meachum looked for a new location for his school. He settled new schools on steamboats on the Mississippi River because the river was not seen as part of the official jurisdiction of the city (Moore, 1973).

The work done at Candle Tallow moved onto a steamship on the Mississippi under the name "the Freedom School." Teachers came from the northeastern states to teach on this steamboat that taught hundreds of black students to become literate. Meachum did not stop with providing education. He also offered jobs to many recently freed blacks as they were studying at his school. Other freedom schools were started in the basements of churches and at other secret locations. The freedom schools continued at least until

February 19, 1854, when John Berry Meachum died in the pulpit. It is unknown what became of the school after Meachum's death.

There were also adult education campaigns aimed at equality and rights such as the campaign for women's suffrage. This involved educating women about their rights. Virginia Louisa Minor started the Missouri Women's Suffrage Association in 1867.

In the late 1800s, as a response to the inadequate and substandard schools that African American children were sent to, African American parents in St. Louis built a school at their own expense and donated it to the Board of Education. The efforts by African American leaders and parents to force the all-white St. Louis school board to provide greater educational opportunities for black children can be seen as representative of the value that African American families in St. Louis place on education. In 1875, Sumner High School opened in St. Louis as the first high school for African American students.

Stuart-Wells and Crain (1999) point out that before Missouri passed a compulsory school attendance law in 1905, there were more black children in St. Louis enrolled in schools than there were white children with similar economic status. It was thought that compulsory school policies would prevent adult illiteracy by emphasizing the education of the child. As adult illiteracy became recognized as a national problem, states began to orchestrate programs to address literacy needs. From 1910 to 1920, there were many community-based efforts in states across the United States to begin an adult literacy campaign. This was spearheaded by the creation of the "Moonlight Schools" in Kentucky by Cora Wilson Stewart. The purpose and goal during this time were to teach adults functional literacy so they could serve in the armed forces and also achieve greater participation in church activities. While state campaigns occurred, there were no federal efforts or commissions established at this time. It is significant to note that Missouri was not a state that participated in a recorded state-level campaign during these years (Dauksza-Cook, 1977). People in the state may have been concentrating their efforts on public education for African American children during this time.

Early adult education efforts—formal and informal—were characterized by community-based adult education. For example, in 1907, African American women Carrie Bowles and Josephine Stevens founded the Booklovers Club which was a women's club devoted to studying topics such as sociology and sculpture. During

World War II, the club became more visible in social activism and supported the March on Washington Movement.

During the early part of the twentieth century, at the national level, there were disjointed legal efforts on the part of individual states but there were no central clearinghouses or organizations to coordinate adult education efforts (Dauksza-Cook, 1977). In 1924, a National Illiteracy Conference was held, and the following year, a "national illiteracy crusade" was undertaken, supposedly as a result of the conference the year before. Relative economic and social stability allowed people the time and resources to explore questions surrounding adult education. During the 1930s, social programs focused on relief programs. While there were some adult education efforts associated with the Civilian Conservation Corps (CCC), the state-run programs were designed to help people find work.

The 1960s ushered in a plethora of tutoring programs for adult education in St. Louis along with other social programs and movements. Programs such as the Volunteer Improvement Program's tutoring program, the Literacy Council, the Maryknoll Center in Valley Park, Cochran House, Neighborhood Associations, and the Sisters of St. Joseph of Carondolet were started by volunteers for a variety of spiritual, economic, and moral reasons. Of course, the histories of adult education and K–12 public education in St. Louis are entangled legacies. Much of the struggle for adult education has been accompanied by the struggle for educational equity for children in the public school system.

Public accommodations were also segregated in Missouri, installing automatic borders between white and black citizens of the state. In the years following the *Brown v. the Board of Education* (1954) decision, Minnie Liddell spearheaded the fight against segregated schools in St. Louis. Liddell started a parent activist group called Concerned Parents of North St. Louis. This group filed a class action lawsuit against the Board of Education of St. Louis and the state of Missouri, arguing that the U.S. Constitution had been violated when her son was bussed to an African American school further from their home. The court case became known as *Liddell v. Board of Education of St. Louis* (1972, 1999; Heaney & Uchitelle, 2004). This initiative became known as the first phase of desegregation in St. Louis that included an intradistrict plan to desegregate the city schools.

The second phase of desegregation included a court order that was composed of three main parts: city-to-county voluntary transfer program, a magnet school program for the St. Louis program to facilitate county-to-city transfers, and a quality education and capital improvements program for the St. Louis Public Schools (SLPS). Thus, the largest desegregation plan in the nation started in 1983 (Heaney & Uchitelle, 2004). Currently, the legacy of discrimination endures as teachers struggle for equitable pay, decent working conditions, and resources for teaching. The well-cited "achievement gap" between African American students and their European American counterparts, the overrepresentation of African American students in special education, and the lack of culturally appropriate texts and materials, among other reasons, lead to the high numbers of students in this district who drop out of school. This history of public education provides the backdrop for understanding the struggle for adult literacy education in St. Louis and elsewhere.

The history of adult literacy education in St. Louis, as in many places around the country, has been characterized by a struggle between community-based and institutionally run adult education programs. Community-based programs often were held in community centers and met adults' immediate and local needs. They often had high numbers—in terms of both adults they served and a volunteer basis. They did not, however, have a reliable and stable funding basis. In 1963, the University of Missouri–St. Louis Extension Service provided funding to support consolidation of many of the community-based programs into a state-run adult education program, under the directorship of Don Mocker. In 1966, the funding from the Department of Elementary and Secondary Education (DESE) was transferred to the SLPS system. At this time, the extension included twelve adult education programs.

Del Doss-Hemsley, a young African American woman, became the second director of adult education in 1966 and remained as director until 2000, over thirty years later. Del Doss-Hemsley commented that at the time, she thought her job in adult education was a short-term job because everyone thought they were "going to work themselves out of a job" and the problem of adult illiteracy would be solved through offering educational programs. The transfer of adult education from the university to the school system was met with challenges. Del Doss-Hemsley explained, "I had a heck of a time trying to expose people in administration in the public schools to what adult education is. During my tenure, questions of the place of adult education were constantly raised. It was a question of where does adult education fit in the system? (interview, Sept. 2006)" Adult education in St. Louis evolved, and continued to evolve, around a set of questions: did the school system fail the adults, or did they fail the school system? If adults were not successful in the school system the first time, what guarantees are there that they will be successful in adult education? What is the appropriate place for adult education? Should adult education teachers be caring, committed adults, or do they need to be certified teachers?

Under the direction of Del Doss-Hemsley, adult education under SLPS continued the process of consolidating services and resources under the auspices of the district. Some community-based programs saw the district-run adult education program as a threat to their autonomy and chose to continue to operate independently of the district. The legacy of racism in the city often reared itself in European American teachers and tutors not wanting to be assigned to schools in sections of the city that were predominantly African American. Thus, adult education sites became segregated. There were other adult education programs that offered GED training but also charged a fee, whereas adult education in the school district was provided free of charge. St. Louis Public Schools Adult Education and Literacy allowed community-based programs to maintain their name and to use the human and material resources of the district (e.g., teachers, professional development, books, and supplies), and, in exchange, the number of adults who were provided with services and the volunteers were counted under the SLPS AEL program. The program grew to one hundred programs, 2 hundred staff, and over one hundred volunteers. The program continues to be the largest program in Missouri.

During this time, programs were using books and readers from elementary schools and some community-based materials, but the publishing market for adult education materials had not yet been created. Adult education teachers were often K–12 teachers or adults who were committed to the cause of eliminating illiteracy and could, according to Del, "think on their feet and were innovative." There was no certification process for adult education teachers, a subject of debate that would continue to reemerge over time. Teachers were required, however, to attend an annual professional development workshop, held in Jefferson City. Explaining and maintaining the identity of adult education within the school district were continual struggles that reemerged with each new school district superintendent. Over the next several decades, community-based programs continued to consolidate with the district and other sites were formed.

Other adult education services emerged during this time period as well. The International Institute was founded in St. Louis in the 1960s as a resettlement agency for immigrants and refugees. It soon became apparent that the adults at the International Institute needed literacy education, which raised the question of who was best prepared to teach immigrants and refugees who speak English as their second language. Eventually, Adult Education and Literacy in SLPS started to provide English for Speakers of Other Languages (ESOL) teachers to adult education sites. The International Institute continues to provide specialized instruction in ESOL to more than two thousand adults in St. Louis annually. Classes also provide literacy education, general education, basic computer training, prevocational training, citizenship education, GED preparation, and Test of English as a Foreign Language (TOEFL) preparation. Classes are offered morning, afternoon, and evening with open enrollment and exit. Most classes are modular in design and operate on a year-round basis. Volunteers help in classroom and on Saturday field trips.

On October 20, 1970, members of the First Congregationalist Church of Webster Groves, Missouri, held a memorial dinner for Frank C. Laubach. Frank Laubach was a Congregationalist missionary who was primarily interested in promoting peace. He created a literacy tutoring method summarized by the phrase "Each One, Teach One," because he believed if all people could read and become more engaged in their community, there would be more peaceful relations between cultures. Following the dinner, a group of church members formed the St. Louis Area Literacy Council. The Literacy Council continued to grow and collaborate with the St. Louis Public Schools Adult Education and Literacy program, became a member of another coalition of literacy providers in the Greater St. Louis Metro East areas called the Literacy Roundtable, and continues to serve St. Louis.

In the 1980s, LIFT-Missouri (Literacy Investment for Tomorrow) was established as a statewide resource center for literacy. Receiving its funding from the federal government and corporations, LIFT, although independent of the district-run adult education programs, offers professional development opportunities for AEL teachers and staff. LIFT continues to provide quality training and on-site technical assistance for educators and tutors; provides accessible resources for teachers, tutors, and program administrators;

integrates web-based technology into adult education and literacy; establishes effective collaborations among literacy providers, supporting agencies, and the business community; maintains a database of statewide literacy providers; utilizes academic expertise and research to improve program effectiveness; and trains parents to be involved in their children's schools.

In the mid-1990s, with the support of United Way funding, the Literacy Service Center was established to bring agencies (some under the district programs and other, independent centers and agencies) together to work on literacy issues in the community. The center was housed at the Adult Learning Center at Kensington and Academy Streets and served as a centralized referral and resource center for approximately thirty agencies. When the funding for this center ended, some of these groups joined with the Literacy Roundtable. For the past ten years, members of the Literacy Roundtable have continued to meet to support literacy efforts in the region.

ADULT EDUCATION AND LITERACY IN ST. LOUIS, MISSOURI: THE PRESENT CONTEXT

In 2000, Bob Weng became the director of Adult Education and Literacy in SLPS. Bob Weng maintains positive state and national visibility. In 2007, he served as president of the Commission on Adult Basic Education (COABE) and continues to serve as a member of the Governance Council of Pro-Literacy America. Other staff at the center serve on the Missouri Valley Adult Education Association and the Missouri Association for Adult Continuing and Community Education Boards. COABE's national adult education conference has been scheduled for 2008 in St. Louis and will attract top educators from across the nation to St. Louis, highlighting SLPS as a leader in adult education. Mary Ann Kramer served as co-chair with Lorene James in planning the conference. SLPS AEL is active in the Literacy Roundtable, the ABC's of Literacy forums and conferences, and other local, state, and national literacy efforts.

The mission of the Adult Education and Literacy program in St. Louis reads, "The mission of the St. Louis Public Schools' Adult Education and Literacy Program is to provide quality educational services to adults as they pursue a better life for themselves, their families and their community." The AEL strategic plan states that academic achievement of adults is a crucial factor in children's academic success at school. To enter AEL, learners must be sixteen years or older and out of school and enter a program in GED preparation, beginning literacy, ESOL, family literacy, workplace literacy, or academic upgrade.

There are forty-seven local Adult Education and Literacy providers in the state of Missouri: thirty-two public school districts, ten community and/or technical colleges, four community-based organizations, and one Department of Corrections. Each local program serves one or more school districts. AEL collaborates with many community partners, including having over fifty class locations provided by community partners. In addition, AEL works with and holds classes in the Missouri Career Centers, Job Corps, the Urban League, the Human Development Corporation, businesses, churches, community education centers, resettlement organizations, and corrections centers.

Even though statewide funding has decreased, SLPS funding has increased due to student performance. The core funding for the AEL program is based on a formula calculated from student performance from prior years. The formula is based on the number of contact hours and student progress according to National Reporting System (NRS) levels and GED attainment. The program budget comes from a competitive award from the federal government's Workforce Investment Act and from state appropriations for AEL.

The SLPS Adult Education and Literacy program is a successful model, providing adult education services to parents, residents, immigrants, job seekers, refugees, and others in St. Louis. The improved academic skills of St. Louis residents will be reflected in improved job readiness, parental academic skills, and civic involvement, which benefit the St. Louis area and St. Louis Public Schools.

St. Louis has the largest Adult Education and Literacy program in the state. Adult education in this district relies on federal funding for three-fourths of the budget. The remaining one-quarter of the funding comes from the state. Funding is based on student-teacher contact hours and performance. There are generally about a hundred teachers in the program. The program serves the city of St. Louis and six other school districts in the city and county. When a teaching position becomes open, an ad is run in local newspapers. A bachelor's degree is required to teach adult literacy education or ESOL in the state of Missouri. Sometimes the pool of potential teachers includes active tutors, tutors in tutor training, or work-study students. In addition, if potential applicants call and express an interest in teaching, they are encouraged to send in a résumé and told that they will be called for an interview when an opening becomes available. A supervisory field staff interviews the applicant. If a teaching position will be extended to this person, he or she is given an application and signed up for the Pre-Certification Workshop (PCW; formally, the Beginning Teacher Workshop). The PCW is a two-day workshop run through the Professional Development Center contracted by the state's Department of Elementary and Secondary Education office and covers the five subject areas on the GED. It also covers administering and scoring the Test of Adult Basic Education (TABE), learning disabilities, working with adults as learners, individualizing assignments, and certification requirements.

Most of the hiring of new teachers is done during the summer when the PCW is held in the St. Louis area, which makes it cost-effective and time efficient to send the teachers to the local workshop (rather than waiting and sending them out of town). Prior to attending the PCW, the prospective teachers are invited to visit two or three different sites to give them a sense of where they might be teaching and to make sure that the expectations of the teacher and the position are in alignment. After they complete both the application and the PCW, they are invited to come to a district-specific workshop during which they are instructed on the procedures and record keeping for this particular district. Then, depending on the teachers, their skill set, their background experiences, and what position is available, they are assigned in either a second teacher role or a master teacher role. Sites that have close to twenty students per contact hour are eligible for a "second teacher." This structure affords the opportunity for new teachers to be mentored by a more experienced teacher. At the same time, it decreases the student-teacher ratio and increases the effectiveness of the instruction. New teachers will sometimes substitute teach before they are placed in their own classrooms.

The field staff tries to make a good match between the teachers and the sites. There are many different factors that would make such a match, but past patterns have indicated that someone who has a background in elementary education might fit well in a family literacy program. People who have a business or training program background might fit well within a workplace literacy program. Once a teacher has been hired and is placed in a classroom, there are numerous points of contact between the teacher and the central adult education office. Throughout the state, all new teachers have a field coordinator as well as a mentor teacher who is assigned to them. The new teachers are required to meet a few times a year with a field coordinator. The field staff will meet with new teachers and orient them in their classrooms. There are four field staff in the district—two who work during the day and two who work at night. This is an on-site orientation unless the teacher is placed as a second teacher, in which case the master teacher at the site would provide that orientation for the teacher.

To maintain their adult education certification, the teachers must participate in twenty hours of professional development annually, which may include teacher certification workshops or in-services. In addition, they must teach 100 hours per year. First-year teachers attend the Pre-Certification Workshop. Second-year teachers attend the Intermediate Teacher Workshop, an in-service, and teach 100 hours. Third-year teachers participate in an Experienced Teacher Workshop. The Experienced Teacher Workshops might include topics such as multiple intelligences, reading instruction, and classroom management in the adult education classroom. The in-service professional development consists of workshops that are offered through the Professional Development Center or are local professional development opportunities that have met with state approval. It is important to note, for the first time in 2006, all school districts have the option to conduct their own professional development that will allow the teachers more opportunities to participate in workshops that connect to their specific educational contexts. St. Louis Public Schools Adult Education and Literacy has decided to pursue this opportunity.

There are ten permanent positions in the district: the literacy coordinator and nine teachers. A permanent position includes working up to forty hours per week and receiving benefits as a ten-month employee. There are three administrative positions that are staffed by full-time, twelve-month employees. The rest of the teachers are considered part-time or temporary, teach up to twenty-eight hours per week, and do not receive any benefits. The teachers are paid on a salary range of $16.00–22.00 per hour depending on the number of students they have in their class per contact hour. The teachers are also eligible for performance funding. State performance allocations to local districts began in 2001–2002. These are based on the progression of students from one level to another (based on the TABE and Comprehensive Adult Student Assessment System [CASAS]) and GED attainment. Allocations for the 2006–2007 year are based on 2004–2005 performances. That same year, performance allocations were made to teachers. A portion of the performance funding from the DESE is allocated to teachers based on the performance of students in their classes. This was done to encourage teachers to be more diligent in reporting the accomplishments of their students for input into the data system. Teacher performance allocations are based on 20–25 percent of the state allocations and are paid the next year to teachers still actively employed in the program. The allocations are determined by the NRS level; level 1 receives an allocation of $50, level 2 receives an allocation of $35, levels 3–5 receive an allocation of $15, and GED completion receives an allocation of $35. When a student had several teachers, the allocation is adjusted accordingly.

Students' educational progress is measured according to the degree to which they have advanced in terms of educational functioning level. There are four levels of basic education, two secondary education levels, and six levels for ESOL. Each teacher needs to maintain a minimum of eleven students per contact hour, or his or her site runs the risk of being closed. The teachers are required to administer a standardized pretest when students enter their classroom. The teacher may choose to also assess the adults' learning with locally developed performance assessments as well. The teachers use the TABE with students who speak English as their first language and the CASAS with students for whom English is a second language. Both tests are normed and criterion referenced. Both satisfy the NRS requirements for testing for program accountability and both use adult-oriented contexts, including functional life skills and workplace context for test items (Kruidenier, 2002b). The TABE and the CASAS measure reading comprehension through a series of multiple-choice questions about what test takers have read.

Both of the assessments have items that test for knowledge of certain word analysis or phonemic awareness skills when they are measuring a more inclusive part of the reading process. Neither the TABE nor the CASAS assesses oral reading fluency. The TABE measures spelling by asking students to read a sentence with a missing word and to choose the correct spelling of the missing word from a short list of words. Neither the TABE nor the CASAS provides norm-referenced scores for written products. Both tests include a script for the teachers to administer the test to the student in a standardized manner.

TUTORS

Tutors serve an important function in adult literacy education. Tutors are recruited, trained, and placed primarily to work with literacy students (students reading below a sixth grade level). They are placed in adult education classrooms and work under the direction of the adult education teacher in the classroom. Tutors come from all walks of life (as do the teachers). They may be college students or people who have recently retired from business, industry, education, or any number of professions. They are generally people who want to "give back" to society, understand the importance of education, and have become aware of the adult literacy "crisis" in their community. There is always a need for tutors. Tutors are recruited on an ongoing basis through word of mouth, through universities, and with flyers at resource and community fairs and events in collaboration with other literacy providers. Adult Education and Literacy in this district is a member of the Literacy Roundtable and works in cooperation with other literacy service providers in recruiting volunteers through the use of a hotline number in partnership with a local news station.

All tutors must attend a tutor-training workshop before they can be placed in an adult education classroom. Training is offered ten times a year at the central office. The training consists of a five-hour foundation training followed with on-site observation and orientation with the classroom teacher. Placement is mutually negotiated based on tutor availability and student need. Supplemental trainings are offered throughout the year that tutors can select to attend. The topics usually advance their tutoring skills in reading, writing, math, life skills, and ESOL. Advanced tutor trainings are also offered.

ADULT EDUCATION STUDENTS
Currently, high school dropout rates average 25 percent and in urban high schools reach 60 to 70 percent (Fine, 1991). A disproportionate amount of these students are African American, many of whom have difficulty reading and writing (Bickel & Papagiannis, 1988; Perry, Steele, & Hilliard, 2003). Currently, the National Adult Literacy Survey (NALS) reports that 46 percent of adults have a limited ability to perform a variety of real-world literacy tasks. The adult education and literacy center in St. Louis is the largest provider in the state.

During the 2004–2005 year, there were approximately 5,070 adults (with at least twelve hours of attendance) enrolled in adult education in the city of St. Louis. Approximately 24 percent of these students were ESOL. Six percent of the total students were ages

16–18, 36 percent were ages 19–24, 44 percent were ages 25–44, and 11 percent were ages 45–60. During the 2004–2005 academic year, 288 students obtained a GED, 1,451 students advanced one or more National Reporting System levels (2–3 grade levels), and 89 students obtained citizenship.

ESOL learners are a subset of Adult Education and Literacy students in the United States. There are 57,000 residents in St. Louis (ages twenty-five and older) who do not have a high school diploma or GED. Fourteen thousand residents speak English "less than very well." Many of these individuals are the parents or other caregivers of children enrolled in the K–12 system. Adults in the St. Louis AEL program who speak English as the first language display the following academic characteristics: 8 percent beginning literacy, 23 percent beginning basic education, 29 percent intermediate low, 29 percent intermediate high, 7 percent low advanced, and 4 percent high advanced. The majority of the students (approximately 90 percent) come in between the levels of 2 and 4 (i.e., eighth grade or below) according to the NRS. This means that the majority of the students coming into the program are considered to be "literacy students," which, as mentioned above, means that they are reading below a sixth grade level when they enter the program. A complete description of the NRS levels is included in the glossary (see appendix 4).

Adults in the St. Louis AEL program who do not speak English as their first language display the following academic characteristics: 28 percent beginning literacy, 24 percent beginning basic education, 20 percent intermediate low, 14 percent intermediate high, 12 percent low advanced, and 2 percent high advanced. ESOL learners come to programs with a wide range of educational backgrounds— from those with no formal education in their first language to those holding doctoral degrees. Findings from a national evaluation demonstrated that half of the ESL population enrolled in adult education had completed at least high school, compared to only 17 percent of the AEL group (Fitzgerald, 1995). According to the National Assessments of Adult Literacy (NAAL) and the Missouri State Assessment of Adult Literacy (SAAL), the average literacy of adults in Missouri is slightly higher than the national average—this includes African Americans, older Americans, and women.

Adult students are recruited to the program through flyers and word of mouth, at resource and community fairs and events, and through an ongoing movement that seeks to raise consciousness about adult education as a civil right.

CURRENT ORGANIZING FOR ADULT LITERACY EDUCATION

The ABC's of Literacy: Acting for a Better Community Conference (ABC's) was organized by members of the Literacy Roundtable in March 2004 as a way to bring multiple stakeholders together throughout the community. The conference ended with small-group discussions identifying how literacy education could address issues such as jobs, health care, child care, and affordable housing. From the expressed interests, the ABC committee decided to hold a series of forums to further raise the consciousness of the public regarding the urgent need to organize around literacy and social justice. The topics of the forums were advocacy, adult education movements, and the link between civil rights and education. These forums were held at the public library and were largely attended by people enrolled in adult education programs, their teachers and tutors, and others in the community. The forums were structured in a way to maximize dialogue and problem solving in small groups. Many of the forums featured adult students talking about their experiences. Often, groups were asked to work on real problems of addressing literacy needs such as identifying statements about literacy that could be used in an awareness campaign. During one forum, people shared their experiences with organizing and activism and talked about different ways of getting involved in the community. Students were asked to join others on a particular action such as signing a petition, becoming a student leader, writing letters, contacting elected officials, and attending a public speaking workshop to address high schools and other public audiences.

During the summer of 2005, a core group of twenty adult education students and ten adult educators from several different adult education sites took part in a thirteen-hour student leadership program led by Voices of Adult Literacy United for Education (VALUE), a national organization whose mission is to strengthen adult literacy efforts in the United States through learner involvement and leadership. VALUE is the only national organization of adult students led by students. The idea and planning for this student-led organization were started at Highlander Education Center.

Highlander is important to understanding the activism and organizing that are currently occurring in St. Louis because of the role it has played since 1932 in providing a space for workers, grassroots leaders, community organizers, and researchers to address pressing social, economic, and environmental concerns. Activist Myles Horton started Highlander in 1932. Highlander's work is rooted in the belief that the people must shape political and economic policies in a democratic society. Highlander uses the popular education model of learning where people go through a cycle of dialogue, critical analysis, action, and reflection in a problem-posing, problem-solving educational process.

Over the course of its history, Highlander has played important roles in many major political movements, including the southern labor movements of the 1930s, the civil rights movements of the 1940s–1960s, and the Appalachian people's movements of the 1970s–1980s. As mentioned, VALUE—the national organization started and led by adult learners—came out of Highlander. After attending VALUE, the adult education students went back to their adult learning sites and started to work on student leadership projects. Part of student leadership is building public awareness around the many issues that surround adult literacy education in the community.

This model informed the problem-posing, problem-solving model of education that took root in many classrooms in the St. Louis area. Teachers and students jointly generated local problems that they were interested in solving using the tools and resources in their adult education sites. Examples of site-based projects included a car wash to raise money for a field trip, the construction of a buddy system or peer mentoring in the classroom to encourage retention, security and safety at adult education sites, fundraising for bus tickets and transportation to adult education sites, and public speaking and outreach in the community about the importance of staying in high school. Several of the adult education teachers in this book were part of this process.

CASE STUDY CHAPTERS

In the following chapters, we present case studies of each of the teachers. Each teacher's case is represented in a chapter. We have intentionally grouped the chapters so that the reader will notice the diversity of practices that exemplify teaching for literacy acceleration within critical frameworks. At the end of every three chapters, we present a cross-case analysis that summarizes and brings out some of the similarities and differences between the cases. This structure is repeated three times. In the following chapters, we invite you to experience the adult education teachers' beliefs, practices, and reflections specific to literacy education.

Part 2

Cases of Adult Education Teachers

4

Designing Communities of Practice

CAROLYN FULLER

In order to know where you are going, you have to know where you come from. And you have to know about the people in the past; if you look at Frederick Douglass, this is a man who taught himself to read and write. But, if you look at some of his writing, it is extraordinary that a man with no formal education could have written some of the text or some of the speeches that he wrote. And when they [adult education students] look at that, and they kind of marvel at it—"Oh here is a man who had no formal education, his mistress taught him some alphabet and from that he is able to write the kind of speeches that he wrote?"—it lets them know that here you are sitting in a GED classroom, you know, you can advance, too. — Carolyn Fuller, interview

Carolyn Fuller, an African American Adult Education and Literacy (AEL) teacher in her late thirties, draws on the narratives and artifacts of Fredrick Douglass to help her General Educational Development (GED) students design a storyline for themselves that includes positive messages about who they are and who they might become within the context of education. Carolyn's instruction attends to the dual goals of accelerating her students toward obtaining their certificate of high school equivalency and setting up the conditions in their classroom where they can envision themselves as active, engaged, and critically conscious citizens. As she does this, she draws on a range of critical black thought, not all of which is considered traditionally academic. In doing so, she opens up space for multiple voices in her classroom.

The AEL classroom where Carolyn teaches is located in the basement of a full-service community center. The community center is located in the primarily African American north end of St. Louis. North and south in this city are signifiers for the racial divide based on residential segregation that exists. The rival gang members in the classroom reflect the existence of gangs in the city. There are pockets within this section of the city that are economically depressed.

Carolyn is the primary teacher in the AEL classroom. Carolyn's professional history includes previous work as a probation officer and working for the FBI. She has a BA in criminal justice and an MS in political science. She participates in the Literacy for Social Justice Teacher Research Group (LSJTRG) and teaches English and composition at the local community college. As mentioned above, Carolyn accelerates her students to obtain their certificate of high school equivalency as well as become socially responsible citizens. On average, Carolyn has 107 students each year who are in her class for twelve or more hours. Of these students, she has a 51 percent retention rate. Her greatest level of impact is a level 5, which means that the greatest percentage of progression occurred with students at this level versus other NRS levels (for full definitions of each level, see the glossary in appendix 4). She has had several students follow her to this site from another site because they liked her techniques as a teacher.

All of the students in Carolyn's classroom are African American. There is a fairly equal distribution of males and females in the classroom, with ages ranging from seventeen to seventy. Their reasons for dropping out of school are as numerous as the students in the class. Some have dropped out because they were targeted for gang violence, others had to take care of siblings, and still others missed a certain number of days and were not allowed to return to school. Their literacy levels range from third grade to twelfth grade, although the bulk of students come in between a sixth and eighth grade level. The number of students in the class varies depending on the weather, the time of the month, their children's activities, and other life obligations. Most of the students in the classroom are from the immediate community surrounding the center, and, consequently, the students know each other—oftentimes having gone to high school with each other. "They will talk with each other about what is going on in the community and in each other's lives," Carolyn noted.

Carolyn's goals for her students include passing the GED test and obtaining their certificate of high school equivalency, and she also believes her role as a teacher includes teaching her students what she refers to as "life lessons" and how to be agents in their social worlds. Carolyn commented on the failure of traditional school models and how she designs the curriculum in her classroom. She stated,

The traditional approach does not work for this at-risk population. If it did, they would have stayed in school. If the traditional approach does not work, we have to try different approaches. We have to look at barriers that prevented them from moving forward in the traditional approach. Some of the barriers include levels of inattention and a lack of congruence between the school curriculum and the adults' lives.

Continuing on the purpose of education, Carolyn stated, "Many of them will say, 'I've never been taught this.' They have never been taught the purpose of education in terms of betterment of their everyday lives. A lot of them are in day-to-day survival mode."

The adult education class meets Monday–Friday from 9:00 a.m. to 2:00 p.m. A sign reading "Adult Basic Education" with letters cut from construction paper hangs from the ceiling before you enter the classroom. The classroom can seat up to twenty-five people. The tables are arranged in rows. At the front of the room is a moveable chalkboard, Carolyn's desk, and filing cabinets. Around the room are artifacts of the GED—for example, a GED robe hangs close to the chalkboard at the front of the room. At the back of the room is a wall filled with GED certificates and the photographs of students who have passed the GED. There are a few computers in the classroom, but they are dated and not hooked up to the Internet. Carolyn has limited access to a copy machine and does not have a printer hooked up to any of the computers in the classroom.

Carolyn integrates relevant and engaging materials—materials that include her students' life stories as well as their language use—into the curriculum. The structure of the classroom follows the same pattern each day. Carolyn puts an issue on the board for the students to write about. These issues may come from current events or from events that are relevant to her students' lives. The students write their essay and then share what they have written with the entire class. Next, Carolyn begins "Current Events," which includes the reading and discussion of a current newspaper article that includes local or world events. Carolyn passes out copies of the newspaper article, and either she reads the article or the students will read aloud. The class discusses the issues embedded in the articles, including the multiple perspectives, the conflicting information, the information excluded from the article, and what the author assumed about the intended audience.

Reading literature follows current events. The readings are usually taken from a piece of literature that Carolyn believes is relevant and engaging to her students. Carolyn chooses the materials or questions based on what will be relevant to her students' lives. She sees her role as "giving her students a new perspective," something that is lacking in their lives. She takes more of a traditional teacher role—and does not disrupt the power dynamics between the traditional teacher and student roles. This may be because of her "tough" population and tacit theories of what it means to educate. She sees her job as teaching her students life lessons that they have not learned before and, as she repeated again and again in the interview, "giving them the skills they need." Her literacy curriculum is primarily literature and text based (rather than workbooks). However, sometimes she does rely on traditional materials such as photocopies of worksheets from GED preparatory materials. Carolyn explained the books that her students have found the most engaging:

These books are The Coldest Winter Ever by Sister Souljah [2000], No Disrespect by Sister Souljah [1996], and Makes Me Wanna Holler by Nathan McCall [1995]. These books deal with urban settings, a character who they can relate to because the character has issues similar to them. If I try to introduce a lesson, or a reading where it does not relate to them personally, they lose interest quick.... Then, we will have a discussion about the book. Many of the students have gone to the library to explore other authors who can write about similar experiences. The book clubs stimulated their desire to read. Many of them have told me that they have never attempted to read before being introduced to this particular set of writings. So the readings have made them desire reading more. And I think that is critical because Souljah really did try to get a very important message across in her writing. Even though to some people it is radical, but she is really trying to reach a certain population. I think she has been very effective at it.

Carolyn takes an explicitly ethical stance on her social responsibilities as a teacher. She frames this explicitly ethical stance in terms of teaching her students "life lessons." Her beliefs and practices reflect what Ladson-Billings (2001) wrote: "teaching well ... means making sure that students achieve, develop a positive sense of themselves, and develop a commitment to larger social and community concerns" (p. 16). Carolyn speaks with authority and conviction when she is talking with her students in the classroom.

As Carolyn discussed the importance of finding relevant and engaging materials for her students, she brings up the purpose and function of rereads in her classroom ("We've read over and over again"). A large part of Carolyn's classroom community is a shared experience with literature. She has several books that she has found resonate with her students' life experiences and future goals, and she will read aloud or ask her students to read sections from these books. The rereads in the adult education classroom function in much the same way that rereads function for children as they are becoming literate. The rereads provide a familiar story structure which provides a detailed book introduction for students who are reading much below the level of the text. For students who can read the text but may have comprehension or fluency difficulties, it provides them with multiple opportunities to make connections between the texts, their lives, and other texts as well as hear a model of fluent reading and practice their own fluency.

By bringing in the book written by Sister Souljah, Carolyn is making space for black feminist thought in her classroom. She is clear that black experiences and ideas lie at the core of the design of her classroom. Collins (2000) writes about the use of *No Disrespect* (1996) as a feminist text:

Rap singer Sister Souljah's music as well as her autobiography No Disrespect *(1994) can certainly be seen as contributing to Black feminist thought as critical social theory. Despite her uncritical acceptance of a masculinist Black nationalist ideology, Souljah is deeply concerned with issues of Black women's oppression, and offers an important perspective on urban contemporary culture. (p. 16)*

By tapping into nontraditional reading sources such as No Disrespect and *Makes Me Wanna Holler* (McCall, 1995), Carolyn grounds the intellectual work of the classroom in the intellectual production of black people in various communities. Carolyn talked about the importance of discussing the literature in the classroom. She discussed how her students made connections with the text and that her students relate with the author:

Souljah really did try to get a very important message across in her writing. Even though to some people it is radical, but she is really trying to reach a certain population. I think she is very effective at it. They can relate to where she is coming from. I think they walk a similar path that she walked. And I guess they feel like, if she made it given all the obstacles in her path, they can make it too.

Carolyn's stance in the classroom illustrates what Collins (1998) describes as key themes in black women's struggle for liberation. Collins (1998) writes, "Black women's activism as mothers, teachers, and Black community leaders, [as well as their] sensitivity to sexual politics are all core themes advanced by Black feminist intellectuals" (p. 27). Carolyn expresses a hopefulness contextualized in struggle that Collins (1998) terms "visionary pragmatism." Collins writes,

Visionary pragmatism emphasizes the necessity of linking caring, theoretical vision with informed practical struggle....Visionary pragmatism more closely approximates a creative tension symbolized by an ongoing journey. Arriving at some predetermined destination remains less important than struggling for some ethical end. Thus, although Black women's visionary pragmatism points to a vision, it doesn't prescribe a fixed end point of a universal truth. One never arrives but constantly strives. At the same time, by stressing the pragmatic, it reveals how current actions are part of some larger, more meaningful struggle. Domination succeeds by cutting people off from one another. Actions bring people in touch with the humanity of other struggles by demonstrating that truthful and ethical visions for community cannot be separated from pragmatic struggles on their behalf. (pp. 188–190)

No Disrespect is a book that Carolyn has read with her class over and over again. Sometimes she copies chapters for the students to read, other times they read the entire book in a book club, and still other times Carolyn reads aloud from the book as the students listen. The student population constantly changes in the classroom, so while there may be members of the classroom who have heard sections of the book before, they seem to take pleasure in knowing a story that is familiar where they can comment, co-construct, and share "insider information" with other students in class who may not have read the book before. Thus, the reread of this narrative functions as a source of power for these students as they become, in Wenger's (1998) terms, the "brokers" in the community of practice, passing along the storyline of the book and of the classroom community of practice. Rereading the text helps the adults to construct an agentic narrative within the context of literature and classroom literacy practices. It provides them the opportunity to demonstrate their leadership in the classroom and talk about books that they are interested in.

As Carolyn teaches for literacy acceleration within a critical framework, she draws on a number of what could be considered critical literacy practices. For example, as the students are reading, she will ask them questions during the reading (her assumption is that they will continue to ask themselves these questions when she is not reading with them).

Carolyn explicitly makes the connection between their reading and discussion of literature and how this will help them to pass their GED test. She tells her students, "The GED is a reading test." She managed to provide a dual support system for her students, one that allowed them to participate in a curriculum that was socially and critically accelerating them toward passing the GED test. On average, Carolyn has fifteen students who pass the GED test per year. Carolyn insisted on the importance of connecting the reading with her students' lives and their social world. She thought this created the conditions where her students could learn to problem solve by critically examining the problem solving of characters in the text. Ladson-Billings (1995) stated,

By drawing on perspectives of critical theorists, culturally relevant teaching attempts to make knowledge problematic. Students are challenged to view education (and knowledge) as a vehicle for emancipation, to understand the significance of their cultures, and to recognize the power of language. As a matter of course, culturally relevant teaching makes a link between classroom experiences and the students' everyday lives. These connections are made in spirited discussions and classroom interactions. Teachers are not afraid to assume oppositional viewpoints to foster the students' confidence in challenging what may be inaccurate or problematic. (p. 94)

In other words, Carolyn's intention is to build relationships through literature so that her students can learn to problem solve in the text and in their relationships (debriefing notes, March 2004). While she uses literature as an entry point for conversations, she expects that her students will transfer such processes into their daily lives. For many of Carolyn's students, this is the first chance they have had to see themselves in the text and to relate to a piece of literature. Indeed, one of the graduates from her class, a thirty-something African American male who is currently attending a community college, reported that *No Disrespect* was the first book he had read in thirty years (field notes, March 2004). It is important to point out that Carolyn engages her male students in a feminist book by bringing them into the discussion and debate about life choices and structural conditions of men and women. In essence, she links the struggle of men and women of color as a common struggle—and teaches implicitly that feminism is a set of issues and actions that is relevant in the lives of men as well as women. She does this by making sure that all voices in the classroom are heard. Carolyn asked her students to identify agentic roles in the literature they read which they might then transfer to their own lives. She explained,

It is what Oprah would call an "aha" moment. Because what they'll do is they will see how this is happening in their life and how they can make a change because a lot of times the characters are able to move out of the circumstance, so it lets them know that if the character can move out of the circumstance, that they can do it, too.

This moment of revelation is similar to what Adorno described as the revolutionary potential of literature to make personal and social changes in people's lives. Her students see the characters in the book as agents, transforming their lives, and they want to change the conditions for themselves. Mills (1954) stated it this way:

If adults start to see situations in their private lives as concrete manifestations of broader social and political contradictions, they will see that changing their individual lives is impossible without political action. Hence, to the extent that adult [education] is effective, it is going to be political; its students are going to try to influence decisions of power. (As cited in Brookfield, 2005, pp. 173)

She also specifically links the struggle for women in general and black women in particular to their reading of the book. She stated,

You know when you look at the plight of the African American female and you can see that she was seeing the same thing: that the numbers are just stacked up against them. A lot of black women, you look at the single parent rate, um, the marriage rate, their rates are different and their quality of life is different and a lot of it is based on education. And I think that was what Sister Souljah was trying to say. In order to increase your quality of life, you have to educate yourself. That is what I saw in my classroom.

Authority is an important part of Carolyn's stance as a teacher. She talked about authority in this way:

What I discovered is if they do not see you as an authority figure, they will not listen to you and they will not respect you. And once they do not respect you, it is all over. The students come in here who have already had problems in school so they bring the same type of mind-set when they were in high school and they were put out. If they do not see you as someone worthy of respect, someone they should listen to, they will cause havoc and then they will start to roam.... So I had to come across as an authority figure first to let them know, no this is not play. This is for real and that you have to respect me and you have to respect other students. And then that gets their attention and they get a mind-set that this is serious and I am here to learn and not to play.

Establishing respect in this classroom is an ongoing negotiation because new students constantly come into the classroom. This stance resonates with what Delpit (1995) has written about authority in African American communities. She writes,

In many African American communities, teachers are expected to show they care about their students by controlling the class; exhibiting personal power; establishing meaningful interpersonal relationships; displaying emotion to garner student respect; demonstrating the belief that all students can learn; establish[ing] a standard of achievement and "pushing" students to achieve the standard; and holding the attention of the students by incorporating African American interactional styles into their teaching. Teachers who do not exhibit these behaviors may be viewed by community members as ineffectual, boring, or uncaring. (p. 142)

Carolyn explains how students who have been a part of the classroom community for some time will often orient new students to the norms and culture of the classroom. This helps them to feel they have a leadership role and are taking authority over the classroom community. As the students' competence and leadership skills are developed, the educator releases some of the support and structure. In this way, Carolyn is teaching leadership skills for her students, an important responsibility of building networks of leadership within the community. Youngman (1986) writes,

Adult educators bring to the education situation a necessary expertise and they initially assume a position of authority and leadership. They take responsibility for making their expertise available in a way that will further the learners' interests. They participate in a collaborative process which aims to raise the level of awareness and competence of the learners and hence their position is not static. (p. 207)

When Sister Souljah visited a university in St. Louis, Carolyn encouraged her students to attend her talk. Several students went to the talk and asked Souljah to sign their book after the presentation.

One morning, Carolyn chose an article on the controversy surrounding a local homeless shelter. The students debated whether or not homeless shelters should exist or whether people should go out and get jobs. The discussion continued for about half an hour, and then Carolyn asked them to write their thoughts. Discussing important social issues with multiple perspectives and viewpoints is an important aspect of critical literacy. Sometimes, Carolyn reported the students do resist this type of reading, discussion, and writing because it does not remind them of what school should look and sound like. To address this discomfort, Carolyn will often remind her students that the GED is a reading test and there are many examples of current events materials on the test.

Carolyn uses many different genres of texts in class—newspapers, speeches, literature, GED preparatory materials, and magazines. Carolyn discussed using Martin Luther King Jr.'s speech in class to analyze the content and the way in which the speech was delivered.

We looked at the MLK [Martin Luther King Jr.] speeches, not just the traditional "I Have a Dream" speech, and we read the lengthy speech that he had written, and the message he was trying to deliver. We analyzed these speeches and talked about how African Americans have advanced our society.

This connects to Carolyn's goal of providing historical role models for her students. In this example she asked her students to analyze the speech, a genre approach to literacy instruction that proceeds from function to form. Angy, an English for Speakers of Other Languages (ESOL) teacher (who we will meet in chapter 12), used the "I Have a Dream" speech to teach her English as a Second Language students. She combined this speech with an analysis of songs. This genre approach to teaching writing is characterized by an emphasis on the purpose, goals, and audience for writing.

Carolyn emphasizes free writing and essay writing in her classroom. In the next excerpt, Carolyn explained to her class why she emphasizes reading and writing in her classroom.

We work on increasing writing scores. That is why we write essays every morning. What happens when you apply to the university with a score of 440 on your writing? They are going to say that is an unacceptable score. Or they will put you in a remedial course…. Knowing how this test is structured, we now can develop a strategy for passing it … right? And, working on our essay writing will move up the test scores…. I use one of my current students as an example. When Donehsa came into the class, she had very low writing scores. But she came to class every day and participated in the writing lessons and her scores moved up by 100 points. She had moved up well into the 500s. It tells us that the technique of writing every day works. At first they were just writing and getting their thoughts on paper, and now they are writing with structure.

It is important to note that Carolyn embeds her explanation of reading and writing in terms of advancing toward the GED test, which is the stated goal of most of her students when they enter her classroom. She uses this common cultural tool as a way to engage students in her method—which, in essence, not only accelerates them toward obtaining their certificate of high school equivalency but also sets up the conditions for critical, democratic thought and action.

In this classroom lesson, Carolyn drew on the successes of a member of their community of practice to demonstrate how her pedagogy has led to the tangible results many of her students are looking for—passing the GED test. Carolyn teaches writing in her classroom through a variety of means. She often writes a prompt on the board and asks her students to write about it when they get to school. For example, she wrote, "What qualities does a good leader possess?" After they have read and discussed a section of the newspaper, Carolyn asks them to share what they wrote about the prompt that was on the board. Her students read their writing. Shawn stated that good leaders are reliable and lead by example. Another student stated that a good leader listens to people. Another student stated that people like leaders they can identify with. As the students are talking, Carolyn writes these ideas on the board. She is making their knowledge an official part of the classroom curriculum. Through sharing in the community of the classroom, the students hear what their peers are discussing and get new ideas they want to add to their writing. When all ideas are exhausted, Carolyn does a mini-lesson on some aspect of the mechanics of writing, such as punctuation, and then gives the students time to revise their writing based on the discussion before handing it in to get feedback from her.

On some days, the class reads the newspaper and discusses an article, and a writing topic emerges from their discussion. Carolyn explained, "We go to a newspaper, because we also try to get them in the habit of writing.... 'What is your view about what is going on in Liberia? What do you think the editor meant when they wrote that?'"

Carolyn encouraged her students to think critically about the author's intention as a writer. She asked them to think about what information was left out and why and how this impacts their lives. She teaches about voting rights within the context of historical movements within the social studies curriculum. Carolyn actively encourages her students to vote and participate in the political process. Carolyn described that her students often feel disconnected from the political process. She stated:

They say that they don't feel like their vote made any difference. But I tend to use the example of the senatorial race that we lost in Missouri. If we had more participation from city voters, she [Jean Carnahan] would have been able to maintain her seat. And they saw that. It is a misconception that the vote does not make a difference. And that is what we are trying to let them know, that this is a misconception. Even for this presidential race coming up, don't let something that happened in the past hold you back from voting.

[Did they go out and register to vote?] Yes, they came in and said that they were ready, they are gearing up for the next presidential, the national election. Initially, they don't think their vote makes a difference. So we go back and look at a historical perspective and study the Civil Rights Act where people lost their lives over the right to participate to struggle to vote. So it is critical. It is not something that should be taken lightly. And all of the restrictions that were placed against blacks because they did not have the right to vote. So not voting is really doing a disfavor to the people who came before us. That's how I see it and that is what I pass along to them. And it gives them a new perspective because no one has sat down and told them this before.

Carolyn also invited a professor of political science to come to the classroom and talk with her students about their rights as voters and participating in the political process. In addition to voting, Carolyn also encourages her students to get involved in politics at the community level. She encourages this by regularly bringing current political events into the classroom. She often brings in newspaper articles that address these topics, and the class will read and discuss the article. She stated:

I bring out ideas during the reading, to the students, ideas they may not have thought of before. There are a lot of different things going on in the reading. Sometimes we are learning life lessons and we are using those types of lessons to help the students in their personal lives.

During this time she sees herself as a facilitator. Carolyn asks her students to read world events politically and critically. In essence she is politicizing her students. In doing this she connects current experiences to a larger historical context, which can be summarized with her statement "In order to know where you are going, you have to know where you come from." Similarly, she provides what Perry, Steele, & Hilliard, (2003) refer to as "counter narratives" about black achievement and success.

This includes correcting misconceptions about history. Carolyn stated, "They think that African American history started with MLK." She readily includes an Afrocentric perspective in her teaching. When studying the conquering of the Americas, she will ask her students, "What part did Africans play in this?" She reminds her students that Africans were sold into slavery by other Africans but they didn't have the concept of slavery as a lifelong enslavement process. She also reminds her students that "through misinformation they have been taught that the entire European system was inherently evil and that is not necessarily the case."

Carolyn encourages participation in the political process inside and outside of the classroom. She encouraged and supported her students to attend the ABC's meetings and participate in the Voices of Adult Literacy United for Education (VALUE) workshops, which focused on building student leadership to organize around literacy education. These actions inside and outside of the community bind the learners together, which adds to the community of the classroom. Carolyn often has students who obtain their certificate of high school equivalency come back to the class to share their story with the rest of the class.

In terms of her own activism, Carolyn is a member of the LSJTRG, a voluntary professional development group, and was president of the Opportunities for Women Club. With a master's degree in political science, Carolyn readily brings political issues and current events from around the world into her classroom teaching. Often this comes in during her "current events" time in the morning or during the social studies part of her day. One of her goals is to make the political process and the political workings of the system transparent for her students. On any given day, her class may engage in a discussion about funding issues in the school district, gay marriage, federal policies, or the war in Iraq. In this way, Carolyn is steadily supporting her students as they cross the boundaries of their adult education classroom and the communities in which they live.

5

Reflexive Teaching

SARA BRAMER

I am just as much of a learner as they are. — Sara Bramer, Interview

Sara is a European American woman in her mid-thirties who grew up in rural Missouri. Her bachelor's degree is in human environmental planning with a minor in family studies. She is married and has two children: one adopted child who is African American, and another, biological child who is European American. She worked as the Even Start program coordinator before working as an adult education teacher. She has been teaching in adult education for ten years. She teaches in a family literacy program where most of her students are reading between a sixth and a tenth grade reading level. She described her role as an adult education teacher: "my piece is to help adults increase their literacy level so they can hopefully reduce or stop the dropout rate of younger children and to increase the literacy levels at home so children are more successful in school."

Sara's classroom is located in an old, privately owned house that was rented and turned into an educational institution that included various classes such as Head Start and Even Start. Sara consistently strives for a classroom environment that is responsive to students' physical as well as intellectual needs. This manifests itself in the organization of the classroom, the bulletin boards, and the full bookshelves. Sara and her family literacy colleagues strive for high quality even though in the last ten years they were moved four times by the cooperating school district in which they were located for various reasons, including the school district using the building for other purposes. When adult education sites are forced to relocate, coordinators and sometimes staff are forced to look for a new location that will meet the realities of their participants' needs (e.g., transportation and early childhood education). Nonetheless, the family literacy center where Sara's adult education class is located was recognized with an award for being one of the best Even Start programs in the state by the Missouri Family Literacy Initiative.

Sara has a retention rate of 75 percent. Sara averages forty students per year with twelve or more hours. Approximately two students from her class earn a GED each year. Her greatest level of impact, according to the Tests of Adult Basic Education (TABE) scores, is at level 2: 67 percent of her students increased to a level 3 during the 2002–2003 academic year.

Upon entering Sara's classroom, there is a long table in the center of the classroom and approximately ten chairs around the table. There are desks and chairs scattered around the room. Two big windows bring light into the room. Under the windows are two long bookshelves full of high-quality literature—adult, children's, and adolescent. There are also magazines, newspapers, and dictionaries on the bookshelves. Supplies are kept in closets that have doors decorated with examples of student work. Sara's desk is located in an adjoining room. While the students are in the classroom, Sara takes a seat like the rest of the students or is walking around working with students. Sara described meeting with the students mainly one-on-one versus in small groups because they attend so many different groups throughout the week as a part of the family literacy program. She describes that she has a "team" of people she works with at the family literacy sites—which was quite unlike the other teachers in the book, who were working in relative isolation. She uses a combination of traditional materials (GED preparation materials, workbooks, and nontraditional materials such as children's literature, African American literature, poems, and newspapers).

As a member of a voluntary professional development group called Literacy for Social Justice Teacher Research Group (LSJTRG), Sara participated in a reading and discussion group around the book *No Disrespect* written by Sister Souljah (1996). Carolyn Fuller (who we met in chapter 4) regularly used this book in her classroom, and she shared this with the members of the teacher group who read and discussed the book. During the book discussion, the teachers talked about issues relating to the oppression and agency of black women, including housing conditions, violence, and poverty. Part of the discussion included a discussion of the term "projects" and the history of low-income housing in St. Louis. Sara had learned in this professional development context that the term "project" was ideologically loaded and could be viewed as offensive to African American people. After the discussion, Sara decided she wanted to use the book in her class.

With approximately ten students in class, all African American and all women, Sara introduced *No Disrespect* (1996) and a lively discussion ensued. Before they read the story, they had a discussion about racial positioning, including Sara's position as a European American woman teaching African American students. Sara reflects on her teaching practices,

I'm always very honest with my students. I have always believed that I am just as much of a learner as they are. And I told them that I knew very little about the St. Louis projects—when they were established and where they were located. And, so the discussion just took off from there. We talked about the word "project," and I asked them, "Why do you think they chose that name [for the projects]?" and they responded, "Why do we get lumped into that?" And they asked questions, and they were answering their own questions.

The discussion with her class lasted close to an hour, and as a result they never started reading the book. Sara explained, "Even though it wasn't part of the plan, it led them to asking for more information the following week, and it fostered more questions. They were happy to see that it was relevant to their lives." This flexibility allowed her students to see they had ownership and choice in the curriculum. Shor (1980) writes, "Teachers need to come to class with an agenda, but must be ready for anything, committed to letting go when the discussion is searching for an organic form" (p. 101). They did read from the text the following week, and students located and learned vocabulary words that were unfamiliar to them.

Before we even began the reading, I told them, "Please don't be scared by a word that you choose; please feel comfortable in having a voice here, to feel safe here, that we are not here to intimidate someone or to belittle someone, we are here to learn together." And I was very honest that there were some words in the reading that were new to me. I think that helps students feel comfortable that I am not sitting there trying to teach only. She is learning as well as I am. We are learning together as a team, as a family.

This captures how Sara teaches literacy within a critical framework. This approach has emerged over time and with experience in the classroom. When Sara first started teaching, her colleagues didn't think she would last very long at the site because she was a small European American woman with blonde hair and blue eyes who grew up in rural Missouri and spoke with a slight Southern dialect, whereas all of her students were African American and grew up in the city. Her colleagues said about her, "They will push her over in a second and she'll be scared to death and leave." But Sara didn't leave. Instead, she actively tried to learn about African American culture on her own and from her students. However, when she started to integrate aspects of African American history and culture into the curriculum, she received messages that she was overstepping her boundaries as a European American woman. She stated:

I have tried to bring in information with regard to African American history and it became a sore spot, not with students, but with fellow staff members who said that I am really not in a position to talk about that because I've never experienced that. It was like I had to prove myself.

These cautionary comments forced Sara to take on a model of following her students' lead, learning from her students, and setting up classroom conditions in which "we can educate each other."

Sara recounts the struggle she had as a European American woman trying to authentically initiate racial dialogues with her students. Sara recalled:

I've had situations where I think students are sometimes uncomfortable talking about race because I am a white teacher and they are predominately African American. But I tell them that I am there to interact and learn and "that I am not here to judge you and I hope that you're not here to judge me and that we can learn from each other and grow from that."

Additionally, Sara explained the importance of developing a teaching stance where she made it obvious that "she wasn't trying to be the oppressor by bringing in information about African American history and culture. I was not stating that the information I had was the ultimate truth."

Sara learned a number of ways to authentically position herself as a European American woman who grew up in the rural United States. Dialogue became a constant thread of her classroom where she could open up with her students and learn from them so she might herself grow as a person and as their teacher and make their voices heard in the room. Sara discussed "reading" her students' "facial expressions, body language, and the comments they make" to help her to understand how they are feeling in her classroom. Sara stated, "I use quite a bit of open-ended questions in the classroom." These open-ended questions are questions that do not have one answer and cannot be answered with a "yes" or "no." Rather, they are questions that foster authentic dialogue among participants in the educational process. In Sara's words, "I think that is how we become allies together and make some progress for whatever that progress will be." Sara stated:

I have always been very open to gaining information. I do not ever want to come across when I'm trying to teach a subject of someone else's culture to be all-knowing and like I researched it and know all there is to know. Because I do not. I do not live in that culture. I will not ever live in that culture because of my own personal skin coloring and where I grew up ... but that does not mean that I cannot be open to what they have to offer and learn something new and try something new, and I think that is what has kept me alive in the population here.

Over time, Sara has become more of an insider in her school and with her students. During the interview, she even integrated aspects of African American Language (AAL) at the level of vocabulary into her speech. Sara consistently and repetitively positioned herself as she talked about her role as a teacher.

She refers to the program she works with as "deeply literature based." She has seen that her students are engaged and motivated to read books that are culturally relevant to them. As a result, she chooses materials written by African American authors to facilitate her students' development as readers, writers, and thinkers. She notices that her students seem to connect intellectually and emotionally with the authors. For example, she has used the books *Rites of Passage* (Wright, 1995); *I Know Why the Caged Bird Sings* (Angelou, 1983); *No Disrespect* (Souljah, 1996); *Having Our Say: The Delany Sisters' First 100 Years* (Delany, Delany, & Hearth, 1994); and *Man with No Name* (Amos, 1994). However, Sara recognized the complexity of culturally relevant materials, that is, just because a book is written by an African American author and chronicles the lives of African American people does not mean that it is going to be relevant to the lives of the students in her classroom. Indeed, her students did not relate to the book *Man with No Name*. As she stated:

I thought [the book] would be an inspirational and motivational kind of book for students, especially those who have been here a while and kind of lose focus and track of their whole goal. And privately or individually it is a good read for them, but reading it aloud has not done as well [for them].

Sara explained that when she has students who keep hitting certain roadblocks—in either their personal or academic lives—she will say to them, "I want you to take a look at what he [Wally Amos] has to say."

While Sara chooses books that she thinks will resonate with their lives, either culturally or in terms of the message in the book, she recognized when books are not engaging for her students because she listens to her students' feedback and has the flexibility to modify her plans. She shares the authority of choosing books with her students by providing book talks on a range of books and inviting them to choose which book they would like to read. Reading from these books generally involves round-robin reading and then discussion of the passages in the book. As a class, they will pull vocabulary from the literature, and their spelling tests come from the words that the students choose. Sara wants her students to become "active readers who highlight, ask questions and write their ideas in the margins" as they are reading. Since most of her students seem to be in the same reading range, she does not have to find books that are at multiple levels. She often uses materials that are written at a lower level but are high interest, including books that would traditionally be considered young adolescents' books. Sara noted that using relevant literature helps to build community in her classroom as students are more willing to talk with each other about their experiences and make connections to the literature.

Depending on her purpose and goal for the reading, Sara will read aloud, the students will participate in a round-robin type of reading, or they will read silently. A discussion of the literature generally follows each of the readings. She describes why her students love to hear her read aloud: "no one has ever dramatized the spoken word before.... They are just amazed at how I change my voice for a man and a woman and get into the character and how it's alive, and that is pure joy." Aside from creating motivation for experiencing literature, Sara is modeling fluency and sociodrama with her students.

Sara chose *Rites of Passage* by Richard Wright (1995), which is an adolescent book but has content that many of her students can relate to from their own life experiences.

The book that went over with the best response was by an African American author. It was Rites of Passage *by Richard Wright. I did not tell them right off the bat that I found this [book] in the section for middle schoolers because I was afraid they would say, "I am too old to read middle school books." I waited until I got folks hooked into the book and the storyline and they begged every day, "Are we going to read the book today?" We took vocabulary out of the book. And I played all kinds of games with vocabulary and print structures from the book. We talked about the dialect in the book. The students found the dialect difficult to read even though they talked the words everyday. And they were sort of amazed after I did tell them that this was found in the middle school section in the library. They were surprised that it would be that thrilling of a book and that risqué for that age group. And they wanted to go read more. The book was hard enough to challenge them with their vocabulary and length, but yet still be of interest and relevant to their adult lives.*

Sara emphasized the importance of her students reading literature written by authors of their own racial and ethnic group. She also emphasized the importance of explicit strategy instruction while teaching literacy within a meaningful context. She discussed integrating vocabulary instruction into the literature discussion. She also talked about using children's literature with her adult students because they have a sense of purpose as they read the books because most of them want to go home and read with their children. Additionally, she chose literature that contains social issues that are important for the adults in her classroom. Other adult education teachers express reluctance about using children's literature in their adult education classrooms because they were afraid that it would be demeaning to their students. Sara explained how she used the children's literature in a way that supported her adults as readers and also supported them in their desire to read more with their own children.

A lot of times, even when I have adults without children or their children are much older than the children we serve (as a part of the family literacy program), I talk about how they have children in their life someway. And if someone comes to visit and has a child, it is helpful to have some books available which can help calm the child down, give some sort of entertainment for that child. I found that [adult] students are really amazed at the artwork and illustrations within the book itself, especially the students who are interested in graphic arts. I don't necessarily always choose very low-level books. There are some children's books with pretty big vocabulary. If they are going to be talking with other children, they need to understand what the book is about.

Sara explained that there are several different ways she might use children's literature in her classroom. If a socially sensitive issue comes up in the classroom discussion (e.g., death, drugs, gangs, and homelessness), then she may choose a few pieces of children's literature to explore the topic with her group. This allows them to "rehearse" how they might have a conversation with their children at home, or, as Sara stated, "It helps parents have an easier transition to talk about those issues with their child." Sara noted that her students are often very interested in graphic design and/or artwork, so they are consistently amazed with the artwork in children's literature. Sara models how to read aloud with her class, and then they practice. They enjoy this, Sara explained, because "they have some reason to use that later on in their daily lives." The adults like this type of real-life connection. On some days, she will bring in a stack of children's literature and the adults will choose a book they think might be a good fit for their child. They will read it silently to familiarize themselves with the content, then practice reading it aloud to the class to get feedback and talk about the book. As a way of responding to what they read, Sara may facilitate a discussion or she may have her students draw a picture to respond to what they thought the author was trying to communicate. Sara valued the role of discussion and multiple perspectives.

It is OK to disagree with one another. I appreciate and I like that there are different sides that are seen by students, and if they do not see the different sides, I try to be that other side to broaden how to look at a passage of writing. It helps them to grow socially.

Sara also recognized the importance of building a safe learning community for adults, especially when talking about socially sensitive issues. She stated:

I want this to be a safe learning space for them to hear points of view that they have never thought about before. No one has ever challenged their point of view. I want them to be a little more accepting of differences around them.

Another way of connecting with her students' lives is by asking them to bring their family histories into the classroom. Sara described how, in the past, she used to use the book *Having Our Say: The Delaney Sisters' First 100 Years* (Delany et al., 1994) as a way into a discussion of family histories. Her class would conduct genealogical research on their own family history. The problem, Sara pointed out, was that oftentimes their family histories were painful or had aspects that they did not feel like sharing in class. Or, there was a case where someone had shared something in class and it was talked about outside of class, which was a breach of confidentiality for the student.

Sara also encourages the learners in her classroom to learn from each other and redistribute the authority of who is traditionally defined as teacher and as learner. She stated, "They are learning from each other, and I think that is the most important key and this is what keeps them interested in their own personal learning." Similarly, Sara deliberately positions the adults in her classrooms as teachers and leaders.

Sara is very conscious of her students' lives outside the classroom. She recognizes the struggles that her students go through in their history with schooling and to come back to school. Sara talked about the myriad of reasons why her students dropped out—or were pushed out of schools. She stated, "First and foremost, this is a district that has not recognized teen pregnancy. Students have told me that counselors or teachers give them guidance to '[drop out of school] and get your GED. It's easy.' They strongly encourage them to drop out." While Sara acknowledges that men and women both have obstacles to attending adult education programs, she notes, however, that women have the added issues of lack of family support, child care needs, and multiple responsibilities to many different family members. Further, family members may feel intimidated by a woman wanting to become more literate and independent. Child care issues often prevent women from attending programs. Aside from these issues are those of disabilities, race, poverty, sexual harassment, and health issues—any one of which makes it difficult for many women to attend and persist in adult literacy classes (Greenburg, 2004; Horsman, 2000). On top of all of the obstacles to attending GED classes is what Sara called a "fear to succeed and a fear of failure." That is, there are students who are ready to take and pass the GED test but who do not go.

Sara discussed the many ways in which her program extends support to students trying to get their GED: assisting with the application fees to take the GED, providing child care while they are taking the GED, establishing a scholarship program, providing transportation for them to get to the GED site, and arranging for a small group of students to take the test together so they have a support system. They have even called individuals the morning of the test to make sure they are awake. Sara stated, "If a person is truly ready inside as well as academically, they will go [to take the test]." While Sara advocated for all of these supports, she acknowledged that there was a fine line between support and dependence, and she wanted to create a self-extending system in which the agency the person exhibited in the adult education program (by coming to class, engaging in discussions, learning the academic materials, etc.) is extended into his or her life beyond the classroom. As a result, education can be personally and socially transforming.

I would say that they become more proactive in their lives. We see that inter-actions with the schools and with their children increase once they have been in this program, or, they may go to the physician for themselves or for their children. They go and ask the doctors questions they want to ask. They may ask for a brochure on a topic to learn more. They may ask for a support person to go with them which they never would have thought they could do. They become more active in their learning.

Sara's humility about her knowledge and her appreciation for the complexity of understanding a situation based on many different points of view challenge her students' assumptions about knowledge, truth, and experts. Students start to see knowledge as constructed rather than received. On coming to see how knowledge is constructed, Belenky, Clinchy, Goldberger, and Tarule (1986) wrote, "It is in the process of sorting out the pieces of the self and of searching for a unique and authentic voice that women come to the basic insights of constructivist thought: All knowledge is constructed, and the knower is an intimate part of the known" (p. 137). Indeed, once the adult learners in Sara's classroom learn they can question truth and knowledge, they begin to do so in all aspects of their lives—at the school, at home, and when they visit their doctor's office. As Belenky et al. (1986) wrote, "Once a woman has a voice, she wants it to be heard" (p. 146).

Like many of the teachers in this book, Sara uses many different types of texts in her classroom. She incorporates magazines, newspapers, movies, poetry, and songs. She will generally bring in materials that she thinks will speak to her students' lives. They especially like incorporating songs because music is such an important part of African American culture. They are often surprised when Sara points out that songs are poetry set to music. She stated, "They get so excited about it because they see a draw to their real life and a love that they didn't realize that were creating poems [when they write or listen to music]."

Sara admitted that she is much stronger at teaching reading than at teaching writing. She attributes this to the fact that she does not enjoy writing or see herself as a writer, and so she struggles to teach writing. However, when she did talk about writing, she emphasized the importance of her students getting their ideas down on paper and then teaching mechanics, spelling, and grammar within the context of a purposeful piece of writing. Sara emphasized, "These are adults. They have lived their lives, and they have information to share from their experiences." These experiences, Sara noted, can be the basis for students' development as writers.

The design of Sara's writing instruction has a twofold purpose. She aims to accelerate her students as writers and facilitate and encourage students to use their voices. She described how she used children's poetry in her adult education classroom. She integrated many different types of writing into her classroom, including poetry.

I use a lot more of the children's poetry for adults than I do heavy-duty adult poetry, or it is poetry that is related to relationships. Or, I choose poetry that is by certain types of authors to capture their interests. Poetry is often difficult for them. If they did not have a great situation in school, [then] I want them to see that it can be a joyful [experience] and you can learn some valuable lessons from it. We pick it apart and I ask, are there words you don't understand? What images is the poet trying to draw with his or her words? I might have students draw pictures of what they think the poet is creating with words.

Sara reminds her students that "there is some poetry on the GED test." In addition, Sara described how poetry enables her students to discover words and sounds and rhythms of language; it invites her students to appreciate the imagery of language, and it challenges learners to see themselves and their worlds in new ways (Kazemek & Rigg, 1986; Wood Ray, 2002). Many of these strategies can be used to make reading-writing connections. Sara explains to her students how many writers intend for their work to be heard and performed through linking poetry and music. Sara will ask learners in class to bring in their favorite song and share it with the class. This allows learners to share personal, and sometimes generational and cultural, connections with each other—establishing links and connections between learners. Sharing songs—whether they are memorized or written down—provides a valuable literacy opportunity for adult learners.

Sara also used the newspaper as a writing prompt but focused on the political cartoon or comic sections of the paper. Political cartoons, as Sara noted, are also on the GED test. She explained her process of working with comics:

> I would look at different newspapers and I would cut some of the comics out of the paper—comics that are not totally unfamiliar to the student. Then I would bleep out a frame of the cartoon, whatever was said. If I have a large enough of a group, I would break the large group into small groups and give each group a different comic strip. Before we would start, I would use an example on the board. Here is the beginning of the comic strip, here are some keywords, this is the beginning of the comic, [here are] transitional words, here are some conclusion types of words. They would then have to come up with the beginning, or the middle, or the ending of the comic. They would write their own comic words for those characters. This works well even for individuals who have very little ability to read.

In Sara's class, writing can be used as a tool for social activism. She observed that her students are most engaged as writers when they have an authentic purpose and a goal for their writing. Sara explained a time when her students used their writing to change the conditions at their center. Her class had just finished a unit focused on health and nutrition. The adults in Sara's class started to make connections between what they were learning during the unit and the quality of the food they and their children were being fed for lunch at the center. They noticed and documented the high-fat, high-sodium, processed foods that they were offered for lunch. After conducting research on the menu at the center and talking with people who worked in food service at the center, the adults drafted a petition that asked for healthier meals for their children and circulated it to the staff and adults enrolled in the program. They presented the petition to the staff, and their demands were met. Healthier meals began to be served at the center. During this process, Sara's students had many opportunities to practice writing by taking notes on the food being served, writing down the responses of the food-service personnel, and writing and revising a letter and petition.

Sara also discussed another innovative way of teaching her students writing—through the analysis of children's writing. She explained this process:

I ask them to bring in their children's writing. Then I break them into small groups, and in those small groups I ask them to talk about the child's writing, what it looks like, what it is saying to them, what kind of questions could you ask about the writing, and so on. Then I would bring them back as a large group and have them share what they learned in their small groups. These are adults, and they have information that they can share from their experiences. I am facilitating. I am not the one with the answers. They are learning from each other. This keeps them interested in their own personal learning.... Do they have writing from their own childhood? They can share this writing with the group, show them what it looks like, and see if others get the idea of what they were trying to say, and how they were taught as a writer. They might ask each other, what would you do differently with your child?

Sara explained that she designed much of her teaching to be responsive to her students' lives. She makes sure that she communicates to her students that "their writing is valued." They have time to free write and to write in dialogue journals, where they communicate back and forth with another peer in class and use writing as their form of expression. She emphasized that the main point of these writing exercises was to communicate—to get their ideas down on paper—and then they could attend to spelling, grammar, and punctuation when they revised the writing. She tells her students, "We are trying to connect what is in your head with what you write on the paper."

Sara believes that teaching is a form of social action. She describes how her students become more proactive in their own lives—and she thinks that is part of the purpose of adult education. Part of social change, Sara believes, is when her students leave her classroom with a positive experience with a European American teacher. She stated, "They may have a whole different view of white teachers, and that is where I contribute to social change." Reflecting on her role as an adult education teacher, Sara stated,

I listen a great deal to see what they are interested in, what they are talking about, and try to make connections to what is real to them, and I think that if we are going to be revolutionary, that is what it might look like. I don't know if all adult education teachers do this.

Sara is a member of the LSJTRG, actively seeks out professional development experiences for herself, and demonstrates her commitment to ongoing learning and professional development.

6

Cultivating Voice

VIVIAN JETT

Literacy is not what I teach, but what they do and what they learn and how they go about changing things. — **Vivian Jett, Interview**

An African American woman in her sixties, Vivian Jett has been an adult education teacher since 1994. Vivian holds a bachelor's degree in business administration. Vivian grew up, lived, went to school, and now teaches in St. Louis. Vivian described being a student who participated in the court-ordered desegregation program that was intradistrict. She was bussed to an all-white school also in the city and went to school with all white children. Before becoming an adult education teacher, Vivian supervised in a personnel office as a labor relations and employee development specialist. In this role she trained employees for the federal government. She was going to volunteer to be a literacy tutor but was encouraged to apply for a teaching position. Vivian was hesitant to apply for the teaching job because of her lack of experience as a formal educator. However, it was pointed out that she had been teaching employees in the federal government for many years. She agreed and applied for the job. Her real start with teaching, Vivian explained, was forty years ago when she taught her nieces and nephews to read. She would work with her nieces and nephews, and before she knew it, more and more kids from the neighborhood would show up. "That is really how I initially learned to teach people to read."

Vivian does not consider herself an activist but is heavily involved in volunteerism in her community. She started her community work when she was fourteen years old when her brother was the director of the YMCA. She then moved into teaching Sunday school and directing a softball league and a social club for girls. She also helped to build homes in St. Louis for low-income families and did a "number of things in the community that I thought would make it better for the community." She stated,

I think you have to give something back to the community. I was very fortu-nate when I went to school. I went on scholarships and grants, and the com-munity supported me.... I was able to go to college because the community supported me, and I think it is important to be active in the community and to give something back.

Vivian's background is in labor relations and employment training. She currently teaches adult education classes at Redevelop-ment Opportunities for Women, a resource center for women, many of whom are in shelters or transitional housing. The classes are located in an unmarked office building in midtown close to small offices and across the street from a large stockbroker's office. There are multiple rooms used for adult education: a resource and library room, a room used for early childhood education and for Parent and Child Together (PACT) time, a small room used for testing or for one-on-one tutoring, and a central classroom. The main classroom has a big table in the center of the room and smaller tables around the room. The room is generally cramped for space because of its size and the number of students and tutors in the room. On the walls, there is a blackboard, motivational signs and posters, post-ers with famous African American men and women, family literacy signs, and pamphlets and flyers announcing upcoming events. On any given day, one could walk into Vivian's classroom and find her at the blackboard teaching a whole-group lesson, sharing ideas and resources with a tutor, or sitting next to a student and guiding his or her learning.

The majority of Vivian's students are women who are home-less. It is important to understand the context of homelessness to understand the way in which Vivian accelerates her students as read-ers and writers and does so within a critical framework. The women in Vivian's program have become homeless (without a permanent shelter) for many reasons. Some of them have been homeless for a few days, and others for years. Fifty-seven percent of the home-less population consists of family members who have become home-less after fleeing from an abusive relationship. Other people become homeless when someone loses a job and a family can't pay their rent or mortgage. African Americans are disproportionately represented among the homeless. However, homelessness affects all classes, ethnicities, and cultures, and is clearly linked to poverty (Nunez & Fox, 1999). People who are homeless deal with tremendous stressors such as fulfilling the immediate needs of food, shelter, and safety. As a result, literacy education often moves down the list of priorities for people who do not have a permanent shelter (Trumpener, 1997). However, the women in Vivian's program have made a choice to attend adult education classes in conjunction with attending to other aspects of their lives.

Most of Vivian's students are reading between a fourth and ninth grade level. She also has a high number of students who enter between the second and fourth grade reading levels. All of the people who come into her class, Vivian notes, "are looking for a GED." On average, four of Vivian's students obtain their GED each year. Level 4 was her highest level of impact because 45 percent of her students moved to a level 5 during the 2002–2003 academic year. Vivian has a 72 percent retention rate in her class.

The program where Vivian teaches is a family literacy program that includes four components: adult literacy or GED classes, early childhood education, parenting classes, and PACT time. Vivian is aware of the many reasons why the students in her class dropped out of school: they had problems in school, were the victims of domestic violence, had teachers who were racist, were on drugs, had parents who did not emphasize attending school, or acted out as bullies and were not able to go back to school. Vivian stated that "their experiences in school were not good, and they got to a certain point and they knew that they were not where they wanted to be. They felt inferior and they dropped out."

Vivian expresses her care for her students through establishing high expectations and attending to the relationships that are an inherent part of the learning process. Vivian stated, "My students forget I am the teacher and open up with me." Her relationships with her students who come from the same city as the one in which she grew up are fundamentally rooted in this sense of shared positionality. Maher and Thompson Tetreault (1994) define positionality as "locating the self in relation to others within social structures, such as the classroom that re-create and mediate those relationships" (p. 202). Put another way, Collins (1998) writes, "Black women intellectuals use their insider-within location in building effective coalitions and stimulating dialogue with others who are similarly located" (p. 38).

Vivian also holds high expectations for her students by expecting that her students will obey the rules of the classroom. One such rule is no cursing. Vivian tells her students, "I come from the same neighborhood as you do. You do not want to curse at me because I have the same flash points as you." Vivian reflects on relating with her students and says, "It's important for students to know I've seen and been through a lot. It helps them know that I can relate to them." These examples provide insight into Vivian's role as a "community teacher" (Boyle-Baise, 2005; Murrell, 2001). Community teachers are teachers who are familiar with the working knowledge and cultural background and resources of the communities from which their students come. Such teachers actively work to use community resources as part of the curriculum design of their classrooms.

Vivian is very cognizant of women-centered issues such as domestic violence, caring for children, and homelessness. She wants her students to be safe in the community of her classroom. To a certain extent, she includes these social issues in her classroom curriculum. However, she is more focused on academics than on critical social issues. This is, in part, because there are social workers onsite who can help her students to deal with these issues.

"I always try to change them to understand that literacy is not what I teach but literacy is what they do and what they learn and how they go about changing things," Vivian explained. Oftentimes, students expect a traditional model of literacy teaching when they enter the classroom. "I think you have to change the students' attitudes towards literacy itself," Vivian stated. To change their expectations of literacy instruction and also support their continued success in the adult education classroom, Vivian designs a curriculum that meets the personal and cultural needs of her students. One student, Vivian recounts, came into the classroom and could not get electricity in her new apartment because she owed the electric company a large sum of money. She had moved to a different state and never had the electricity turned off. When she returned to St. Louis, the electric company would not turn on her electricity until she paid the back amount.

Vivian explained, "I told the student that she needed to write the company a letter. She also went to Legal Aid and got a lawyer. The lawyer took the case, and the electric company resolved the issue by asking for documentation that she had been living in another state." The issue was resolved, and the person got her electricity turned on. "I tell them, if you have a problem, you have to have a paper trail and you have to be literate and this means you have to talk and write and understand what is going on." Vivian sees this happen often with electric bills and cell phone bills.

They have to learn to live within the community and be literate in terms of getting jobs but also know how companies are trying to get money from them. Reading and writing is not just for getting a GED. A GED is opening doors, and you have to learn these things to open doors and move on.

In terms of the purpose of adult education, Vivian stated,

They have a lot of expectations from their GED. Then they get their GED and they don't know what to do next. So I try to instill in them that the GED is opening some doors. You have to figure out which door you will go through. Just having a GED does not make a big difference in terms of money.

This statement reflects her taking the authority granted on her as a teacher to liberate her students from the false consciousness associated with the GED mystique—that is, the direct relationship between the GED and upward social mobility (e.g., Boesel, 1998). Indeed, studies have demonstrated that a GED provides little to no economic benefits for those learners who have a low skill set (Tyler, Murnane, & Willett, 2000).

I think adult education for those students is teaching them that they have to determine what is their most important goal and get their priorities in order. The younger students are worried about boyfriends and housing, but I try to teach them that their education is their first priority. They have to be independent and once they get their education, they can start to work on other problems. If they resolve the education problem, the shelters will work with them. What I am trying to impart to the students is education is important. And I have a couple of students who dropped out of school and then got their GEDs before their class graduated from high school. You can do that with the sixteen and seventeen year olds. I have one young lady who came back and told me that she said to her friend who was a senior, "The only thing I am missing is the senior prom because I got my GED and I am going to college." She is still in the shelter, and she is a very bright young lady. We try to teach them that they can move on and they can structure their own lives. I guess the biggest issue is that they think it is someone else's fault, but when you get to a certain age you have to realize that it does not matter whose fault it was—it is your problem now. And we teach them to solve their problem, and the first decision is adult education or getting some kind of education.

Vivian strives to teach her students to value themselves so that others in various spheres of their lives (social, familial, religious, and economic) will also value them. However, she stresses as a black woman speaking to black women that when they are in her classroom, "their education is the first thing."

Vivian creates a community of learners that recognizes the competing demands that women have on their time—battling addictions (e.g., drug, alcohol, and gambling), keeping their family together, making sure their children attend school, continuing to pursue their own education, looking for work, and looking for housing, to name just a few. Together, this creates a collective knowledge based on the learners' experiences in the political economy and Vivian's position as a middle-class black professional in the same economy. Such an analysis recognizes the reality of the economy that the majority of jobs available to black women are domestic and service jobs (e.g., Beggs, 1995; Critzer, 1998). Collins (1998) writes,

The employment vulnerability of working class African Americans in the post World War II political economy, the relative employment equality of poor black women and men, and the gender specific patterns of dependence on the informal economy all have substantial implications for U.S. Black women who find themselves among the working poor. (p. 62)

Education, in this analysis, is seen not as an end goal but, as Vivian Jett put it, as "opening doors."

Vivian makes connections with her students personally and culturally. Vivian teaches African American history during African American History Month and does it by making interdisciplinary connections (language arts, social studies, math, and science). During this month, she encourages her students to draw on their strengths outside of school in terms of singing, performing, and preaching, and then works with her students over the course of the month to prepare them for a celebration-performance. This performance marks the culmination of their learning and growth about African American history. At this performance, students will recite speeches or poems they have memorized and will sing or dance to a variety of African music from spirituals to blues to hip-hop. Students will also read from their favorite piece of literature or share something they have written. While she does this during February, she extends what is often referred to as a "holiday approach" to culture because she deepens and extends the analysis, discussion, and interdisciplinary connections between subject areas as students are learning about African American history. Vivian brings African American culture in the form of traditions, discourse patterns, routines, and experiences into the classroom on a regular basis. Vivian described how a conversation might come up in class, and then she would ask her students to go home and find materials to add to their discussion. She described this process:

I will ask them who Condoleezza Rice is and it is their job to go home and find some information about her. The next day, someone will come back with an article and we will read it and discuss it as a class. The last time we talked about her we talked about affirmative action, because even though she is a Republican she talks about how affirmative action helped her to get where she is. We talked about the Supreme Court Justice Clarence Thomas, because for the first time he started to talk about how affirmative action helped him. So that is what we usually do when I see something in the news that is worthy. We will talk about it in class. We talked about [the blues singer] Oliver Sain from St. Louis, and most of the students have never heard of him or how influential he was in St. Louis.

Vivian uses a range of different literacy practices in her classroom. Vivian explained that "there are two systems" of teaching people to read:

One is a holistic system. You teach students to read and then they get the concepts of what they are reading. But I think you have to teach words and the sounds of words because if they cannot understand the meaning of the word, they miss the whole concept of the sentence or the paragraph.

When we asked Vivian how she teaches reading, she stated, "I teach reading working on sounds: learning sound-letter relationships, putting together sounds, and then sounding out the word. When a student misses a word, I spell it for them and have them look at the word. I find that they know the word once they spell the word." When asked if she combines phonics within a meaningful context, she said,

I think so, but I am not as much of a holistic teacher. I think when you read as a group, that is wholistic reading. When a student is reading, and they do not

know a word, or they will pass a word up or say it wrong, they will go two or three lines and realize what the word was and that they need to go back and figure it out. So we do that when they are reading out loud. But when I am reading one-on-one with a student, if they miss a word, I will stop and ask them to reread the whole sentence again. I would rather have them pronounce the word and know how to pronounce it. Then I find that once they know, they are sitting with me one-on-one, they start paying attention to the words. They know that I am going to stop them, so they try to figure out the word. I think they can read a lot of the words but they are being lazy. Sometimes they know it just can't possibly be what they are saying, but they just pronounce the word incorrectly and move on. But if you call them on it, they pay a little more attention to the words. So I guess I use both methods (phonics and whole language).

Vivian goes on to talk about how even her advanced readers will substitute words as they are reading. They "will read over and see a word, so they are reading something that is just not there." Her theorizing about the reasons that her students substitute words as they are reading shows the edge of her thinking about strategy instruction, a point we will return to in the cross-case analysis.

Vivian uses many different literacy materials in her classroom, including workbooks, *Jet* magazines, newspapers, and condensed novels. When she brings in a newspaper article, for example, they will discuss the article in class, and students will read in a round-robin fashion. She always asks for volunteers so her lower level students do not feel put on the spot. She also groups her students into three reading groups. Vivian discussed the use of groups in her room. It was this description that was most illustrative of how she teaches literacy. Vivian explained the grouping for reading instruction in her classroom:

Normally I will have three different reading levels. Students reading eighth grade or higher are in a group and the material in that group can be at any level because basically it is a GED level and they will just read whatever the material is. When I am at the second level, it is usually the sixth and seventh grade. Normally the reading there is at the level of the lowest student. If I have a student who is reading at a sixth grade level, that group will read at the sixth grade level. The last group is third through sixth grade level. With that group, the lowest students are usually reading at the third grade level. If I have a student who is reading lower than that, I will just work with them one-on-one.

Vivian made the point that she makes sure that the reading materials that she uses are at an independent or an instructional level for everyone in the group and that they are not reading frustration-level materials. If, for example, she has a pre-GED group where the lowest student is reading at a fifth grade level, she will make sure that she provides the entire group with fifth grade–level materials. This helps the lowest reader process texts efficiently—in terms of both comprehension and decoding—and allows readers who are at higher levels to practice fluency and comprehension. This acknowledges, tacitly, that individual readers may have more than one zone of proximal development. Vivian also uses DEAR (Drop Everything and Read) time in her classroom to emphasize the importance of silent reading for the adults in her class and also to provide a model for parents to encourage their children to read at home.

Vivian explained that in her two top groups, she may use GED materials in addition to magazines, newspaper articles, and condensed novels. The lower level groups are mainly reading from the reading books or one of the books from the basic adult reading series.

Vivian talked about the various roles she plays as a teacher with each of these groups:

My role is to see that they stay on task in their reading. What I find is that the more reading they do, the more comfortable they get. When I first started the groups, they were pretty uncomfortable. However, after a couple of weeks of working in the groups, they were comfortable with each other. They read aloud and silently. [Do they help each other?] A lot of times, they will stop and correct each other with their reading. I ask students to try to figure out words on their own. If a student is struggling and does not have many independent reading strategies, another student can help them figure out a word.

Just as Vivian strives to make their reading relevant and meaningful to their lives, she does the same with writing. Vivian emphasizes writing for meaningful purposes and for real audiences—and, above all, for the women to express their voice through writing.

Writing instruction was a clear strength for Vivian as a literacy teacher. In her classroom students engage in a variety of writing practices, including essays, responding to readings, free writes, interactive writing with the teacher, and writing in a range of different genres. Vivian clearly realized that her students have a wealth of life experiences to draw on as writers, and she sees her job as pulling those life stories from them and helping them to see the connection between oral and print literacy. Vivian emphasized the importance of getting her students writing and then focusing on grammar and mechanics after they had their ideas down on paper. Vivian explained the dilemma that is often apparent for students who do not perceive themselves to be writers. She stated:

They do not like to write. They have gotten to the point where they like to read but they do not like to write. They do not want to write anything because they think that they do not write well and it is difficult for them to write. They just do not like to write. When I say it is time for writing, I get all kinds of groans. After forty-five minutes, they have three sentences and I say, "You will have to write tomorrow because you did not write today." Once they find out that they will have to write anyway, then they put something down. So I try a lot of times to [assign writings] about things that they like. If you ask them a question about something they do not know, they just will not write. But if you ask the question or give the topic they are interested in, they can talk about it all day. But when you ask them to write about it, the words go away. What I try to teach them is if they can talk about it, they can write about it. Why don't you write what you said? They have a problem transferring the spoken word to the written word.

Like other teachers in our study, Vivian is focused on her students communicating their ideas, rather than on the mechanics of the piece. This notion of idea development is linked to the concept of voice in feminist theory and pedagogy. Voice represents the emerging consciousness of ideas and thoughts. As Maher and Thompson Tetrault (1994) write,

The writing process provided a necessary bridge between the personal language of journals and the issues of feminist theory. Their insistence that students find a personal voice to interpret [their lives] enabled students to make connections that had eluded them before. (p. 95)

This is important because often the voices of women, people of color, and homeless people have been silenced or rejected as part of society as well as within the classroom curriculum (e.g., Lee, 2001; Schaafsma, 1994). In this process of asking for, hearing, and encouraging the use and development of voice, students move from "received" to "constructed knowers" (Belenky, Clinchy, Goldberger, & Tarule, 1986) as they claim their knowledge, their experiences, and their futures. The learners in her classroom become more conscious of their own voice and how this relates to public and collective voices. Macedo (1994) argues that voice is a "human right" (p. 4). Further, he notes that finding one's voice requires struggling with preconceived notions of who is an authority, whose knowledge is valid, and who gets to speak. Vivian creates a classroom climate in which otherwise silenced voices are given the chance to emerge. Vivian discussed the concept of voice in relation to standard English and linguistic variation in her classroom.

They have plenty to talk about. I think the problem is converting their oral language to standard English. I encourage them to write as if they were speaking. Then, they have some writing that you can revise and convert to Standard English. I usually get them to write, just write. I am not as concerned with the nouns and verbs when they write as I am about them writing something that we can read and understand. There was a woman who did not want to write at all, and now she has been in class a year and is getting ready to take her GED. Now when I ask her to write, she says, "Oh, I know how to do that." It is a matter of getting them confident in writing. They start off thinking, "I just do not like writing and I cannot write." And my job is to get them past that, and the only way I can do that is to have them write. The hardest thing is grading because if you grade it as it is written [they wouldn't get a good grade], so then you have to say, "This is a great idea." You have to be careful when you talk with them about writing. I might say, "This is a great idea," or "We need to work on the language skills to get the writing where it needs to be." I also have to be careful when I am grading their writing. I do not give letter grades. I find that if you give a poor grade and give them negative feedback, such as "This is a very poor specimen of writing," they tell you, "I told you, I could not write." Basically this confirms what they already thought about themselves as writers. Instead, I find something positive about what they have written, and then I move from the positive.

While she focused on affirming and promoting student voice, Vivian does not underestimate the extent to which her students need to have control over the codes of power in society. On this, Delpit (1995) writes,

I suggest that students must be taught the codes needed to participate fully in the mainstream of American life, not being forced to attend to hollow, inane, decontextualized subskills, but rather within the context of meaningful communicative endeavors; that they must be allowed the resource of the teacher's expert knowledge, while being helped to acknowledge their "expertness" as well; and that even while students are assisted in learning the culture of power, they must also be helped to learn about the arbitrariness of those codes and about the power relationships they represent. (p. 45)

Generative writing in Vivian's class includes a discussion on a socio-political topic that is important to the students' lives. At the close of the discussion, Vivian asks the students to give her a sentence that summarizes their discussion. Vivian writes the sentence on the board, and asks the students to copy the sentence and then add another sentence to what they have already written. Over time, the students are asked to write more and more independently. Vivian talked about how she assessed her students as writers and, as importantly, how they monitored their own progress.

They keep a writing folder so they can monitor their own progress as writers. They get more comfortable assessing their own writing. One student told me that she shared a piece of her writing from class with her fourteen-year-old daughter, and her daughter said to her, "This is terrible." The woman told her daughter that her teacher thought it was a good piece of writing. The woman's daughter said to her, "Your teacher lied to you. That was terrible." The woman came back to class and told me what her daughter said about her writing. I told the woman that her daughter was probably talking about the grammar and the spelling, not the ideas. I told her, "I'm commenting on the content and the ideas." She has made a great deal of progress as a writer and can talk about this progress.

Like the other teachers, Vivian also noted the importance of making her students feel successful in her classroom. Vivian explained, "I try to put them into a situation in which they can succeed." Vivian explained that the higher level students will work with the students reading at a lower level and that gives them responsibility in the classroom. Other students like to make sure the classroom is clean or quiet. For others, coming to class every day is their position of authority.

I let them assume the responsibilities of the classroom. I let them be the leaders. And when that happens, they all have a better feeling about the class. I try to find a way that everyone can have an important contribution to the classroom, and I think that gives them a sense of authority.

Taking responsibility and leadership in class are types of authority that could lead to an authority based on voice and respect for diverse ways of knowing. As Maher and Thompson Tetrault (1994) write, "Once teachers begin to view their students also as a possessor of authority, the process of knowledge construction changes" (p. 129). Vivian often invites speakers to come in and talk about a current event or a subject that the students think is important. Recently, the class has talked a great deal about the school system because of budget cuts, changes in administration, and the teachers' strike. She said that her students are "generally pretty critical of the city school board." Vivian leaves space for critical social issues in the classroom. However, she is conscious of her role as a member of the class. On this, she stated, "I don't try to tell them what is right or wrong or what they should think." Rather, she brings in newspaper articles. Recently she brought in one that compared St. Louis Public Schools (SLPS) with the surrounding districts, and they reflected on why the SLPS consistently ranks lower than the other districts. She positioned her students as agents when she said, "Most of the parents want the school district to be better for their children because they didn't have a good time with education and they are really trying to do something for their children." This concurs with the findings of a study conducted by Rogers (2004) that demonstrated that when it came to their children's education, adults enrolled in AEL programs were active participants in the educative process.

Vivian does not consider herself a revolutionary in terms of seeking to change social structures or encouraging her students to do the same. She does want her students to be able to "deal with the gas company, the electric company." She stated that she sometimes stays away from discussing social issues in her class because they do have other classes in their family strengths program that deal with social issues. So she spends most of her time on academics. She tries to relate to them personally and to get them to understand the importance of education, but says, "I don't see myself as getting them involved in the community. There is not time to do that consistently." She does, however, want her students to be involved in the community—as she said,

I think they have to understand that they have to take a part and have a voice in what is going on. They need to go to schools to understand what is going on. They need to go to community and neighborhood associations and find out who is building where.

Vivian, like the other exemplary adult education teachers, valued sharing authority and power with the adult learners in her classroom.

7

Designing Relevant and Engaging Instruction

CAROLYN, SARA, AND VIVIAN

Stepping into the classrooms and hearing the practices and beliefs of exemplary educators Carolyn, Sara, and Vivian demonstrates the complexity of teaching for literacy acceleration within a critical framework. As Carolyn, Sara, and Vivian discuss their "wisdom of practice" garnered from years spent in the adult education classroom, we are reminded of the importance of context in shaping adult literacy education. In the context of recent debates about the professionalization of adult education (Sabatini, Ginsburg, & Russell, 2006; Smith, 2006), it is important to note that neither Carolyn, nor Sara, nor Vivian was professionally educated as a teacher. Carolyn had worked as a parole officer and for the FBI, Vivian as a trainer of employees for a business, and Sara as a child care provider. They bring diverse backgrounds and work-life experiences with them into the classroom, which impacts what they are positioned to know, how they see their students, and how their students see them as educators, adults, and women.

Sara and Vivian both teach in family literacy programs. Vivian teaches at the Redevelopment Opportunities for Women (ROW), a service organization. Women who attend adult education classes at the site also attend a number of other classes ranging in topics from life skills to parenting. To a certain extent, this frees Vivian's time to focus on academics. Vivian also knows that many of her students will not be in her classroom for any length of time, which makes it difficult to follow an open-ended inquiry around critical social issues from day to day. It also demands that Vivian keep a certain amount of professional distance (perhaps more so than other adult education teachers) between her and her students because her student population is so transient. Consequently, following Cervero and Wilson's (1994) notion of the adult education teacher as a "broker," Vivian serves as what we would call an "academic broker." That is, she focuses primarily on literacy acceleration and academics because she knows that her students are getting what Carolyn refers to as "life lessons" in other parts of their program at ROW. Although both Sara and Vivian work in family literacy programs, Sara's students tend to be more long term because they are in more stable housing. Vivian's students are in either shelters or transitional housing. As a result, Sara can build on an ongoing thread of inquiry that focuses on critical social issues in her classroom. Carolyn's class is housed in a full-service community center, but her students may or may not utilize the other services located at the community center. Carolyn focuses on teaching her students "life lessons" and doing so while teaching for literacy acceleration. It is important to emphasize that the context of the classroom is shaped by the geographic location, the students, the teacher (and the histories of participation they bring with them into the classroom), the texts, and the instructional contexts, which complicates what "relevant" and "engaging" instruction might look and sound like to adult education students.

Carolyn, Sara, and Vivian all practice culturally responsive teaching, which validates learners' life experiences, attends to the whole person (employee, parent, learner, and community member), and uses the vast cultural resources of the communities as they design curricula. They all noted that relevance and engagement are the cornerstones of setting up the conditions for literacy acceleration within a critical framework. Engagement is always socially constructed from interactions, relationships, materials, and interactions. In other words, while sociopolitical topics may provide interest and engagement, this engagement needs to be sustained with reading strategies for problem solving and comprehending texts. In a discussion about the importance of engaging students in their classes, Carolyn and Vivian talked about a method called "hook and hold." Carolyn explained, "You hook the students when they come in and then you hold them by designing a curriculum that engages them."

Students need to be engaged in the texts they are reading and in their experiences before they can accelerate. Much has been written on designing culturally relevant curricula (Ladson-Billings, 1995, 2001; Moll & Gonzalez, 1994; Moses, Cobb, & Cobb, 2002; Perry, Steele, & Hilliard, 2003; Richardson, 2003). We know much less about *how* culturally relevant instruction leads to student engagement and achievement. Carolyn and Sara suggested that when students are engaged in curricular materials and lessons where they can see and hear themselves and others like them as well as think about issues, themes, and narratives that relate to their experiences, a positive emotional energy is constructed alongside the cognitive context.

According to Ladson-Billings (1994), culturally relevant instruction is instruction "that empowers students intellectually, socially, emotionally, and politically by using cultural referents to impart knowledge, skills, and attitudes" (p. 18). Culturally relevant instruction for African American students would include recognizing the historical legacy of language, literacy, and literary traditions that inform current cultural traditions. Instruction might include Afrocentric topics, contrastive rhetoric and discourse analysis, uplifting themes, narratives and accomplishments of African American people, and incorporation of African American Language (Morgan, 2002; Smitherman, 1977) into classroom literacy lessons (Perry et al., 2003). Culturally relevant instruction was used as a starting point for making connections between accelerative and critical frameworks because students need to see themselves in the texts they are reading and writing.

Carolyn and Sara share a definition of culturally relevant instruction that includes the importance of students seeing themselves in texts and curricula systematically representing the history of achievement, accomplishment, intelligence, and culture that people of color and women bring to their educational experiences. Their cases provide us an opportunity to think more deeply about the complexity of literacy learning that is both personally and culturally relevant. Indeed, one can imagine the tension between trying to use historically and contemporary relevant materials (e.g., the abolition of slavery, civil rights, and the African Diaspora) that may not be personally engaging, and using personally engaging materials that may not have cultural significance (e.g., cars, jobs, and shopping). Oftentimes, good-intentioned European American teachers will describe their dismay when their African American students are not interested in a lesson they thought was culturally relevant. When they describe their lessons, it turns out that the lessons they thought were "culturally relevant" turned out to have a sole focus on slavery. This focus assumes that African American culture can be reduced to slavery rather than the enduring themes, narratives, and contributions African American people have made to this society. This distinction between levels of engagement is described in the research literature as engagement that is either situational or personal (Hidi & Harackiewicz, 2000). Situational engagement is interest in an object, event, or person that is most likely fleeting. On the other hand, personal engagement is an enduring quality or set of interests which transfers for people across contexts. The goal of (critical) literacy teachers is to provide a scaffold that supports turning situational interests into personal interests which will be associated by long-term motivation and engagement with the issue. This demands that the teacher knows (1) herself and what she is positioned to know based on her background experiences, (2) the complexity of her students' cultural diversity (the diversity that exists both within students and across students), and (3) how such diversity is or is not represented in her curriculum design.

In listening to Carolyn and Sara discuss their literature-based classrooms, it is clear that Sister Souljah's book *No Disrespect* (1996) serves as a window for understanding the similarities and differences of teaching for literacy acceleration within a critical framework in each of their respective classrooms. *No Disrespect* is a book that provides the students with a complex array of narratives and counternarratives of African American life. At once, the book presents stereotypical images of African American women and men (which the class uses as a point of departure in talking about their own ways of making meaning around similar events that occur in their lives) but it also develops a metanarrative provided by the author's foresight on her own experiences and how her decisions are rooted in the systemic racism that exists in society. After reading this book, many of the students (in both classrooms) comment that Souljah has given them the opportunity to reflect on their own decisions based on the decisions she has made.

Both Sara and Carolyn have used *No Disrespect* in their adult education classrooms. While they used this book for similar reasons—to engage their students with literature, to open up multiple perspectives, and to evoke discussion—the use of the book was different in each classroom. Neither of the teachers had multiple copies of the book, an issue we return to in conclusions. *No Disrespect* is a book written at approximately a tenth grade level, which means that many of the students in Sara and Carolyn's classroom would have independently decoded the words but would have needed some support in terms of making predictions, making inferences, and visualizing what is happening in the book. Both teachers provide a rich book introduction before their students start to read or listen to the book. Carolyn provides multiple types of literate engagements with the book—from read-alouds, to partner reading, to listening to the book read aloud, to reading silently and then having a book club discussion. Sara primarily used this book as a read-aloud—in part because she did not have access to multiple copies of the book. Both of the teachers co-constructed different literary experiences with their students, based on their positionality in the classroom.

Sara used *No Disrespect* (Souljah, 1996) as an artifact to have a cross-cultural and cross-racial dialogue about her positionality as a European American woman vis-à-vis the book with her students. While the book was not completely consistent with the complexity of cultural backgrounds in her classroom, it provided a place of departure for her students to get to know each other and Sara (their teacher) better. Using this book pushed Sara out of her comfort zone as a European American teacher. Indeed, her use of the book marked her own learning as a teacher. Had she not read and discussed the book within the context of a racially diverse professional development group, she might not have taken the risk to use the book in her classroom. Indeed, the books Sara mentioned using in her classroom prior to Souljah's book were books that were much less controversial than Souljah's activist-feminist text.

Sara's case illuminates the complexities of a European American teacher learning to teach within a culturally relevant framework. Sara's experiences of struggling with her space and place as a European American teacher learning to be a culturally relevant teacher, the challenges she confronted along the way, and her responses to these struggles are educative to other teachers facing similar challenges. Rather than acquiesce to the colleagues at her site who challenged the appropriateness of a European American woman teaching African American history through literature to a group of African American students, Sara took a critical and reflective look at herself. She contemplated what she was positioned to know and how she might best design a curriculum that reflected the diversity of her students' cultures (Guy, 1999). This refocusing helped her to more clearly situate herself as a European American teacher who is on the journey of becoming a culturally relevant teacher.

Carolyn is an African American woman who grew up in the same metro area where many of her students grew up, who attended public school, and who worked in a prison setting where she primarily sees young, African American males. Carolyn brings a partial insider status to her choice of literature for her students. It is important to reiterate the partial nature of this insider status, though, because Carolyn is an outsider to the community of the classroom as well. In many ways, her life experiences and values are quite different from those of her students. Carolyn does not try to hide these differences in her teaching. Rather, these differences become a space of discussion and sometimes debate, especially within the "Current Events" and "Literature" portions of her day.

Carolyn consistently uses literature she thinks her students will find relevant to their lives. Indeed, she uses Nathan McCall's *Makes Me Want to Holler* (1995) and Sister Souljah's *No Disrespect* (1996) and *The Coldest Winter Ever* (2000) as anchor texts in her classroom which serve to build community and pull a common storyline through the class—week by week and month by month. Based on her position as perceived by her students, she uses these texts as a way to "teach life lessons." What is clear in both Sara and Carolyn's classroom is that the relationship between literature and discussions is bidirectional. That is, discussions they have in class can find their way into discussions of literature, or literature can serve as a point of departure for discussions that connect to the adults' lives. Either way, literature is jointly negotiated within the interpretive community of the classroom. Their literacy practices also offer us insight into the boundaries of culturally relevant practice. Both Carolyn and Sara talked about abandoning a book if it did not seem to be relevant to their students' lives. Sara discussed how Wally Amos's book (1994) was not appropriate for her mainly female student population. Carolyn Fuller read *Makes Me Want to Holler* and her students thought that it was "too academic." Both teachers are sensitive to the boundaries between personal and cultural engagement. They also recognize the importance of teaching new genres of literature in their classrooms—to provide windows for their students to look through to theorize about their own experiences in relation to other people's experiences.

A less discussed aspect of culturally relevant education is the way in which one person (let alone a class of people) is a complex intersection of multiple cultures. Indeed, culture is complex and includes language, geographic location, class, ethnicity and race, religion, sexuality, gender, and all of the associated ways of interacting, ways of representing (self and others), and ways of being. Thus, when Vivian, Sara, and Carolyn discuss the importance of making learning relevant to their students' lives, they do so while recognizing that they can never be completely relevant to all aspects of students' lives or to all students in their classroom at any one point in time. Rather, the texts (spoken and written) that they choose to bring into their classroom serve as a broker for negotiating culturally relevant spaces—that is, as learners and teachers interact with the cultural spaces of literature, they can reconstruct spaces that reflect who they are as people and the multiple positions they bring with them to any interaction. Carolyn, Sara, and Vivian have given us glimpses into what culturally relevant instruction looks like at particular moments in time in their classrooms. However, they also give us insight into the flexible and unstable nature of culturally relevant instruction, that is, it is an instructional space that is continually being learned, unlearned, and relearned. They also give us insight into what happens when a book or literacy event does not connect with their students' lives—an aspect of becoming a culturally relevant teacher that we seldom hear about.

While Vivian did not talk much about the use of literature in her classroom, we know from our observations of her class that she does have multiple copies of hi-lo (high-interest, low-readability) novels (New Readers Press) in her classroom. Vivian relies on a range of materials—including photocopied workbook pages, magazine articles, literature, and newspapers. Newspapers, work materials, papers, and business forms are all considered part of the "local literacies" (Barton & Hamilton, 2000) that people use in the process of getting things accomplished in their families and communities. These local literacies are often touted as authentic materials—important to incorporate in the adult education classroom to connect with adults' experiences. In Carolyn, Sara, and Vivian's cases, we have seen that the newspaper was used in very different ways.

For example, Vivian uses the newspaper as a resource. After a topic has come up in class, she will ask her students to learn more about the topic in the newspaper and bring what they have learned back to class. Sara teaches genres within the newspaper that her students may not be familiar with—such as political cartoons. Newspapers, in Carolyn's classroom, are a part of her everyday lesson on current events. Each of the teachers incorporates critical literacy questions into their reading of the newspapers (e.g., "Why did the author write this?" "What is her position in this article?" and "What are other ways this issue could have been represented?").

Each of the teachers uses the newspaper in complementary ways in her classroom. What is clear is that positioning the reading of the newspaper as a literacy practice means complicating the authenticity of the practice. First, reading the newspaper (any part of it) is not an authentic task for all students. Some students in their classrooms have never read the newspaper and have very little experience with newspapers. Other students may be familiar with particular sections of the paper (e.g., sports or classified ads) but may be unfamiliar with other aspects of the paper (e.g., obituaries, political cartoons, or book reviews). In sum, it is not just the presence of authentic materials that matters but also the interaction between the teacher, the learner, and the materials. Rather, materials that have traditionally been viewed as authentic can be utilized in a critical or noncritical manner.

It is important to emphasize, within the current context of adult literacy education that creates an artificial division between "literacy" students and "GED" students, that Carolyn, Sara, and Vivian all see themselves as literacy teachers. That is, they recognize that regardless of where their students are as readers—at a second or tenth grade level—they all need to be accelerated as readers. They each address their students' literacy development despite the fact that most of their students already know how to read and write (and are doing so above a sixth grade level). Indeed, each has developed a set of instructional techniques that will help to accelerate their students as readers and writers. These include book introductions, flexible grouping, rereading texts, and strategy instruction.

Carolyn, Sara, and Vivian all want their students to have functional reading and writing skills, though they differ slightly on the ultimate use or context of these proficiencies based on their students' needs and the complexity of the contexts in which they are teaching. Vivian is focused on reading and writing for the empowerment of women. Carolyn is concerned about how reading and writing can help her students survive and obtain their GED. Sara is focused on how reading and writing can promote family literacy development which encompasses parenting skills. Each teacher sees the importance of attending to larger critical social issues while, at the same time, accelerating her students as readers and writers.

Carolyn, Sara, and Vivian, as with all of the adult education teachers in our study, have had to learn about the complexity of the students in their classrooms. This automatically positions them as learners as they are constantly observing and theorizing about who their students are, what motivates them, what their purposes and goals are, and how they can design curricula that attend to all of these issues. Carolyn, Sara, and Vivian teach us that there are many different ways in which teachers can also be learners. First, teachers can learn from their students. We hear Sara actively positioning herself as learning from her students' background experiences when she stated, "I am just as much of a learner as they are." Similarly, Vivian stated, "My students forget I am the teacher and open up with me." They each discuss opportunities where they open up a space in the design of their classroom for their students' expertise to be foregrounded. Sara actively invites her students to share their cultural and racial experiences with their peers in the classroom. She also invites parents to share knowledge and strategies related to parenting with each other. Carolyn often positions students who have been successful in her classroom as experts. She calls on these people to provide their narratives of success (whether it is passing a section of the GED test, getting a job, having a child graduate from high school, or writing a strong essay) to the rest of the class. Similarly, Vivian calls on her students' local knowledge as rappers, preachers, spoken word poets, and so on during the African American history celebration. Further, in literature discussions, each of the teachers set up the contexts in which multiple perspectives on an issue can arise in the classroom—which, again, sends a message to students that their perspectives are encouraged and necessary to the classroom community. Each of the teachers has experimented with her literacy practices. We hear this "inquiry stance" embedded in their talk about their instructional practices. For instance, we hear Vivian say, "I found that when my students ..." Her use of the verb "found" suggests that she is constantly observing and theorizing about what works and what does not work based on her students' feedback. This inquiry stance was built into how Carolyn and Sara described their instructional practices as well. Carolyn recently tried book club structures, Sara has increasingly discussed race in her classroom, and Vivian experimented with a grouping structure in her classroom. Each time a literacy teacher tries out a new practice, a boundary is pushed. This opens up a new set of possible designs in the classroom.

As we have seen in these cases, adult literacy teachers can develop ways to support students' cross-cultural investigation by looking deeply into matters of race, class, and gender. In doing so, they are supporting their students' experimentation with new literacy practices as they traverse the boundaries between home/community and school.

In Vivian, Carolyn, and Sara's chapters, we have seen that they fall on different points of the emergent framework presented in chapter 2. In Vivian's classroom, for example, curriculum may include materials to help learners develop the reading, writing, and speaking proficiency to do a particular job (e.g., finding a job or housing). In Carolyn's classroom, she may focus on developing the same skill set, but both the process and her intended goal are different. In her classroom, the curriculum would also include a set of questions to promote discussion and analysis about the current economy, labor rights, or developing more jobs in the area. Depending on the student, the context, and their comfort and familiarity with a topic, Sara, Carolyn, and Vivian move in and out of the various fields in the emergent framework.

RETHINKING PRACTICE

1. Carolyn, Vivian, and Sara's instructional practices have offered us insights into the complexity of culturally relevant instruction and the importance of local contexts and the interactions between the reader, the text, and the context. Think about your own classroom. What are the purposes and goals for the literature you use in your classroom? What diversity exists in your classroom? How can literature be used as both a "window and a mirror" for students to see themselves and others' experiences in the curriculum?

   Select three books that you think might be culturally relevant for your students. What, specifically, makes these books culturally relevant? Does one need to be an insider to the culture to use this book? What other information do you need? What are the possibilities and responsibilities for adult education teachers who are committed about teaching within a culturally relevant framework?

2. In the preceding chapters, we have focused primarily on culture and race. However, we know people are more complicated, and a finer grained analysis of the fabric of oppression and liberation is necessary. What are the multiple positions you occupy as a teacher? Make a list of all of the various positions your occupy—including race, class, age, occupation, gender, sexual orientation, language background, history with schooling, and so on. Which of these positions are privileged or hold "high status" in this society?

Which are considered "low status" in this society? Share with other teachers. What did you discover? How is your teaching stance determined by your multiple positionalities? How does this intersect with your students' positionalities? Try this with the students in your classroom.

3. Having multiple copies of literature and texts is important in an accelerative literacy classroom. However, in classrooms where resources are limited, copyright laws prohibit making multiple copies of copyrighted texts, and teachers may not have access to copy machines. Therefore, multiple copies of texts may be hard to come by. What are some creative ways in which you can expand your collection of multiple copies of texts?

4. Flexible grouping, or differentiated instruction, is an important strategy of an accelerative literacy curriculum. In Vivian's case, we heard her talk about how she established reading groups in her classroom. The next step might be for her to move toward a flexible grouping arrangement that responds to continuous enrollment and mixed skill levels. What are the different ways in which Vivian might organize reading groups in her classroom? When and why might she change the groups? How might you organize the learners in your classroom into flexible groups?

For further reading on differentiated instruction and flexible grouping, see the following:

Fountas, I., & Pinnell, G. (2001). *Guiding readers and writers: Grades 3–6*. Portsmouth, NH: Heinemann.

Tomlinson, C. (2000). Reconcilable differences? Standards-based teaching and differentiation. *Educational Leadership, 58*(4), 6–11.

Part 3

Cases of Adult Education Teachers

8

Teaching the Codes of Power

DOROTHY F. WALKER

Why did the author tell you this and not something else?

— Dorothy Walker, Interview

Dorothy F. Walker is a lifelong educator and citizen of St. Louis. In her eighties when she participated in this research, Dorothy is an African American woman who has taught for over thirty years in the St. Louis public schools. Dorothy's mother and father were both teachers. Her father obtained a graduate degree and taught in a one-room schoolhouse in rural Missouri. Her parents were strong advocates of reading, art, and music. Dorothy stated, "We always had books and magazines to read at home." Dorothy's mother insisted that all of her children graduate from college. Dorothy graduated from Vashon High School in the city of St. Louis with the class of 1939 and went on to get an education degree from Harris Stowe College (a historically black teaching college), also in St. Louis, in 1943. Dorothy was married to Milton Walker for thirty years. However, at that time, women were not allowed to teach if they were married. She postponed her career in education and pursued a career as a mapmaker for the government. As Dorothy noted, her mapmaking job ultimately helped her to "teach with a global understanding of the world." Dorothy returned to teaching in 1962 and taught for twenty-four years in the K–12 system. She taught third, fourth, and eighth grades. After retiring from public education, she taught Adult Education and Literacy classes with St. Louis public schools for another ten years. She started as a substitute after she retired from K–12 teaching and then stayed on to teach for another nine years in a family literacy program and in several adult education programs housed in elementary schools. Prior to formally teaching in adult education, she had volunteered in adult education classrooms. Dorothy is a committed educator who continued to teach long after her retirement and has literally inspired generations of educators, students, and social activists in her lifetime.

Dorothy's case is written primarily about her teaching in an adult education class that was part of a family literacy program. However, because of her many years of teaching experience, she does, at times, reflect on and draw on her experiences of teaching adults and youth from other contexts. In this classroom context, Dorothy has, on average, nineteen students enrolled in her class throughout the year who average twelve or more contact hours. Dorothy generally has one student each year who obtains his or her GED certificate. The students in her class have a retention rate of 79 percent. Her greatest level of impact is level 4 on average; 33 percent of her students moved into level 5.

Dorothy believes that good teaching begins with the establishment of relationships between the teacher and the learner. Dorothy emphasized getting to know her students—their hopes, desires, past experiences with school, weaknesses, and ambitions—through dialogue. After these relationships are constructed, her teaching philosophy can be characterized as individualized instruction within a culturally and personally relevant framework. She uses a combination of traditional and authentic literacy materials and places priority on teaching reading and writing for a purpose. When she can, Dorothy teaches writing within a personally meaningful context. She also explicitly teaches the genres of writing necessary for students to accelerate as writers.

Several strong themes emerged in Dorothy's case as an adult education and literacy teacher. First is her emphasis on recognizing homes and communities as situated contexts for learning (Cope & Kalantzis, 2000a; Lave & Wenger, 1991; New London Group, 1996). Second is her belief in explicitly teaching what Delpit (1995) refers to as the "codes of power"—whether the code of power is Standard English or the ability to construct a sermon or participate in school structures—to her students. As Delpit and Dowdy (2002) point out, the fabric of powerful discourses in society is often invisible, and consequently it is difficult for people of color and women to gain access and control over such powerful discourses.

Dorothy's adult education class is held at an elementary school in the city of St. Louis. The elementary school is a neighborhood school established in 1903. Ninety-nine percent of the children and families who attend the school are African American. Located on the second floor of the building, the adult education room is a large, well-lit room. When one enters the classroom, there is a table with a coffeepot, tea, snacks, and current magazines such as *National Geographic, Jet, Sports Illustrated, Essence, Newsweek,* and *Time.* Students are welcome to help themselves to a hot drink during break time. Often during this time, students will peruse the magazines and read an article that is interesting to them. The tables in the room are set up in a U shape. Each table holds three to four adults. There is a four-shelved wooden bookcase in the back of the room. In this bookcase are about fifty GED and pre-GED books, as well as job skills books with titles such as *Real People Working in Communication, Real People Working in Education, Real People Working in Science,* and *Real People Working in Sales & Marketing.* On the front table are a few high-interest low-readability books, placed next to binders full of program materials. The walls are decorated with colorful motivational posters such as "Families Reading Together," "Be a Star," "The Question Is Not Can You but Will You?" "People Can Alter Their Lives by Altering Their Attitude," and "Books Go Everywhere." On the side wall by the door are more posters, the family literacy schedule, a newspaper article, a United States map, and a world map. There is a "Wall of Respect" with African American leaders hung on two walls. On the back wall, above the brown metal cabinet, is the food pyramid guide. There are math manipulatives on the desk for the students to work with during math time. Dorothy's desk is located in the corner farthest away from the entrance to the classroom. On Dorothy's desk is Marie Clay's (1990) book *Becoming Literate: The Development of Inner Control.* She also has a "work readiness series" and program manual on her desk. A row of PLATO computers lines the side wall.

Dorothy is knowledgeable about the students' cycles of change (Fingeret & Drennon, 1997) and attempts to find out the underlying reasons why students are in the classroom and how this may impact other aspects of their lives. Before administering any formal test to students who enter her classroom, she starts by talking with them. She stated, "The first thing the teacher has to do is evaluate her students and see what they bring with them. I have a regular conversation with them because I want to know what their goals are and what they want." She goes on to say that this conversation is easier for some students than for others who may not believe and trust in the adult education teacher immediately. When she does administer a test, Dorothy talked about the importance of emphasizing their strengths as a starting point in instruction (Cambourne, 1995; Johnston, 1997).

Humanistic in her philosophy toward teaching, Dorothy said, "You are not teaching things; you are teaching people." She also stated, "I simply believe in human beings. I believe that everyone has a right to learn to be able to take care of themselves." While she couched education in this discussion in terms of rights, she talked about the importance of individuals taking responsibility for themselves. The purpose of adult education, according to Dorothy, is "to build hope and self-esteem for individuals who don't have any hope." Assessing for Dorothy is learning about the entire person, what motivates them, why they are here, and what their histories with school and education have been. She motivates her students by appealing to what their strengths are and what they want to learn outside of school.

Dorothy's theories and practices of teaching reading and writing within a critical framework came out as she discussed teaching three adult education students—Lance, Bobby, and Samantha (all names are pseudonyms). Through each of their narratives, we will hear the themes embedded in Dorothy's interview.

Lance was a thirty-three-year-old African American man who was born and raised in the city of St. Louis. He attended public schools and was placed in a remedial reading class when he was in the fifth grade. He talked about his reading in class in terms of the other children laughing at him and pointing out when he "bluffed and stumbled" over words. He dropped out of school in the twelfth grade. He was missing a few history credits and had to drop out to get a job at a grocery store to support his college-educated mother and his siblings. Lance was a minister in the church where he grew up. He served his church by delivering sermons, teaching Sunday school and Bible lessons, and helping with fundraisers. He also drove a tractor-trailer for a delivery company for many years. Lance was also an active participant in his community through organizing block meetings to decrease the amount of crime in the neighborhood and to deter drug dealers. He returned to adult education a decade after he dropped out of school. He stated that he wanted to get his GED, but he also revealed that he had trouble reading and understanding directions when he was driving the tractor-trailer. Above all, Lance wanted to become an ordained minister in his church, but he needed to pass an ordainment test which included reading, writing, speaking, and listening. As Dorothy dialogued with Lance, she learned about his history of participation with school and his dreams, interests, and weaknesses. Dorothy wanted to capitalize on the literacy practices that he was already proficient with from his life as a preacher in the community. She asked him to bring all of the texts and materials that he used to develop a sermon, and she helped him to study for his ordainment. She described the process of teaching Lance reading and writing within the context of a student-determined goal—one that was socially meaningful.

We would work with the Bible. He would have his Sunday school book that he would get and we would work from that. I would have him read, and then I would have him discuss. And it goes again to history because some of the places in the Bible are on the map. And I was helping him in his interpretation of things. You need an explanation for people and in order to explain, you need to understand. I'll tell you the worst situation I had with him is when he was trying to become ordained and they [the other ministers at the church] had written out this series of their commitments. Now whoever wrote these out, they left so much out, it was terrible. They wrote it the way they thought it. And as we began to do this, I told him, "This is not right ... this is wrong." I said, "It needs to be different." So he went back and got the printed book that has all of this in it. And I showed him, "Do you see the way it is written in this book? It is not what is written there." Not what you have what they told you to learn.... Part of his presentation, he was reciting it the way it was in the book, and they told him don't do that. Say it the way we wrote it.... And he told me, "Ms. Walker. I know now that is important that I have to read something else to understand because they wanted me to recite something and it was all jumbled up." And we had a lot of discussions on the pronunciation of what you had to say. So, if you are going to be a minister, you need to be clear and read it right.

In drawing on the community texts that are relevant to Lance, Dorothy is not only teaching Lance how to read and write within a culturally authentic framework; she is also teaching him the strategies and resources of critical literacy along the way. Indeed, as Dorothy brings multiple texts to Lance's attention and shows him how to compare the accuracy of the information ("Do you see the way it is written in this book? It is not what is written there") and the gaps in the information ("They left so much out, it was terrible"), she is teaching for critical literacy (Luke & Freebody, 1999).

Luke and Freebody (1999) proposed a model of critical literacy that includes four resources that readers call on as they read. These include being a code breaker (How do I crack this?), text participant (What does this mean?), text user (What do I do with this, here and now?), and text analyst (What does this mean to me?). As Dorothy teaches Lance to read the texts provided and to design his own sermon, she is modeling each of these literacy practices for Lance. Above all, Dorothy emphasized the importance of reading and writing for understanding. She stressed this by emphasizing the real audience that he would have in front of him as a preacher. She stated, "If he cannot understand it, no one else will be able to understand it."

Dorothy helped Lance practice the sermons he was going to give, read and reread what he had written, and practice on his deliverance. While he was doing that, Dorothy taught him critical reading questions that he could use as he was preparing his speeches without her support. While he was reading, Dorothy would ask him, "Did that make sense?" and "Did that sound right?" These questions are what Clay (1993) would refer to as prompts that develop a system of monitoring for meaning which can develop into a self-extending system. Lance learned to monitor and self-correct his reading and writing with the support of Dorothy, but then he transferred this strategy to when he was reading scriptures and developing sermons on his own. This self-extending system is developed both at the textual level as learners interact with texts and also at the social level where they put the texts to use within social practices. Similar to other humanist educators, Dorothy explained the self-extending system in this way: "you don't expand your thinking by someone telling you something. You have to think for yourself so that when situations come up with problems that you have to solve, you are able to solve the problems." Similarly, Mackie (1981) writes that "to be literate is not to have arrived at some pre-determined destination, but to utilize reading, writing and speaking skills so that our understanding of the world is progressively enlarged" (p. 1).

Dorothy described the process she went through in teaching Lance how to develop his sermon. Throughout, she called on questions that evoked a critical interrogation of the text, the audience, and the social practices of the sermon. We have italicized sections of her talk that particularly emphasize critical literacy.

Once you have read some part of the Scripture, say you have read the Twenty-third Psalm, or Thirty-fourth Psalm where it says, "I will rejoice in the Lord. I will always sing his praises." So if you took the Scripture, and you ask, What did that just say? I will rejoice. In the Lord. What? Always? I will always sing his praises. Why are you rejoicing? Why are you singing his praises? You are developing from that point of view. So usually we will develop three points of whatever it is. So you are explaining whatever you are saying. Then you ask, Who said this? And then you find your way into history. You have to go back to your Bible and find out why David was saying this at the time. Why was David saying this? I will sing his praises always. Why are you singing his praises? And this is how you would develop his sermon. And see, Lance was good: once he began to think about it along those lines, he was good.

We hear how Dorothy explained how she taught Lance to read and write his sermon calling on critical literacy practices. Specifically, she asked Lance to examine multiple and conflicting texts ("You have to go back to your Bible and find out why David was saying this at the time"), examine the historical and cultural contexts of the texts he was using ("And then you find your way into history"), investigate how readers are positioned by the values in texts ("You are developing from that point of view"), question the meaning behind statements ("Why are you rejoicing? Why are you singing his praises?"), and encourage multiple passes through a text ("You have to go back to the Bible"). As she models critical literacy processes with Lance, she is also explicitly teaching the genre of the sermon to Lance. Dorothy is aware that when Lance stands up in front of his congregation, he will be judged based on the quality of his sermon. Delpit (1995) writes,

Teachers do students no service to suggest, even implicitly, that the "product" is not important. In this country, students will be judged on their product regardless of the process they utilized to achieve it. And that product, based as it is on the specific codes of a particular culture, is more readily produced when the directives of how to produce it are made explicit. (p. 31)

Once Lance learned the linguistic tools that went into the design of a sermon, he was able to take these linguistic tools and redesign his own sermon with the specific background and needs of his congregation in mind (Cope & Kalantzis, 2000b). Dorothy's stance to teaching literacy has been articulated by Delpit (1995), who writes that students "must be encouraged to understand the value of the code they already possess as well as to understand the power realities of this country. Otherwise, they will not be able to work to change these realities" (p. 40). As students are taught how textual resources are strategically put together in a design which is recognized as a genre (e.g., a newspaper article, a letter, a sermon, or a speech), they can begin to activate their own cultural resources which are specific to their local contexts and redesign the genre based on their needs, interests, and desired outcomes.

Dorothy was sensitive to the gains that her students made as readers and writers, not all of which could be measured using formal assessments such as the Test of Adult Basic Education (TABE). In Lance's case, a woman from his church came up to Dorothy Walker and told her that Lance's sermons at church had improved a great deal, his message was clear, and everyone understood what he was saying. Lance ultimately took the ordainment test and passed. Dorothy stated,

Lance got to the place where he learned after he began to develop his sermons and he began to read his sermons himself, well, when you do all that, you can deliver it. You can always deliver it without the script, if you have done a good job. They [preachers] generally have notes, but they often move away from their notes. That is the same way in reading. When you are reading with adults and there is a story that they have read, say it is a scientific story, the first thing you do is question them: why did the author tell you this and not something else? I like the GED books for that reason. You have to do more reasoning in them. They used to be the paragraphs they gave you. You could go back and find a sentence. You cannot do that now. You have to have a sense of reasoning to know why the article is so important.

In this description, we hear how Dorothy used a combination of authentic and traditional literacy materials to teach her students reading. Regardless of the text, she incorporates critical literacy questions into her teaching. In the above example, she noted that when her student is reading from GED preparatory materials, she will ask her students, "Why did the author tell you this and not something else?" In this way, she is prompting her students to think about in whose interests particular texts work, who has written the text, and how the text might be different if someone else had written the text.

Dorothy did note that she thought the current GED materials are more relevant to students' lives because they include topics such as health and nutrition, parts of the body, or driving places, and thus help to close the divide between relevant and irrelevant materials. As Dorothy teaches reading and writing within a culturally relevant framework, Lance learns the design of the sermon. He is also learning skills which are associated with success on the GED, such as outlining his ideas, reading critically to gather the author's intention, gathering background information from multiple sources (e.g., speeches, poetry, and the Bible), making inferences, writing the speech, presenting the materials, and delivering the speech to the audience in a compelling manner.

Teaching literacy within a critical framework, for Dorothy, includes attention to adults learning how to participate in society. Dorothy made the point that sometimes adult educators get so caught up in the academics that they forget about the citizenship part of education. She stated, "I hope that [students] have accomplished what they can and go and be good citizens. I want them to be able to take care of themselves and not rely on anyone else to take care of them." A good citizen, according to Dorothy, is "someone who lives in harmony with the persons around [them] in this world and are able to live with moral issues and they are able to think for themselves and not forget about others." She believes parents can model good citizenship for their children. This notion of citizenship includes helping the adults move from private (school or home) to public contexts (community, teachers, etc.) to expand their proficiency with reading, writing, speaking, listening, and being a participating citizen. Indeed, Dorothy directly connects learning in the classroom with learning outside of the classroom. Sticht (1997) writes, "To the extent possible, learning contexts, tasks, materials, and procedures [should be] taken from the future situation in which the learner will be functioning" (p. 3). In this framework, "Literacy is developed while it is being applied" (Sticht, 1997, p. 2).

Dorothy supported Lance as he developed his voice as a preacher in his community. As we will see with Bobby and Samantha, two adult education students who Dorothy talked about at length, she also cultivated boundary crossings between the private and public domains and explicitly taught the dominant forms of power so her students would have access to them.

Bobby was an African American man in his mid-thirties who had dropped out of school in the fourth grade because he needed to stay home and take care of his grandmother, who was blind. Bobby's parents worked on a farm picking cotton in the Deep South. Bobby attended elementary school in the same school where he now attends adult education classes and where his son, Bobby Jr., currently attends school. Bobby Sr. is a single parent and is very involved in his son's education. Dorothy learned all of this information about Bobby as she engaged in dialogue with him.

Dorothy explained that while Bobby is a literacy student (reading below the sixth grade level), his comprehension skills are excellent. While Bobby's acceleration in reading and writing has been slow, she cited a number of other ways in which he has accelerated. She recalled Bobby's self-reports of his progress (which she actively attended to): "he said, 'I have learned a lot—how to hold my temper, to talk to other people, to teach my son how to talk with other people, learned to get along with his brother, to listen to my son's teachers better.'" Indeed, as part of Bobby's adult education program, he observed and participated in his son's (Bobby Jr.'s) elementary classroom. During this time, Bobby Sr. learned how his son's teacher was teaching, which helped him to accelerate as a reader and writer and made him more able to reinforce at home what Bobby Jr. was learning in his classroom. For example, in engaging in an authentic dialogue with Bobby—similar to what Edwards (1999) refers to as "parent stories"—Dorothy learned about family traditions, trips that Bobby Sr. and Jr. took together, household routines, and literacy practices at home, including Bobby Sr. buying a television that had closed-captioning so that Bobby Jr. would learn how to read by watching the TV. These generative themes became instrumental as Bobby began to critically examine his life and his son's life within the context of his past school experiences and the community in which they live.

Dorothy's adult education class was connected to a family literacy program, and as a result, she actively attended to the ways in which intergenerational literacy impacted the adults' literacy skills as well as the children's literacy skills. In the context of intergenerational literacy learning, adults gain a sense of personal control as a result of the ease with which they can negotiate otherwise foreign boundaries. As Bobby Sr. moved from his child's classroom back to the adult education classroom, Dorothy debriefed with him by answering questions and demystifying the cultural capital associated with the school. In this way, she explicitly taught him the "codes of power" of the school. The literacy learning, however, did not move only from the school to the home. Dorothy was very clear that she believed in bringing family and community literacies and resources into the classroom. In this way, the family literacy practices informed—indeed, transformed—the school literacy curriculum

(Edwards, 1996; Paratore, Melzi, & Krol-Sinclair, 1999; Shanahan & Rodriguez-Brown, 1995).

Language experience stories are useful for teaching beginning readers and writers of all ages. In this approach, a student is asked to tell a story from his or her own life experiences, and the teacher records the story as the student tells it. The teacher then asks the learner to "read" the story back. In the case of beginning readers, the reading is more of a memorization of the story that they have just told. The teachers accepted the memorization as a first stage in emergent reading and identify sight words, or what Clay (1993) refers to as "anchors," to build a literacy lesson around. These sight words take on meaning and relevance because they are in the context of a story that has come from their own experiences. Dorothy explained her interpretation of a language experience approach:

In a language experience story, you talk with the adult about some experience in his or her life that is important. Something they have experienced. It is either good or bad, but it has excited them. They give you the sentence and I ask them, "How did this happen? When did this happen?" During this time, you [the teacher] are writing this story. After they have talked with you about it, then you ask them for a sentence to summarize their story. There are several things going on as we do this. This may be the first time they have thought about these issues. That is the reason for experience stories with adults who can't read. The adults who read and write, you want their experience story, too, but they write their own experience story. As you begin to talk about it, they begin to write about it, and you may help with organization through mapping or through using Venn diagrams.

In using the language experience approach, generative themes and questions emerge from the learners' reality: their history, their culture, and their social and political lives. Macedo (1994) explains that as people start to name their experiences, they start to explore and question their participation in the making of these experiences. Such analysis can lead to an increase in dialogue, action, and reflection.

I would have him write his story. If he went on a field trip with his son and his teacher and they came back, he would dictate it to me, where they went, and everything. And how he would tell me what streets they traveled and I would write it for him, and then we would work on him being able to read whatever it was he said.

In her explanation of the language experience story, Dorothy hinted at the importance of raising Bobby's consciousness. For example, as Bobby Sr. told her about his histories of participation with school, how he dropped out of the same school where he now attended adult education classes, Dorothy described how he realized, for the first time, the relationship between the school context and intergenerational literacy learning. Instead of blaming himself for having intellectual deficiencies as the school has taught him to do (by labeling him as a "remedial learner"), he started to question the curriculum and the teachers in the school. He also started to develop a questioning stance about why his son was also placed in special education class and how this might have been avoided if he had access to quality instruction. Shor (1992) describes critical consciousness as the process of coming to understand individual experiences and social structures. As students become critically conscious, they start to see the way in which society is historically structured to privilege some groups of people over others. As they recognize the patterns between their lives and the lives of many other disenfranchised people, they begin to recognize the need for critical social action to transform such structures.

This approach is based on a strengths-based approach to adult literacy learning within the sociocultural context of family and community literacy practices. Through the language experience stories, Dorothy can learn more about the types of situated learning that are occurring in the home and community and uses these as strategic contexts for accelerating her students as readers and writers in the classroom. She recognized the shortcomings of standardized tests to provide her with this type of sociocultural information. Along the same lines, she discussed how important it is to frame the TABE results in terms of strengths rather than deficits.

After I have administered and graded the TABE, I talk with the students about the results. I try to talk with them about their strengths first. It is important to talk about strengths first because some of them have already failed. If I have a student who has come to me after I have tested the student, if the weaknesses that the students have will frighten the student, I don't talk about them right away. I talk about other things and then we lead into their weaknesses once they understand their strengths. They need to know that. You can't always build on the weaknesses first because it scares then. You deal with the strengths first.

Dorothy does not avoid controversial issues in the classroom. If and when an issue came up from the newspaper or media, dialogue, their parenting class, or their own lives, she discussed these issues with the learners in her classroom. As far as using the history of African American people went, she stated, similar to Holiday (see chapter 9), that "it's difficult not to integrate the history because it is around us all the time." She discussed how she tries to learn about her students' family histories, which helps to build a sense of community in the classroom.

As we have seen through Dorothy's teaching of Lance and Bobby, her literacy teaching is characterized by promoting African American community development. That is, by supporting her students as they negotiate the boundaries between home and school, Dorothy works to regenerate, develop, and sustain community development. One final example of this in practice that she discussed was with a female student, Samantha. Samantha had three children who attended the school where the adult education class was held. She also had a child who was not yet in school, and so attending classes regularly was a challenge for her. She was married to a man who did not have a high school diploma or GED. Samantha was very good with computer skills and wanted to get her GED. In order to motivate her to keep coming, Dorothy asked her to do certain things for her on the computers in their room (e.g., installing software, linking the computers to the printers, and helping other students get established on the computers). Dorothy paid Samantha with her own money for her computer services. In the process, Samantha earned valuable computer skills and money, and attended the class to study for her GED. This ultimately motivated Samantha's husband to come to class. He, too, got his GED. While Dorothy does have students who get their GED like Samantha and her husband, she thinks that along with preparing them for the GED, she is also preparing them "to live out here in this world."

In each of these cases—Lance, Bobby, and Samantha—Dorothy's work with the African American adults in her classroom functions as a type of social activism that often goes unnoticed. Indeed, Collins (2000) points out that prevailing definitions of activism often deny the importance of everyday activism in black women's lives—activism such as teaching. Activism is often defined in terms of the struggle to transform institutions in society. While this is important, activism also includes struggles for group survival, a struggle that occurs in invisible spheres of life, such as the adult literacy education classroom.

Dorothy discussed the development of her own critical consciousness as a black woman and activist who grew up during the era of Jim Crow laws. Dorothy recalled being discriminated against in her hometown in southern Missouri. She shared the story of how she went into a store to get Pepsodent toothpaste and the salesclerk brought her back a generic tube of toothpaste, not what she had asked for. The European American salesclerk said to her, "You must not be from around here because you take whatever I give you." She said, "In that case, I don't want it." It was at that point that "my mom said it was time for me to get out of there because I was already beginning to resist, to resist the status quo." She provided another example of racism from when she was married. She and her husband were traveling by train and the train personnel would not let them take their seats because white people still needed seats. Even though they had purchased tickets, they were denied access to the train. Incidents such as these sparked her critical consciousness as a black woman and activist, consciousness that she has brought with her through a lifetime of educating African American students.

Throughout her lifetime, Dorothy has been actively involved with her church and with other community groups. As a teacher, Dorothy actively volunteered for professional development opportunities such as participating in the Literacy for Social Justice Teacher Research Group. She continued to participate in voluntary professional development such as regularly attending school board meetings to stay informed about what was happening in the district. Dorothy was also committed to mentoring new teachers into the profession. When she was in her eighties, she accepted a student teacher into her classroom to observe and learn about adult education. She regularly encouraged new adult education teachers to collect life experiences so that they could relate to the experiences of the adults in their classrooms. She stated, "Teachers who teach adult education really should be very knowledgeable about not only the academics of what they are teaching but about outside experiences as well. Collecting out-of-school life experiences," Dorothy continued, "is important for teachers because then their knowledge is expanded and they are able to communicate with adults because they have had some experiences that adults have and there are experiences there for sharing." It was in this spirit of lifelong learning and teaching that the 1st Annual Educating for Change Curriculum Fair was dedicated to Dorothy Walker.

9

Literacy Education as Activism

HOLIDAY SIMMONS

The whole dynamics of the classroom is social change.

— Holiday Simmons, Interview

Holiday is an African American poet and a social worker and brings many experiences with social activism into the adult education classroom. On any given day, you could walk into Holiday's classroom and see a student-centered curriculum in action, one that is problem based and reflects her students' lives and concerns. On the purposes of adult education, Holiday stated,

I definitely want my students to reach tangible goals like employment or get into a higher educational institution because a lot of them are in poverty. In addition to that, I want them to have a higher sense of empowerment and knowledge of social issues, specifically along the lines of race, poverty, and gender. I really want them to go out and be fighters. And they already are because they are here [in adult education].

Holiday had been teaching for two years at the Adult Learning Center in the northern section of St. Louis. The building where the Adult Learning Center is located previously hosted a K–5 school. The building has three designated classrooms used for adult education—one that is Holiday's primary base, one for a second teacher or for additional students, and one used as a critical literacy lab (CLL), which is an innovative structure piloted at the learning center. Holiday teaches in a large room with tables situated so that four students can comfortably work in the space. Two walls are lined with blackboards and bulletin boards that contain motivational posters and messages, and the third wall has windows with bookshelves underneath that hold materials and books for student use: typical adult education textbooks (Contemporary, Steck-Vaughn, New Readers Press, etc.). The teacher's desk is located in the back of the room with file cabinets and a coat rack. Holiday rearranges the tables as she thinks will best afford positive interactions among students and between students and herself.

Like many of the other educators in our study, Holiday was not conscious of adult education before she was offered a position in adult education. Initially, she was an English for Speakers of Other Languages (ESOL) family literacy coordinator and a full-time student in a graduate-level social work program. Her undergraduate degree is in women's studies, African American studies, and environmental science. She comes from a family of educators and cites her family—particularly the women in her life, her mother and grandmother—as her primary influences in learning how to teach.

Her philosophy of education is rooted in justice and following the lead of the learner, concepts she learned from the feminist educator and activist bell hooks, the revolutionary Brazilian adult educator Paulo Freire, and her parents. Combined with a learner-centered philosophy of education, teaching for acceleration within social justice frameworks, Holiday stated, "The whole dynamic of our classroom is social change." It is significant that Holiday used the phrase "our classroom" rather than "my classroom" because it reflects the dialogic nature of her classroom and her feminist or womanist orientation as a woman-teacher-activist in the classroom. "Womanism," a term coined by Alice Walker (1983), brings a racialized and often class-located experience to the gendered experience suggested by feminism.

Holiday's current focus in her graduate studies is on community development, and she discussed the connection between social work and education. Further, she saw the various roles that adult educators take on as they deal with students as learners and people on many different levels—social worker, educator, confidant, mentor, and friend. She stated, "You're getting to the core of people's lives, and it makes you reevaluate your own life." This focus translated into an emphasis on the community of the classroom. A focus on the whole person and on community is rooted in the philosophy of feminism. Indeed, hooks (2003) writes,

Looking at ourselves holistically, seeing our emotional well being as rooted both in the politics of race and racism as well as in our capacity to be self

defining, we can create the self-esteem that is needed for us to care for our souls. (p. 20)

Like bell hooks, Holiday sees the importance of attending to all aspects of a person's being. On describing the community of the classroom, Holiday stressed the connectedness and associated emotionality that she cultivates in her classroom. She stated, "There are times when we have all cried together, we've all held hands and prayed together."

Holiday defined the core purposes of education as "empowerment," "activism," and "knowledge of social issues," along with obtainment of the GED. Part of her literacy instruction is embedded in the critical literacy lab. Holiday explains the purpose and function of the CLL. The purpose of the lab is to integrate the values identified with feminist teaching methodology (Maher & Thompson Tetreault, 1994), critical literacy (Freire, 1993; Freire & Macedo, 1987), liberation theology (Deelen, 1980), and popular education (Freire; Purcell-Gates & Waterman, 2000; Shor, 1980) within a comprehensive approach to literacy instruction which includes the primary reading components of phonemic awareness and phonics, vocabulary, fluency, and comprehension. This approach also includes guided and independent writing in a range of genres for a range of purposes and audiences.

The students who participate in the lab are voluntary Adult Education and Literacy students. All of the students are African American and range in age from sixteen to eighty-seven. Students were grouped based on their Test of Adult Basic Education (TABE) scores: (A) 0–2.9 and (B) 3.0–5.9 grade levels. Holiday described the CLL:

The [critical literacy] lab is where we target the low-literacy students (students reading below a sixth grade level). The group is broken in half: a group consisting of zero- to third grade–level students, and fourth through sixth grade–level students. Within the group, we focus on different techniques such as fluency, phonics, phonemic awareness, and vocabulary.... In the literacy lab we read for two and a half hours. I give context, but the bulk of the time is doing the actual action of reading. [The focus of the classroom is on] African American literature. It was an eight-week session broken into two-week subsections, using different genre chapters from books and songs.

The critical literacy lab is, as mentioned above, in a designated classroom to promote critical literacy instruction and development, and is identified as such on a bulletin board at the front of the room. Tables and chairs in this room are arranged in a U configuration to afford equal views among participants while providing access to the blackboard or flipchart in the front of the room. A chair is available to the front side of the U, so the instructor can sit while creating a common circle when reading or discussing. Two round tables with chairs are situated in the back of the room for small-group or one-on-one tutoring opportunities. The room has the same floor and wall plan as the other classroom, and the bulletin boards in this room display a combination of motivational reading posters, summaries or brainstorms written on flipchart paper from previous class discussions, and a spiral reading—*Think It, Speak It, Write It, Read It, Live It*—with pictures from the civil rights movement. The bookshelves and windowsill are filled with a combination of reading and writing texts that are not standard for most of the other centers in the program such as spellers, specific comprehension skills booklets, as well as magazines, books, pamphlets, condensed novels, and high-interest/low-level readers from New Readers Press. There is a file box that contains graphic organizers, lesson plan templates, and additional reading assessments. Materials are accessible to students, tutors, and teachers alike.

The literacy instruction that Holiday described in her interview was the basis of our observations of her teaching, which included an eight-week series focused on African American literature. Each week was thematically structured and included poetry, music, short stories, newspaper articles, and novel excerpts. The students who participate in the CLL read materials including lyrics from rap and blues songs, the novel *The Women of Brewster Place* (Naylor, 1982), poetry by Langston Hughes, and selections from Oakland Readers (collections of stories written at different levels by adult education students in Oakland, California).

Each group met for two hours twice weekly. Tutors were actively involved in working with one or more students as necessary in the context of class and with follow-up assignments after group sessions. The course topic ensured relevant content, and teachers facilitated discussions that afforded connections to current events and students' concerns.

Holiday talked about the importance of starting each literature selection with a strong book introduction. The purpose of a book introduction, as discussed in previous chapters, is to "debug" the text (Clay, 1993). Because learning to read is an intersection between the text, the instructional context, and the reader, the book introduction can serve to make a difficult text more manageable and can broaden the difficulty of an easier text by introducing more background information. The teacher's role is to think about the demands of the text and the skills that each of the readers has, and to introduce the concepts, vocabulary words, images, or background information that may cause the reader to struggle as he or she is reading. Holiday talked about this process as she introduced the abridged version of *The Women of Brewster Place* (Naylor, 1982) to her adult education class.

I always start off [a book] with a historical standpoint. For a good hour and a half, we talked about the Great Northern Migration, and, of course, always applying it to our lives. About half the people in class were from the South and then moved to St. Louis as teenagers. They recalled that, but they never knew that it was a movement, they never knew what it was called or that it had a name, or a context to it. So we talked about that and shared personal stories and talked about the push and pull factors, leaving the South and coming to the North. Then we got into the story, we pulled out pieces that related to the broader historical movement. We discussed how the main character cleaned houses and how this was representative of the types of jobs available to women. They made connections to the gender and racial oppression in their own lives, saying things like "Oh yeah, my grandmother cleaned houses."

From a critical standpoint, as they are reading the text, they make connections between the text and their own life or between different texts. In this example, Holiday is making their reading of a piece of literature relevant to their lives by placing it within a historical context. She is also facilitating the formation of what Collins (1998) refers to as a "group-based collective standpoint" (p. 24). Such a standpoint often characterizes black women's experiences and ideas as a group, particularly because black women have collectively experienced similar racial discrimination in the areas of housing, employment, health care, and education. Collins (1998) writes,

U.S. Black women had common organizational networks that enabled them to share experiences and construct a collective body of wisdom. This collective body of wisdom on how to survive as U.S. Black women constituted a distinctive Black women's standpoint on gender specific patterns of racial segregation and its accompanying economic penalties. (p. 24)

From an accelerative standpoint, Holiday is bringing the reading level of the book into range for students for whom the readability may otherwise be too difficult by providing a strong introduction. Further, for students who may be able to read the words but may need support with their comprehension, the book introduction brings the book into range for this group of students as well. Additionally, Holiday integrated fluency practice, phonemic awareness, and vocabulary within the context of a culturally relevant literature unit on African American literature. She supplemented the reading and discussion of literature with songs.

And then the next week, building upon that reading, we did songs, which is basically poetry put to music. The beautiful thing was they first listened to songs such as Stevie Wonder, Bill Withers, and Billie Holliday. First, they listened to the songs, and many of them knew the words, but after they listened to it the first time, they read the lyrics as they were listening to it, and it was just like you could see light bulbs going off across the classroom because they are like "Oh I always said it 'cause I heard it, but I did not really know what he was saying or what he meant." And after that, we reconstructed the lyrics. "What did she mean? What did he mean?" And we analyzed different parts of speech. We underlined the nouns, circled the verbs, things like that. And then, the next two weeks building on songs was short stories.

Holiday described teaching for acceleration within a culturally relevant framework. Specifically, she is teaching vocabulary and phonemic awareness within the context of literature.

Holiday: We studied one of Billie Holiday's songs called "God Bless the Child." I asked the students to take a look at the "ch" prefix that appeared throughout the song in words like "child." Then we looked at words that started with "sh." I asked them to look at similarities and differences of the words. Then, they wrote five additional words from their background experiences that started with either "ch" or "sh." Then they choose a few words to put into a sentence.

Interviewer: And then what would you do for the vocabulary for the Billie Holliday song?

Holiday: We chose words throughout the song to focus on. They would first have to give me the definition off the top of their heads, what they thought it meant, and then we would look it up in the dictionary and I would choose two people to have to use it in a sentence. Everyone would write down the definition, and then I asked them to use it in a sentence.

When we asked Holiday, "How do you integrate the history of African American people into your curriculum?" she paused, and stated, "It's like breathing air; it just is there." Holiday is dually focused on her students' academic progress and the social and structural issues that facilitate or impede that progress. Ladson-Billings (1995) defines culturally relevant teaching as using

students['] culture in order to maintain it and to transcend the negative effects of dominant culture.... Culturally relevant teaching is a pedagogy that empowers students intellectually, socially, emotionally, and politically by using cultural referents to impart knowledge, skills, and attitudes.... This kind of moving between the two cultures lays the foundation for a skill that the students will need in order to reach academic success. (pp. 17–18)

Holiday's insistence on using relevant materials with her students connects their lives outside of the classroom with the learning inside the classroom, which blurs the lines usually drawn between "school" and "home" or "community." She and other teachers in this book, such as Carolyn and Angy, blur the lines between what is traditionally separated as "personal" on the one hand and "political" on the other hand. The phrase "The personal is political" is an often quoted phrase from feminist thought that captures the right of privacy and also the notions that personal choices are inherently political and that political choices have personal implications (Hanisch, 1969).

Holiday incorporated a comprehensive approach to literacy instruction that included a social purpose for the literacy event, comprehension, fluency, vocabulary, and word work. All of this self-extending system is underlined by the importance of developing the students so what they learn in the classroom translates to their daily lives. Her students primarily read aloud, although they do incorporate some Drop Everything and Read (DEAR) time, which is silent reading time.

Holiday truly enjoyed teaching her students as writers. It was an area she identified as her strength as a teacher. She attributes this mainly to the fact that she identifies herself as a writer. Holiday used many different techniques for teaching writing in her class. When she models writing in her classroom, she does so with examples that are culturally and socially relevant. For example, she described teaching her students how to write an essay using the standard five-paragraph format of introduction, body 1, body 2, body 3, and conclusion. On this, she stated:

I used the example of "Dr. Martin Luther King was a great leader." So that was like the topic sentence, and as supporting details, I wrote that he was a great follower, a great preacher, and a great civil rights leader. Then I had them throw out examples of how he was a great follower, how he was a great preacher, and how he was a great civil rights leader. And then, sum it all up again, he's a great leader so he should be honored. Then, we took it to the next step, which was, OK, we've told you he's a great leader, so, so what? I use tangible examples that I thought everyone kind of knew about, and it would go in the diagrams or like the outline. After providing a model and an outline, I ask them to write using this structure. I don't care if there are spelling errors or grammar errors at this point. I tell them that once it is done, then I'll go back and show you individually one-on-one how to revise your essay.

Holiday focused on the purpose and the meaning of their writing, versus on the grammar and mechanics. In this way, Holiday encourages her students to develop their voices. While some of the teachers taught poetry as a genre, something that needed to be learned because there might be a poem on the GED test, other teachers were very passionate about poetry. Holiday shared her passion for spoken word poetry with her students. The following quote by black feminist Audre Lorde (1984) resonates with how Holiday spoke of her use of poetry as a teacher and activist, both in and out of the classroom:

For women, poetry is not a luxury. It is a vital necessity of our experience. It forms the quality of light within which we predicate our hopes and dreams toward survival and change. First made into language, then into idea, then into more tangible action. Poetry is the way we help give name to the nameless so it can be thought.... The Black mother within each of us—the poet—whispers in our dreams: I feel, therefore, I can be free. Poetry coins the language to express and charter this revolutionary demand, the implementation of that freedom. (pp. 37–38)

The teachers in the study discussed a variety of ways of negotiating the reading. Carolyn, Vivian, and Holiday discussed using small groups for the reading. Carolyn used book groups. Some teachers used independent and silent reading. Still others used partner reading in their classrooms. Many of the teachers used the reading strategy of round-robin reading in the classrooms. While round-robin reading is not seen as a good literacy technique in the reading research, the teachers have a reason for using this strategy (Eldredge, Reutzel, & Hollingsworth, 1996). Holiday said that it reminds her students of a church session. Vivian commented that it helps to build community in her classroom. It also reminds the students of their past experiences in school with reading instruction, and while she ultimately wants to move them beyond such approaches, she finds it useful to connect with their expectations first and then to take them in a new direction.

Flexible grouping is an important part of an accelerative literacy curriculum. Holiday used flexible grouping in her classroom. Holiday commented on her choice of groups:

The low-literacy students will be in another room with a tutor. I do group reading with pre-GED and GED level. I think more so than the literacy level is the age level that causes caveats in grouping. We have students from ages sixteen to eighty-seven, and they have completely different frameworks. The younger students have the sharpness, but their motivation is lower. The older students are so motivated ... but they shy away from the computer. The older students love the group lessons because it turns into a church lesson for them. The younger students like small groups. They don't like one-on-one because it bruises their ego, and whole-group lessons remind them too much of high school. Groups of four—they love it.

Holiday deeply believes in the power of the students in her classroom to lead in and out of the classroom—so much so that she positioned herself as an organizer of the leaders in her classroom, which is an idea that comes more from organizing (literature) rather than from education. She stated,

There is already an intrinsic knowledge in people. The goal of education is to pull that out rather than just feeding them these hard facts and asking them to regurgitate it. Our goal is to pull out what is already there and have them walk out of the classroom more enlightened than when they came in, more able to deal with their situation, their environment, their families, their communities.

This statement of commitment about her students reflected Holiday's stance toward teaching and learning in her classroom. Holiday commented that her students have told her on more than one occasion,

"If I had a teacher like you in school, I wouldn't have dropped out." She goes on to say,

They don't use the word "empowering," but in one form or another, they're getting way more than just math, how to write an essay, and I think that is the root of social change. I have no doubt in the world they are going to change something. They're currently changing something. I don't have to wait until they have this GED.

Indeed, the adults in Holiday's classroom are not simply students. They are also workers, preachers, mothers, sisters, activists, former alcoholics, and grandfathers. She recognized the multiplicity of identities of the people in her room and, with that multiplicity, the resources for transformation in and outside of the classroom. As an example, she described how at the beginning of their monthly potluck, she asked the preacher in the classroom to offer a prayer before they ate. One of the office staff in the building at the Adult Learning Center holds an elected position in her ward, and her initiatives focus on getting drugs off the streets and filling potholes. Holiday has asked her to speak with the class about the process for contacting their alderperson and making changes in their community. To summarize, Holiday stated, "Whatever skill they have, I let them be the teachers on it." In this framework, everyone is a learner, including Holiday as the teacher.

This dialogic understanding of teaching and learning is based in humanist philosophy and participatory education and is radical in the sense that it starts from a strengths perspective and assumes that the way toward transformation is already rooted in people. Every curricular design, intervention, and andragogical move in her classroom are rooted in this perspective. Holiday explained how she even organized her classroom from her students' perspectives, that is, she tried a number of configurations with the tables and chairs until her students told her the way that they liked the tables set up. Her recognition of who the people in her classroom (in their entirety) are also echoed in the boundary crossing that she seems to seamlessly do between her activist-educator lives in and out of the classroom.

On being a learner, Holiday stated, "It is a collaborative effort. It is a cyclical effect. The teacher is educating but at the same time being educated. And by the same token, students are given the position of leadership in education." Holiday readily acknowledged her students' out-of-class leadership in the classroom. This recognition creates a connection between the community and the classroom and sends the message that Holiday cares about her students as people, not just as learners in the classroom.

Holiday consistently positioned herself in relation to her students with regard to age, lived experiences, income, educational levels, and so on. She recognized that while she is African American, as were her students, and shares some similar experiences, she grew up in the middle class and is "one generation removed" from many of the experiences of living in poverty that her students experience on a daily basis. Differences in experiences create the potential for an authentic dialogue between the teacher and the learner.

Holiday is an activist in her own life, and the borders between her personal and professional activism were very blurred. Holiday primarily identified herself as an activist-poet. She is involved in the spoken word community which often speaks out on critical social issues. She also combines her art and activism through leading a writers' group for youth who are in juvenile detention centers. It is relevant to note that Holiday's activism outside the classroom includes her in the role of a literacy educator. Similarly, her role as a "formal" educator in the classroom includes her life as a poet-activist.

When we asked Holiday to comment on the tension that some of the other adult educators felt about bringing a social justice framework into the classroom, Holiday responded with her own question: "what is the classroom for, then?" Holiday explained that education is a form of socialization, and children and adults are socialized into a mainstream version of the world where they learn to be factory workers and tools of the capitalist system. A counterversion of education, then, Holiday explained, would teach learners to be agents in their social worlds. This connects to Holiday and other teachers in the study who believe that education is always value laden and ideological, even when it claims to be neutral.

Critical theorists have long critiqued the technical, rational models of education that function to reproduce the status quo. There has been much less work around the visionary project of constructing new possibilities for schools, classrooms, and other sites of learning. Holiday argued for the importance of social change: "social change is not necessarily a march on city hall but the ongoing little things that you never really hear [in the classroom, for example] which is the proactive side of activism."

The students in the critical literacy lab demonstrate evidence of this as they act to make social change that extends beyond the classroom. Students in Holiday's class were concerned because a "For Sale" sign had been placed in front of the adult literacy center. They asked Holiday why their school was for sale. Responding to their inquiries, Holiday brought in multiple documents that discussed the sale of the school for them to read and discuss. She brought in a newspaper article that listed their school as "unused." She brought in a document from the real estate company, and other newspaper articles that discussed the financial status of the school district. The class read and discussed these documents. They were concerned with the inaccuracies in the newspaper article that listed their building as unused. The class generated a list of action strategies they could take in response to this inaccuracy. They decided to write a letter to the editor that exposed the inaccuracy and listed the reasons why they should not sell the school building. Their actions influenced others in the building to act as well, which resulted in a member of the Board of Education visiting the site. Ultimately, the school building was not sold; it was (at least temporarily) removed from the list of buildings to be sold, and the "For Sale" sign taken down.

Holiday sees teaching as a form of activism. Embedded in her philosophy is a critique of education, but she is also reconstructing a new vision of education with her students. As she stated, the "whole dynamics of her classroom is social change."

10

Ethics and English Teaching

JANET OMURTAG

We always try to get them to talk about what is going on in their lives.

— Janet Omurtag, Interview

Janet, a European American woman in her sixties, is an English for Speakers of Other Languages (ESOL) teacher. She has worked at various adult education sites in the years she has been teaching ESOL—including the South Side Catholic Center, Oak Hill Elementary School (a family literacy program), and a hotel teaching workplace literacy. Janet comes from a family of seven brothers and sisters. Janet's mother eventually obtained her GED, and her father obtained a college degree. Her parents emphasized the importance of education with all of her siblings, and, as Janet stated, "It never occurred to any of us that we would not go to college." After college, Janet went to Turkey, taught ESOL in a university for three years, and then prepared literacy materials in a hospital for two years. On her choice of teaching, Janet stated, "I always loved education and wanted to be a teacher because I loved school so much." When she returned to the United States, she taught part-time in an ESOL classroom in a college setting. She then took a job in a public high school and taught English and speech classes for twenty-five years. After retiring from teaching high school, Janet again began teaching ESOL classes, stating that "[teaching ESOL] was meant to be." Janet is a certified high school teacher, has the adult education certification to teach ESOL, and is familiar with the process of second-language acquisition from her own experience of learning Turkish.

Beginning in 2001, she taught at Oak Hill Elementary School in an ESOL family literacy center modeled after Even Start and Families in Schools Programs. She worked at this site for twenty hours a week, Monday through Thursday from 8:00 in the morning to 1:00 in the afternoon. Her students at this site were primarily Bosnian and Serbian. Student enrollment and retention rates were the highest when Janet was teaching at this site, but after a year, she left this site because she didn't want to work as many hours. She then started teaching at two sites simultaneously, a local hotel where she taught workplace literacy classes and the South Side Catholic Center, where most of her students were of Mexican origin. The workplace literacy classes were only offered once or twice a week, and eventually closed because of low enrollment. Janet continued to work at the South Side Catholic Center, which was a community-based program which offered a food bank, employment counseling, adult education, and ESOL classes. She taught at this center for two years at less than ten hours per week. Her students at this site were primarily Latinas who were low-intermediate speakers of English. After this site eventually closed, she began working as an adult education teacher at the city jail.

This case study of Janet focuses primarily on her teaching at Oak Hill and at the South Side Catholic Center. At both of these sites, Janet taught an international, multilevel ESOL student population. Most of her students were not literate in their primary language. The majority of her students were low intermediate or beginners. A couple of students in Janet's classes were more advanced with their English and would be good candidates for passing the GED tests. On average, at the South Side Catholic Center, Janet has thirty-four students with twelve hours or more enrolled in her classroom. She maintains a 69 percent retention rate. Her greatest level of impact is English as a Second Language (ESL) level 1. Seventy-five percent of her students who enter her classroom at this level progress to level 2 according to the Comprehensive Adult Student Assessment System (CASAS) test scores. The CASAS is the assessment used to test ESOL students in Missouri.

Oak Hill Elementary School is a three-story traditional brick St. Louis schoolhouse. Janet's ESOL family literacy classroom was situated on the basement level in a small room with the early childhood classroom located next door in an even smaller room. The adult classroom was divided so that approximately one-third of the space was separated by a divider for administrative use by the project coordinator. A large blackboard in the front of the room was filled with words under review or associated with the current lesson. Word labels were taped on chairs, tables, and numerous other items and fixtures located within the space. Multinational flags, maps, and colorful displays were placed around the room, creating an inviting and inclusive atmosphere. Adult students sat around two tables placed together to provide one large group setting with Janet's desk immediately adjacent. A coffeepot with condiments was always in use on a table in the back of the room.

The South Side Catholic Center was founded in 1937. Janet describes the classroom as very spacious but also run-down. The classroom had shelves on one wall. Another wall was covered with windows that were protected with iron gating. The furniture in the classroom was old, and the wooden chalkboard was broken and dangerous to move. The air conditioner in the room rattled and clanked so loudly that they never used it on high if they wanted to have class discussions. Despite the dilapidated conditions of the classroom, Janet described the hope in the room.

The rooms were filled with books that gave off a feeling of being safe, positive, and hopeful. We enjoyed the light from our windows and were happy to have so many tables and chairs. We found our chalkboard perfect for holding self-adhesive poster paper (and thus were able to keep examples of our work and progress) and thanked our lucky stars we had cool air during days in St. Louis. Best of all, we used our space for individual group work and child care when we had no nursery.

Janet continually emphasizes the connections between reading, writing, speaking, and listening in her classroom. She works from a communicative language teaching approach, one that emphasizes the communication of ideas and content rather than accuracy. She incorporates dialogues into her class by asking students about their weekends and encouraging responses in English. Often the students liked to "become the teacher," Janet explains, and ask questions of each other. Janet writes their dialogues on the board. Students copy the dialogues and then practice role playing in small groups. Mini-lessons with small or whole groups on aspects of language and vocabulary often resulted through this process. One standard activity ended the class period: students were expected to fill out their Daily Prescription Sheets (DPS), but often there was time to sing a round of "Farewell, Have a Nice Day" to the tune of "Are You

Sleeping?" Students enjoyed the musical departure from class and learning patriotic songs.

Janet gives dual attention to teaching language as a formal system and as a social practice. She uses a range of methods including language experience stories, dialogues, and more traditional workbooks. As previously noted, Janet focuses on teaching grammar within meaningful language experience contexts. She also uses the commercially prepared literacy materials and sometimes moves from part to whole (i.e., from analysis of grammar and vocabulary instruction to purposeful language activities) or from grammar to meaningful experiences. The textbook, however, never becomes the curriculum in Janet's class. In other words, Janet seems to avoid the either/or position that often characterizes discussions of participatory ESOL teaching. This debate often characterizes teachers either as participatory in their approach by always working from whole to part or as functional in their approach by teaching sounds and grammar outside of the context of meaningful language experiences. Her approach resonates with how Auerbach (2001) discusses integrating grammar instruction within a participatory education framework:

Learning to contextualize grammar instruction (within a relevant curriculum) is an essential skill for teachers.... Anyone who listens to students knows that they see both of these aspects of language learning as critical to enabling them to take action in their lives. (pp. 281–282)

Janet explained that her students are motivated to be in her classroom, and as a result, Janet finds great pleasure in her teaching. Janet discussed the desire that her students have to learn English and claimed, "They all want English." This statement hints at the power and politics of English language teaching. Indeed, English is seen as "one of the most powerful means of inclusion into or exclusion from further education, employment, or social position" (Pennycook, 1994, p. 14). As such, access to English often impacts the social mobility and life chances of adults and children who do not speak English fluently as their first or second language. However, English teaching is also a political project in the sense that the teachers' dominant language carries with it social positions, hierarchies, and inequities of the society itself. As students learn the dominant language, they also acquire ways of thinking and talking about society that are coded through the dominant language. Teachers of English are faced with a constant struggle of teaching language that will allow learners to move forward in their day-to-day lives (survival or functional language skills) and yet, at the same time, recognizing that functional language often serves to reinforce hierarchical relationships and traditional power-knowledge relationships.

Like many teachers, Janet struggles with this ethical dilemma. Taking a humanistic stance, she hopes that as an adult education teacher, she can "open minds and facilitate thinking and learning with a sense of joy. This is really easy when people are coming to you by choice." When we asked her about teaching for social justice, her response was as follows:

A teacher has more than enough to do. Should I be responsible to outreach into the society? I do not think that is my primary role. I have everything I can do to teach English. But the whole American experience with education is to level the playing field. The federal legislation No Child Left Behind (NCLB) is not going to do this. We really want equal opportunities.

Janet's response helps illuminate the complexity of her stances as an ESOL teacher. On the one hand, she comments on the ways in which adult education teachers are already overworked with their responsibilities ("A teacher has more than enough to do"). Rhetorically, she questions whether her role as a teacher should also include what she refers to as "outreach into the society." She then draws on a critical stance to critique the failures of the "American experience" and federal policies in providing "equal opportunities," and argues that teaching English may contribute to a more equitable society. In our debriefing conversations, Janet talked about the many structural factors that frame the issue of equity and language policies in the United States.

Janet is very aware that teaching an international language has ethical implications, that is, issues related to the just and equitable treatment of all humans. Janet has presented at several professional conferences on the topic of ethics in ESOL. Hafernik, Messerschmitt, and Vandrick (2002) point out what they see as distinct dimensions between ethics and social justice in the context of ESOL. One dimension involves an interpersonal component: "the way students treat students, teachers treat students, students treat teachers and even the ways teachers treat other teachers and colleagues." The second component involves "teachers exposing students to social justice issues and developing their critical thinking skills" (p. 6). Janet's language teaching moves in and out of both components of ethics.

Janet worries about the ethics of promoting a critical stance toward language, literacy, and society when many of her students do not yet have citizenship (Auerbach, 2001; Hammond & Macken-Horarik, 1999; Lin, 1999). Because she works with international students, she is always receiving a fresh perspective on the United States from her students. She stated, "One of the things that amazes me is how my students always have positive things to say about America. Yet, they are aware that we are not very good to our old people. They are very insightful." Janet's comment reflects the contradictory nature of her students' understanding of the United States—what Lin (1999) refers to as a "want-hate relationship" with becoming a U.S. citizen (p. 394). Also embedded in Janet's insight about her students' ambivalent stance toward the United States are unstated questions about what this stance means for teachers of English. Some examples of unstated questions are as follows: what are the ethical roles of ESOL teachers in designing critical language awareness in an ESOL classroom? Do students need to master the dominant language (their second language) in order to become critical of it?

Janet is resistant to English-only legislation. Rather than putting the onus of responsibility on foreign-born students alone, Janet argues that everyone in the United States should become bilingual. This position, along with her critique of U.S. policies toward immigrants and refugees and her recognition of students' insight into the injustices in U.S. society, provides us insight into the subtle ways in which she teaches English from a critical stance. This critical framing is less overt than with other teachers such as Angy (also an ESOL teacher), Holiday, or Carolyn.

Janet's emphasis on justice can most clearly be observed through the *process* of her teaching, rather than in the content. Janet is learner centered and consistently starts with her students' experiences. The dialogues she and her students develop generate themes that they can explore further in discussions or in reading and writing. Because the majority of her students are women, the themes often reflect the day-to-day realities of living in a patriarchal, racist, and classist society. Most of the women are living in poverty and are caught in the web of oppression, which includes daily physical, symbolic, emotional, and verbal assaults on their personhood (Carmack, 1992; Horsman, 2000; Rockhill, 1990). These are not personal conditions. Rather, they are conditions that have been woven so tightly into their lives that they seem invisible to the women. Janet helps the women understand that they are not to blame for these issues. In talking about and through these personal and public-political issues, Janet creates a context where students have access to interpersonal and academic discourses.

The community of the classroom is important to Janet. She consciously builds a classroom environment where her students can feel safe as people and as learners. She builds community in her classroom by building relationships with and between the adults in the room. When she worked at Oak Hill, a site that offered early childhood education, some of the women had infants who were too young to enroll in the classes. Janet allowed the women to bring their babies to class so they would attend. This choice demonstrates that Janet recognizes the relationship between women, families, and education. As Rockhill (1995) stated, "Education is women's work but not their right" (p. 171). In attending to the women in her class as whole people, including their roles as mothers, rather than just as students, Janet creates a supportive environment in her classroom where the women can learn. Indeed, Janet recognizes the women's complicated relationship to power; often, they are in positions of leadership in their families and communities but are not granted access to power sharing or political participation. She realizes that there are many different cultural understandings of power but also believes that there are certain ethical principles that can guide practice, such as encouraging everyone's voice in the educative process.

Janet encouraged cooperative learning in her classroom so that the learners can learn from each other as well as from her. Learning often comes in the form of cross-cultural dialogues in which there is an exchange of culture. Dialogue is central in any empowering learning relationship. As Freire (1992) writes, "[Dialogue] implies a sincere, fundamental respect on the part of the subjects engaged in it, a respect that is violated, or prevented from materializing, by authoritarianism" (p. 117). Oftentimes, in a Freirean way, the reading and writing follow the discussion.

Janet is clear that any language and literacy instruction must start with relevant and engaging literacy materials. However, relevance is a moving target, something that changes across her students and among the different sites where she teaches. At the workplace, for example, she uses materials that have a job flavor. While she does use traditional workbooks and the Pictionary series along with relevant materials in her classroom, she acknowledges that her students are not as engaged by the traditional materials. Janet explained that many of the series emphasize phonics relationships over the meaning and context of a story, and students find that boring. However, volunteers are often important in working with these materials. Workbooks that teach phonics are available in several series, and many times it isn't boring and discouraging for a student if a volunteer helps him understand how this type of process is helpful.

Inspired by techniques derived from different learning styles and multi-intelligences, Janet will contextualize the phonics (or word study) lessons within materials that are more relevant to students' lives. She uses books on finances and taxes, the National Public Radio (NPR) writers' series, stories and articles from the Internet, newspapers from the adult education and family literacy programs in the district, and the local newspaper. Janet also collects stories from the Internet to use as the basis for discussion and then reading. She also uses multisensory material to practice colors, designs, directions, and prepositions. Sometimes she uses photographs to start a dialogue which will then lead to reading and writing. Janet stated that she chooses her materials based on "something they said, what is going on in class, what is going on in the world." This approach to teaching language and literacy acquisition has not been unproblematic. Like all adult learners, Janet's students bring their cultural models of what instruction should look like. Oftentimes, their models are based on education that includes rote memorization, language drills, lecturing, copying, and tests. At times, students in Janet's classroom have asked her to be more "workbook oriented."

When Janet does consciously bring a social issue into the context of the classroom, she tries to focus on issues that will not intensify the social divisions that already exist in the classroom or in their lives (e.g., between racial or ethnic groups or between a husband and wife). Janet described how a student brought in an issue about her electricity bill and how she thought her neighbors were hooking up to her electricity. Janet took this issue and facilitated a small-group brainstorming session. The woman left class with a number of different ways to address the problem. Or, the class will dialogue about a topic such as the pros and cons of living in Mexico and the United States. Often the Mexican women in her classroom talk about how they are working to get their families from Mexico to move to the United States. Or she might ask them, "What are some of the customs in your country?" Janet will ask critical questions during the discussion to move the dialogue to a deeper level. When the discussion has run its course, she will then write a summary statement on the board which captures the essence of their discussion. She will ask the learners to read back with her the sentences they have generated as a class. They will copy the sentences into their own notebooks and practice reading and rereading the sentences. Within these sentences, she will teach vocabulary words so that the words come from her students' experiences. She made the point that she teaches with words rather than with phonics rules. She often asks her students to read aloud so she can assess the fluency and intonation of their reading.

Janet loves literature and gets very excited about including literature in her classroom. She struggles, though, with the availability of high-interest, low-readability materials for second-language learners. Also, while students are motivated to engage with oral language and literature, they are often less amenable to engage in writing activities. That is why, in Janet's classroom, students copy a great deal or practice traditional writing instruction that focuses more on structure, spelling, and grammar. Janet noted that her students copy a great deal or practice writing things that they are likely to encounter in their lives such as their names, addresses, information for forms, and so on. While she tries to keep the writing relevant to her students, the process of writing itself is sometimes traditional. Journal writing has widespread use in her classroom.

One assignment that fared well revolved around journal writing. The husband of a Mexican woman in her class was shot, and the crime was reported in the newspaper. With the student's agreement, the class read and discussed the newspaper article and then wrote entries in their journals. Similarly, Scott and Schmitt-Boshnick (2001) shared their experiences of writing about personal topics in a community-based adult education program for women. They write, "The personal issues articulated in group dialogue can be considered an emancipatory process because each woman recognized she has an interest and a need to be connected to other women" (p. 128).

Janet uses a mixture of formal and informal assessments in her classes, all of which are linked with instruction. In addition to the formal CASAS test, which is required at least twice a semester, more authentic and context-based assessments are also helpful for informing instruction. Once a teacher has a sense of the students' basic listening, speaking, reading, and writing skills, individual informal assessments can also be noted on each student's DPS.

Janet asks herself the following questions: is a student improving in pronunciation or fluency? Does she respond without as much help from classmates to a question? Are there signs of improvement in his individual reading? Are the notations the students write in their journals clearer and more controlled? Janet also asks her students to keep their own prescription sheets so they can take responsibility in self-assessment. She also informally assesses her students to hear the rhythm and fluency of their language. Janet described how her teaching day is filled with "teachable moments." For example, if someone drops an ending while she is in a dialogue, Janet will conduct a mini-lesson on endings. "When something is not working, I will make an English lesson out of it and explore why. Everything we do is in the interest of learning English," Janet explained.

Janet does not shy away from addressing racial issues that characterize St. Louis. When a controversial event was happening with the police and one (European American) police officer had resigned and turned in his badge because a partner accused him of being very disrespectful to an African American woman, Janet talked with her students about this event and let her students know that the police have "a less than stellar reputation" in terms of racial profiling. Janet shared her racialized position with students and explained that she comes from a generation in which racial issues were not openly discussed. For her, personally talking about race in the classroom has meant disrupting her own comfort zone. Janet's goal is to "keep the conversation going … no matter where the conversation goes. It is in English, and it helps to build vocabulary and communication skills." If they were interested in learning more about racial dynamics in the city, she might bring in a guest speaker or find another text such as a police report or political cartoon from the newspaper. She and her students will dialogue around a controversial topic that gets her students talking and building vocabulary and language skills. In this way, the students control the flow of the conversation at times in the classroom.

Janet talked about the range of experiences that the immigrants and refugees have and gave a broad analysis of the risks they take in coming to the United States. She discussed how this complicates their critique of the United States as well as the ways in which social and ethical issues might be brought into the classroom. At other times, her students are surprised at how critical she is of the U.S. government and its policies. Janet explained it this way: "I want them to know how wonderful this truly flawed country is…. I want them to think patriotism means you can criticize [the government]. They are not comfortable with that. They think I will get thrown in jail for what I say." She went on to say, "It takes time for them to understand their rights and responsibilities as a citizen." As Maher and Thompson Tetreault (1994) point out,

The mix of people in any classroom, in terms of overt and hidden aspects of their identities and group memberships[,] profoundly shapes the possibilities for creating consciously positional pedagogies.... The instructional context also helps determine the degree of intimacy and trust afforded in the classroom context for discussion of these issues. (p. 216)

These dynamics are heightened as the students become more aware of the politics, power of language, and social identities in society, understandings they arrive at through a process of reflecting on their day-to-day experiences, often in low-wage jobs without health care or benefits; dialoguing about these experiences with other adults; and reflecting on the dissonance in their experiences in the United States.

As reflective teachers often do, Janet reflected on some of the errors she made as a teacher when working with immigrant and refugee groups. She explained how at Oak Hill, one of the adult education sites where she teaches, where her students were mostly from Bosnia, Janet found out that her use of Turkish with Bosnian students was making her Serbian students uncomfortable. When she discovered that many Turkish words were similar to Bosnian words and amused so many of the students, she made every attempt with new troublesome words to see if Turkish was any help. This strategy was not sensitive to the religious realities in Bosnia. With Serbians, the religious culture is Orthodox Christian; with Bosnians, the religious culture is Islam. Janet knew that communicating with students in their first language would promote relationships and trust in the classroom. However, in this case, Janet was confronted with differing cultural and religious beliefs that had ethical dimensions. When Janet learned that adults did not return to class because of her lack of awareness about these linguistic and ideological differences, she discontinued the use of this linguistic strategy.

Janet has confronted the pervasive belief that only English should be used in ESOL classrooms. Janet has made space for first-language communication in her classroom which helped her to understand her students, to draw out themes that were important in their lives, and to support students in their movement toward proficiency in English. She would allow her students to speak in their first language, which serves as a bridge for learning vocabulary, validates learners' lived experiences, increases trust between teachers and students, and makes gains in English language development. This process often helped to build a sense of community and a sense of respect for the first language, and helped Janet to understand her students' motivations, interests, and needs better. Indeed, there is ample research to suggest that the exclusive use of English in the classroom can be detrimental to language learners (e.g., Guerra, 1998; Shamash, 1990).

Janet's stated reluctance to directly address matters of social justice might be fueled by the context of her classroom. She is concerned about her students' safety and citizenship issues. She is also relatively alone in her teaching, that is, she does not have other colleagues who she can collaborate with or get ideas from. She is conscious of who she is in the classroom as an American citizen and who her students are in the context of citizenship. Further, because Janet teaches at a site where there is only one classroom (rather than at a site where there are other social services offered), she may feel more alone and less able to take risks in her teaching than other teachers who have a supportive network, like Sara, Carolyn, Holiday, or Angy, who all teach at centers where there are other teachers and social service professionals.

In her own life, Janet calls herself a feminist, has been very active with the Equal Rights Amendment (ERA), and has even run as a delegate for the ERA. Janet stated: "I was on the front lines, marching." She has introduced her daughters to the importance of fighting for women's rights and often brought them along when she attended marches, rallies, and protests. Janet actively seeks out professional development opportunities. For example, she is a member of the Missouri Association for Adult, Community, and Continuing Eudcation (MAACE) and has presented several times at their conferences on the subjects of ethics and workplace literacy.

11

Recognizing and Valuing Multiple Literacies

DOROTHY, HOLIDAY, AND JANET

RECOGNIZING DIFFERENCE

All three of the teachers presented in this section are fundamentally concerned with student experiences. What comes out most readily in Dorothy, Janet, and Holiday's cases is how they interrupt the authoritative voice of the teacher and the curriculum and open this space up for designing the curriculum together. Part of this is a conscious and political decision. Part of it, though, is a decision rendered because of the lack of resources and materials in adult education. They inevitably draw on multiple literacies in ways similar to how teachers in African American Freedom Schools and Native American boarding schools made do with the narratives and the resources they were provided. As a result, creative and sometimes resistant literacy practices are designed.

Each of the teachers brings diverse life experiences with them as people and educators into the classroom. Dorothy Walker and Janet Omurtag were both teachers in the K–12 system before they became adult education teachers. Holiday Simmons did not have any experience in a K–12 classroom. Most of her teaching and learning experiences came from the spoken word workshops she facilitated with youth in the community. Dorothy lived through Jim Crow segregation and the civil rights movement as well as through a time when women were not allowed to be married and simultaneously be employed as a teacher. Dorothy worked at different government jobs that influenced how she related to and connected with her students as workers and as people who have historically been discounted in society. Holiday is an activist in the various communities in her life. She facilitates spoken word workshops for youth in the community, as mentioned, and she was educated as a social worker. Janet lived overseas in Turkey for many years, and this prepared her with the firsthand experience of immersion in another culture. These rich and varied experiences, like all adult education teachers have, expand the horizons of their classrooms and open possible layers of meaning in the teaching and learning interactions that occur in their classrooms.

Like Carolyn, Sara, and Vivian, the teachers presented in this section also consciously reflect on their positions as teachers in the classrooms and communities in which they teach. Holiday is conscious of her relationships with her students because of her youthful appearance and age and because of the different experiences she has had as a black woman. On the one hand, she explained, she can relate with her students as a person of color, but on the other hand, her experiences are "twice removed" from her students because she grew up in a comfortable, middle-class home. Because of the *difference* between her and her students, Holiday intentionally opens up space in her classroom for dialogue so that they can teach each other. They can teach her, and she can offer them the experiences and knowledge of content and process that she possesses.

Dorothy takes on the presence of an elder in her classroom, and this presence demands the type of respect and attention that one might give someone who has a lifetime of experiences, struggles, and knowledge. Bringing her experiences that traverse a quarter of a century in the city where she still lives and teaches into the classroom, Dorothy acts as a guide for her students who are struggling to get an education. She is, however, unfamiliar with many aspects of youth culture. She recognizes that times have changed for her students, but some of the injustices that held true fifty years ago—such as apartheid practices in education and housing, high rates of unemployment, job discrimination, and violence—still ring true today.

Janet recognizes the privilege she brings with her into the classroom as a European American woman who is also a native speaker of English, and listens to her students' wants and needs as adult learners. She also recognizes the differences that exist between her and her students—cultural, linguistic, and life experience—and recognizes that neither she as an educator nor education alone can be a panacea for society's inequalities. She sees her role primarily as supporting her students as they gain access to English so they can become participatory citizens.

Janet, Dorothy, and Holiday are all conscious about how sociopolitical contexts construct their voices as women and teachers in the classroom. They all focus on the adult as an entire person, rather than as just a student in their classroom. They recognize the multiple and varied experiences the adults bring with them into the classroom, and these experiences become the cornerstone of their literacy curriculum. Janet, for example, begins every class with a dialogue about generative themes in the adults' lives. In the process of dialoguing, she learns more about the issues that are relevant to the adults in her classroom. She allows the women to bring their children into the classroom during instructional time, and recognizes that if they don't have child care, they will not attend classes.

Dorothy admits that she never administers the Test of Adult Basic Education (TABE) to a new student in her classroom before she has time to sit down, talk with the person, and really learn about his or her motivations for returning to school, hopes, and goals. Similarly, her instruction is based on her knowledge of her students' interests and goals, whether that is passing an ordainment test to become a minister or reading with their children. In addition to setting more traditional goals for her students (moving up in their TABE scores, for example), she allows the learners to set their own real-life goals and use literacy in the service of these goals. What she finds—and it is a general theme with all of the teachers in this book—is that in the process of using literacy toward real-life, authentic goals, they become more literate and also accelerate in more traditionally defined school measures (e.g., TABE, CASAS, and/or GED).

The teachers recognize that the adults in the classroom take on many different roles in their communities: leaders, preachers, mothers, workers, and community activists. They operate from the belief that the adults in their classrooms have a wealth of experiences to draw on, and they ask that they bring these experiences with them into the classroom (e.g., Gonzalez, Moll, & Amanti, 2005; Rogers, Light, & Curtis, 2004). These roles inevitably bring with them local language and literacy practices with which the adults are fluent. Local literacies are the ways of using oral and written texts to accomplish everyday goals and social practices (Barton & Hamilton, 2000). Literacies involve not only engagement with written and oral texts but also the associated ways of interacting, being, and representing a range of knowledge that are attached in some way to some form of activity or social practice (e.g., writing a letter to the editor, text messaging a friend, completing an online bank transaction, reading corporate advertising, skimming a popular magazine, negotiating bus schedules, and reading a note sent home from a child's teacher). Every social practice also has a special vocabulary known only to insiders in the social practice. Often the literacy practices are taken for granted both by the experts and by people in official institutions, such as schools. Most people thrive on local literacies for recreation, health, education, work, political activism, and community development. Further, many literacies are connected to a global flow of knowledge.

ORAL TRADITIONS AND MULTIPLE LITERACIES

Holiday, Janet, and Dorothy value and encourage multiple literacies and the associated identities in their classrooms. Richardson (2003) defines literacy as "the ability to accurately read experiences of being in the world with others and to act on this knowledge in a manner beneficial for the self-preservation, economic, spiritual, and cultural uplift. African American literacies are ways of knowing and being in the world with others" (p. 35). Richardson and other African American scholars (Gilyard, 1991; Morgan, 2002; Smitherman, 2000) have stressed the importance of recognizing that African American literacies come out of a tradition of negotiating vernacular and standard epistemologies and ontologies across time and space. Indeed, literacies (both empowering and oppressive varieties) used by African and African American orators during African enslavement and through Reconstruction, post-Reconstruction, the Harlem Renaissance, the civil rights and black power movements, and hip-hop consciousness share a common lineage and struggle. The long and continuous development of the oral tradition from oral narratives, spirituals, gospels, slave narratives, blues, hip-hop, and spoken word poetry is an important part of African American culture. Columbus (2004) writes,

Storytelling from the oral tradition originated from African cultural forms— oral narrative, music, religion, and language. The best known of the verbal performers was the griot, the African storyteller, cultural historian, and educator. Although griots were known for the entertaining ways in which they told stories, their intention was to assist their people in maintaining self-awareness, a role that has continued significance for people of African descent today. (p. 483)

Within the oral tradition, there are a wide range of discursive strategies evoked to convey messages. Smitherman (1977) calls these strategies "black modes of discourse" (p. 103), which may include strategies such as metaphors, call-and-response patterns, signifyin', or indirect discourse. All of these strategies function to convey multiple meanings, oftentimes meanings that convey resistance to dominant ideologies and worldviews.

Black modes of discourse also include the syntactic and orthographic features of African American Vernacular English (AAVE) or African American Language (AAL) (Morgan, 2002; Richardson, 2003; Smitherman, 2000). Morgan (2002) writes, "African American English is the language, discourse, and interactional styles and usage of those socialized into the speech community" (p. 65). AAL and AAVE have their own grammar, morphology, and syntax.

Dorothy, Janet, and Holiday understand that language communicates the values and ethics of a culture. Language constructs the social world and is also constructed by the social world. Language is, as Delpit and Dowdy (2002) remind us, "the skin that we speak" and is intimately connected to identity, collective experience, and community. Thus, the act of denying people the right to speak their primary language is a political act of silencing and subordinating these people. When, on the other hand, their language is welcome in the classroom, people can use their language to make themselves heard and become active agents in their world. Because language, itself, is value laden, when students' languages are welcome in the classroom, the values of their home, community, and collective experiences are also welcome in the classroom. These values are tools of resistance, which conflict with the dominant values of society. Through the oral tradition, people express oppositional knowledge that comes from living through struggles of oppression. Thus, multiple literacies, including the language and literacy practices connected to oral traditions, become a space for critical and radical literacies as well.

As members of the African American community, Holiday and Dorothy participate in this tradition as they incorporate aspects of the oral tradition into their teaching. For instance, Holiday often code-shifts from Standard English to AAVE when she is talking with the younger students in the classroom. She shares her spoken word poetry with her students. She integrates blues music into her literacy sessions. She uses literature that includes black discourse: themes, discourse patterns, and linguistic codes which express narratives of racism, sexism, and class exploitation. The narratives provide a way for students to see their experiences in a format that they know is valued in schools: in books. This recognition helps them to break the silence around their own forms of oppression.

Dorothy models her value and respect for the oral tradition in other ways. Her instructional discourse often reflects aspects of the oral tradition as she meanders in content and form when she is dialoguing with a student. If she is trying to communicate why students need to check their child's bag for homework, her story may take ten minutes and move in and out of past and present contexts, evoking imagery, metaphors, humor, and dialogue as she constructs her narrative. Her narratives, like those of the African griot, function simultaneously to entertain, educate, and pass on the cultural traditions and values from her generation. Observations in both classrooms reveal that the teachers often set up a call-and-response pattern of instructional discourse in which they will make a statement, and the students will respond, sometimes rhetorically, as they talk.

This is important, because at the heart of the oral tradition is the power to name one's reality. People learn quickly that their language is or is not valued. Adults enrolled in the adult education classrooms often have views that their language is incorrect, is not valued, and is simply "slang." Similarly, English for Speakers of Other Languages (ESOL) students are often faced with learning English in a way that denies their linguistic and cultural identities, and relegates their first language to a subordinate position. Such linguistic ideologies are reproduced by language policies, media, popular culture, and other dominant social institutions, including education. This widespread misinformation about linguistic histories contributes to a continued oppression of people as they are informed that their linguistic codes are not valued. A powerful tool of consciousness raising occurs when students become aware that the way they talk is a legitimate and rule-governed language.

While both Holiday and Dorothy recognize and value the oral tradition in their classroom, both in their own modes of participation and in what they encourage the adults to bring into the classroom, they depart in their views of the place of AAVE, or the syntactic aspect of black discourse, in the classroom. Holiday takes an approach similar to that of other educators such as Baker (2002), Lee (2001), and Meachum (2001), who advocate for connecting AAL with literary language and setting up the conditions for authentic language inquiry in which students compare and contrast "standard" and "nonstandard" forms of language. Indeed, Holiday models code switching with the younger students in her classroom.

Dorothy incorporates aspects of black discourse, such the oral tradition, use of metaphors, call-and-response patterns, and so forth, in the classroom. She asked her students to conduct a real-life "experiment" around the issue of Ebonics in the early 1970s, when the term was first coined by sociolinguists at Washington University in St. Louis. Dorothy recalled this time period when everyone was talking about Ebonics, or black sounds, because scholars at Washington University held a conference about Ebonics. During this time, her students came into her classroom and told her that they should be able to speak Black English (BE) in the classroom because the professors at the university said it was appropriate. Trying to point out the different contexts in which BE might not be appropriate (including the classroom), she told her students to call the famous sociolinguists' secretary on the phone in her office at the university. Dorothy told her students, "If she speaks in Black English when she answers the phone, then BE can become the official language of the classroom. If, on the other hand, the secretary answers the phone and speaks in Standard English (SE), versus black English then the students would have to learn to negotiate SE in the classroom." Dorothy gave her students the opportunity to interrogate different languages in different contexts. In doing so, she sets up the contexts for critical pedagogy and the investigation of the production and valuing of differential understandings of language. In this process, students were encouraged to engage in the task of inquiring into their own theoretical and political positions on language use.

The division in theory and practice of Holiday and Dorothy around language ideologies reflects political as well as generational differences. A larger set of issues emerges from the differences in terms of incorporating AAL and black discourse patterns into the classroom regarding whether or not students can be taught for liberation using the linguistic codes of the colonizer. Freire & Macedo (1987) wrote that "to continue to use the language of the colonizer as the only medium of instruction is to continue to provide manipulative strategies that support the maintenance of cultural domination" (p. 117). All of the students enrolled in adult education speak a dialect, creole, or language variation that may be more or less related to Standard English. Indeed, according to geographical, economic, racial, and gender differences, all groups of people speak a unique linguistic variation. Most of the students have also experienced multiple forms of oppression. Freire (1985) wrote,

Any people who can courageously break the chains of colonialism can also easily read the word, provided the word belongs to them. Their new leadership fails to recognize that in the struggle for liberation these people were involved in an authentic literacy process by which they learned to read their history, and that they also wrote during their struggle for liberation. (p. 56)

The ESOL students in Janet's classroom face a similar dilemma. The ESOL learners in Janet's classroom represent a subset of adult education and literacy students. On the difference between the two populations, Bailey (2006) writes, "The key distinction is that in the United States, AEL students use their mother tongue, English, to improve basic skills, gain knowledge, and handle learning tasks. AEL students communicate easily with their instructors" (p. 115). Bailey's distinction is, indeed, partially correct. Oftentimes, ESOL students have already mastered basic skills, in many cases in their own language, and their focus is on acquiring literacy in a second language. However, the teachers' cases presented here extend this analysis as we look across the two AEL classrooms and one ESOL classroom. We see moments of "culturally contested pedagogy," or cultural and linguistic collisions between learners and teachers, in each of the classrooms (Li, 2006).

Janet stresses the importance of meeting the learners' oral communication needs in her classroom. The Equipped for the Future (EFF) initiative set out to ask over 1,000 adult education students to respond to goal 6 of the National Educational Goals ("By the year 2000, every adult American will be literate and will possess the knowledge and skills necessary to compete in a global economy and exercise their rights and responsibilities as citizens"; www.ed.gov/G2k/index.html). Their responses were divided into four goals: (1) access, (2) voice, (3) action, and (4) a bridge to the future (Merrifield, 2000). These four goals reflect the importance to adult learners of having information to resources, having their voices heard in a wide range of contexts, having democratic participation in the communities in which they live, going to school and work, and having access to ongoing advancement for themselves and for their communities. Arguably, there is much overlap between the goals of ESOL learners and AEL learners who speak English as their first language.

Janet, Dorothy, and Holiday are all adamant about the need of the adults in their classroom to have access to the "codes of power" of dominant society. For Janet's students, this means becoming fluent with English in a range of communicative contexts, and for Dorothy and Holiday's students, this means learning Standard English and gaining control over the dominant genres of power (e.g., business letters—more here on "codes of power"). Holiday, in line with her more critical and radical views on the purpose and function of education, would argue that the codes of power can be transformed at the same time they are learned. However, all of the teachers intuitively know from their own experiences that there is a wide corpus of research that demonstrates that initial perceptions and assessments of individuals are based on short speech samples (e.g., Baugh, 2000; Purcell-Gates, 2002). Thus, to varying degrees, language awareness is an important aspect of their literacy and language teaching.

RELEVANT LITERACIES, COMMUNITIES OF PRACTICE, AND CRITICAL CONSCIOUSNESS

Janet, Holiday, and Dorothy, like Vivian, Carolyn, and Sara (all in section 2), focus on what is relevant and authentic in their students' lives in the service of obtaining their GED or improving their English. Their students' immediate goals become the avenue through which they accelerate toward the more traditional goals. Dorothy, for example, explicitly "translated" one of her student's (Bobby Sr.), home literacy practices into schooled literacy practices so that he could support his son as a reader and writer. Similarly, she invited Lance's church and truck driver literacy practices into the classroom and used them to teach various aspects of schooled literacy. Holiday called on her students' connections with blues music (Billie Holiday's "God Bless the Child"), their knowledge of the words of the songs and the artists, and the deep cultural meanings the songs have in their lives. She uses this cultural knowledge as a bridge between their home and schooled literacy practices. Indeed, we saw how she used a song to teach reading and critical response. Janet invited her students to use their first language as a bridge to second-language learning. She also incorporated culturally relevant practices into the classroom by making explicit the places of connect and disconnect between their culture and the dominant culture in the United States.

They also recognize the double bind inherent in working toward their students' immediate goals, which may be more in line with the goals of dominant society (for example, knowing how to fill out a job application to obtain a low-paying service sector job without health care, or how to read a letter sent home from the school that recommends that their child be placed in special education). However, as they recognize what their students already know to work toward these goals, ask critical and thought-provoking questions, and set up the conditions in which the adults can take over control of their own learning, two things are accomplished. First, the students experience success toward their traditionally defined goals. Second, and more importantly, they participate in a new type of education, one that is responsive and critical and leads to a different type of participation in society. Indeed, the teachers intentionally engage their students in critical consciousness-raising dialogues. Consciousness-raising education results in individuals seeing their lives in deliberatively political terms. Holiday discussed how she engaged the learners in her classroom in a discussion of the historical conditions surrounding the great northern migration in the book *The Women of Brewster Place* (Naylor, 1982). They began by discussing various types of oppression and discrimination that people in the classroom had experienced in their lives. Holiday invoked the authority of lived experiences of the adults in her classroom to connect to a history of group oppression to show the universality of their specific oppression. Dorothy asked Bobby Sr. to reflect on why he, as an adult, is sitting in a classroom in the same school where he attended elementary school. This type of consciousness raising offers a challenge to the dominant discourse which attempts to silence such experiences.

We heard Janet reflect on her choice to use the adults' first language in the classroom, a decision with ethical dimensions she was not aware of, because there were cultural and religious differences in the classroom. Janet described how, when she learned her students were offended by her language usage in the classroom, she stopped speaking in this language. Threads of power and ideology are woven through this example. This "error" in linguistic practice could have been used as a space for students and teachers to inquire into the politics and power of language in the classroom and in society. Such points of conflict can serve to strengthen communities of practice.

Janet, Dorothy, and Holiday strive to build communities of practice in their classrooms (Barton & Tusting, 2005; Wenger, 1998). This means that they each understand where their students are in their personal journeys with education, or what Fingeret and Drennon (1997) refer to as the "spiral of change" (p. 65). The spiral of change includes the personal changes that are associated with involvement in adult education. The stages in this spiral of change are prolonged tension, turning point, problem solving and seeking, changing relationships and changing practices, and intensive interaction. A summary of this spiral of change is that adults experience enduring tensions relating to literacy in their lives (prolonged tension). There might be a time when change feels possible or necessary (turning point). This point leads them to engagement in an instructional program in which affective bonds are formed and relationships outside of the program are either supportive of education, neutralized, or discouraging of education (changing relationships). Adults are exposed to intensive ongoing interaction in the diverse social and cultural contexts that exist both inside and outside the program (intensive interaction). The turning point generally involves many social factors in an adult's life: for example, losing a job, having a child, or getting a divorce. When adults enter into adult education classrooms, there are many social factors that have influenced this decision, and, in turn, many factors are influenced by their continued presence in adult education classrooms (Fingeret & Drennon, 1997, pp. 65–67). The relationships and understanding of the complexities of their students' journeys allow teachers to be continually flexible and responsive in their instruction.

Holiday, Dorothy, and Janet each take risks as educators as they negotiate relations of power in their classrooms. The teachers treat the curriculum as a narrative that they design by choosing books that are available to them from the adult education program, reflecting on their personal experiences, eliciting their students' life experiences, and so on. The curriculum becomes a patchwork quilt of voices, sewn together by the histories of participation of both the teachers and the students. In the sewing of this quilt, the teachers are creating a radically new design, one that is transformative from the inside.

RETHINKING PRACTICE

1. Invite your students to engage in a "self-study" of their own "localized" literacy practices. Ask your students to carefully document through writing, drawing, taking photographs, and the like the many literacy practices in their lives. You might ask learners to consider the following questions: in what areas do you consider yourself to be an expert? How

do you use literacies to accomplish this social practice? How did you learn these literacies? What specialized language is associated with this practice? How do others regard these literacy practices? Do they function in parallel with "official literacies," or were they developed in opposition to "official literacies"? In what ways is this literacy practice part of a global network? What are the "flows of knowledge" that are connected with this literacy practice? How might this literacy be a bridge to learning in an "official" setting? You could ask your students to document their literacy practices over the course of the day or choose a particular practice that they consider themselves to be an expert at to document literacy practices. Conduct your own "localized literacy" self-study alongside the learners in your class. Schedule time to share the inquiry.

2. Ask your students to represent their areas of expertise (e.g., mothering, driving, playing drums, knitting, baking apple pies, etc.) through multiple modalities. Invite them to paint, act out, draw, design an interactive media presentation for, write about, and/or sing about their area of expertise.

3. Take a community print walk with the learners in your class. Document through photographs all of the ways in which language and literacy are used in the community to accomplish important social goals. Ask your students, How is language used? How are we used by language? With your students, learn how to construct a digital story incorporating the photographs, written texts, music, and other images.

4. Try a contrastive language analysis mini-lesson with your students. Ask your students to observe and document their primary language in different official (e.g., church, school, and bank) and unofficial contexts (e.g., at a restaurant or with friends). Take note of the formal and informal rules of their language in different contexts. Ask them to bring in their observations to share with the class and bring people's attentions to particular features of the language. Hold a discussion about language variation and context.

5. Talk with colleagues about the ethical dimensions of teaching Standard (or Dominant) English.

For further reading, see the following:

Baker, J. (2002). Trilingualism. In L. Delpit & J. K. Dowdy (Eds.), *The skin that we speak: Thoughts on language and culture in the classroom* (pp. 51–61). New York: New Press.

Hammond, J., & Macken-Horarik, M. (1999). Critical literacy: Challenges and questions for ESL Classrooms. *TESOL Quarterly, 33*(3), 528–543.

Part 4
Cases of Adult Education Teachers

12

Class Actions
Worker's Rights and Literacy Education

Angela Folkes

It gives me a sense that I am teaching for social justice, not just English.

— Angela Folkes, Interview

Angela (Angy) Folkes had been teaching English for Speakers of Other Languages (ESOL) at the International Institute of Metropolitan St. Louis for six years. A European American woman in her early forties, Angy is quick with humor ("I used to be an industrial worker; now I am an industrial-strength adult education teacher") and very serious about her commitment to literacy education and justice. Prior to working at the International Institute, she worked for many years in a machine shop. Both in and out of the classroom, activism is a strong thread in Angy's life. "For me, it is an innate sense to fight for social justice, so you do that on the job every day," she said. "I did this on the shop floor and picket line every day, and now I bring that experience into the classroom."

Angy spent over ten years in various industrial jobs including working as a production worker at a cabinet company; as a sheet metal worker and spot welder of vending machines for a company called Crane National Vendors; as a chemical operator for an oil company; and as an assembler and tester of medical calibration equipment in a health care products company. Angy holds a BA in American culture studies with a minor in political science. After college, Angy was a Young Socialist and became a union activist, which led her to work in industry for many years. She completed her master's degree in Teaching English for Speakers of Other Languages (TESOL) while working full-time in a machine shop. Angy has taken two years of French and three years of modern standard

Arabic, and participated in an intensive Spanish language program in Nicaragua. Angy believes that being a language learner herself helps her to more deeply understand the process the adults in her class go through as they are learning English.

Angy had not professionally taught before she began at the International Institute, but she practiced education on the job by teaching other workers about their rights concerning safety issues, sexual harassment, the rights of women on the job, and how to organize effectively. When her union voted to go on strike against Allied Healthcare Products, Inc., she was one of the leaders on the picket line. She helped to unify the workforce, which was one-third European American, one-third African American, and one-third immigrant. After the strike, she encouraged coworkers to stay involved in other picket lines, participate in broader demonstrations, and educate themselves with labor and social justice videos. She even took a carload of coworkers to Detroit, Michigan, to hear Nelson Mandela and Rosa Parks speak.

Angy comes from a long line of educators. Her grandparents attended college, her mother was an elementary school teacher, and she had many aunts and uncles who were teachers or administrators of schools or universities. Angy described her parents as "news junkies," and consequently, Angy explained, "I grew up watching and discussing the news." Angy attributes her radical roots to her life growing up on a farm in Illinois. "Farming made me end up where I am now, teaching immigrants and refugees because farmers are connected to the global world through markets. I saw how farmers were suffering from the corporate manipulation of grain prices." Angy witnessed the impact of capitalism's global markets on the farm economy and on farm families. Angy reflected on her developing understanding of global issues: "I remember once when I was a kid, playing in the grain wagon full of soybeans and wondering, which country are all of these soybeans going to?"

Angy's awareness of the global connections in peoples' lives informs her approach to English language instruction (Auerbach, 2001; Campbell, 2001). Angy readily invites her students to bring their preoccupations and struggles into the classroom, a telltale sign of teaching English from a critical language awareness perspective. She explained, "I was raised to respect the value of a master's degree and a bachelor's degree but I also learned to respect not having a degree. I have learned to value what each individual brings into the classroom." In this approach, attributed to Brazilian educator Paulo

Freire, students name and share experiences in order to analyze them, construct knowledge collaboratively, and join their voices in addressing them. This model of teaching English connects the challenges that learners face in their local contexts with a global movement.

Angy's commitment for workers' rights and justice is woven into her work as an adult education teacher working with immigrant and refugee populations. Angy teaches a multilevel classroom of students from all over the world. Her classroom is a language- and print-rich environment, and her basic philosophy is getting her students to use language for meaningful purposes. She is student centered in her approach in terms of the focus and the level of her lessons. Angy's discussion of her language and literacy pedagogy was framed by concepts of social justice.

On most days, Angy explained, she is teaching basic life skills but always within a critical framework. Angy often thinks about what her students will need on the job. However, she does not advocate for workplace literacy in which students can simply become better and more efficient, compliant workers. She does want her students to be effective, cooperative workers, but not at the cost of their own safety or democratic participation. She does not seek to create anarchy in the workplace, but points out that blind obedience is not a service to the employers. Naturally, she supports the right to organize.

Upon entering Angy's classroom at the International Institute, the whiteboard is in the front of her room. Angy frequently teaches her lessons using PowerPoint, which is projected onto the whiteboard. She purchased the LCD projector with her own money. There are three long rows of four long tables which seat approximately fifteen people in each row. The walls are decorated with posters, maps, and signs, all of which are written in English. On any given day, one could walk into Angy's class and see Angy standing at the front of the room, asking her students to "repeat a sentence" with her, sitting side by side with students at their table and guiding them with their writing, or observing as small groups of adults work together. She readily changes her role (and accompanying physical positions) in the classroom from direct instruction to facilitation to learning with her students.

Angy views teaching, even at the lowest level, as political, because she is empowering her students, even if she is teaching them the difference between "chicken" and "kitchen." Angy described how even when she is teaching her students what would be considered everyday language and literacy practices such as talking to a teller at the bank or asking the clerk at the post office how to mail a letter, she is teaching them to be active in their community. Angy believes that students at any level of language and literacy learning and development can benefit and learn from an emphasis on social justice. She discussed various methods and techniques that she used to accelerate language and literacy development. Rather than teaching isolated skills, Angy teaches using relevant and problem-based materials and using dialogues that address important issues in her students' lives. She is, however, attentive to the different language levels that exist in her class.

She described using picture stories, a staple of her language pedagogy, in her classroom.

We use picture stories that are stories told with different frames of pictures. There is one about a woman who works in an office, and the boss calls her into his office and asks her to sit on the sofa, and somewhere in the story he pinches her and he asks her, "Do you like your job?" And she says, "Yes I like my job." And he goes, "Kiss me!" And she says, "No." And then he says, "OK, no job." And that is where the story ended. So, I try to take it a frame farther, and open it up for discussion, and make it clear to them that if you do this on the job, you will be fired, and if your boss treats you this way, you can go to the union, and then you can go to your boss's boss and the EEOC [U.S. Equal Employment Opportunity Commission].

The way in which Angy uses pictures stories is a clear example of teaching language within a critical framework. Picture stories (or any stories relying heavily on graphics such as photos, drawings by hand, cartoons, etc.) and language experience stories function in similar ways in the ESOL and General Educational Development (GED) classrooms. Both serve to make connections between the students' lives and their school literacy learning, generate dialogue, and move from the spoken word to the written word. Bardnt (2001) described a similar approach where learners name, make, and connect their lives using "photo-stories." Photo-stories include students capturing their worlds through pictures, making a story from the pictures they create, and then naming their social, political, and economic realities through their construction of the photos. Picture and language experience stories set up the conditions for what Freire called "reading the word and the world." There are many places in the process of constructing picture stories that are participatory:

deciding which themes to focus on, sharing ideas that become the core of the stories, writing the stories, and collaborating to act out the storylines. This process invites the student into the process of producing his or her own texts, rather than simply consuming someone else's ideas.

Picture stories are stories told with pictures and few words. This allows the learners to engage in a dialogue about what they see happening in the picture. As they talk, generative themes arise, which are used as the basis for writing and word study (or phonemic analysis). Angy also made the picture stories into PowerPoint presentations so she can project each frame of the story onto a board and students can "read" the story together as a class. At each stage in the process, students are invited to contribute their ideas and voices, which positions adult learners as co-designers of the curriculum.

Angy also has picture stories that are already created that she used to help her students practice language and literacy development. One such story was about the civil rights movement, particularly Rosa Parks and the Montgomery bus boycott. After reading and talking about the picture story as a class, Angy and her beginning-level class extended the picture story into a play. She supplemented the picture story with various language and literacy activities that connected to the theme of the picture story. The students worked on word scrambles, dictations, and true-false questions. They read and reread the picture story. They rehearsed, role-played, watched a movie about the civil rights movement, made props, and worked in small groups. By the end of the week, the class performed a play for other teachers and students at the International Institute. Throughout the week, they learned language and literacy skills, principles of organizing, and the foundations of civil rights in the United States. This is a good example of how Angy's teaching helps to build alliances between immigrant-refugee and African American groups in St. Louis, alliances that address the impact of institutionalized racism on all people.

Angy integrated technology into her teaching to bring together the pictures with the text. She used PowerPoint to cover each slide in the picture story. She introduced the word on a PowerPoint slide and provided her students several opportunities to practice using the word in context. As a class, they jointly negotiated each frame of the picture story. With beginning students, she read a frame and then asked her students to repeat the frame. They proceeded through the entire picture story in this manner. When Angy sensed that her students had an understanding of the story, she then asked them to reenact the narrative using simple props (e.g., chairs for the bus, a hat for Rosa Parks, and ties for the bus owners). This is a form of reader's theater, in which readers are asked to step into the narrative. This type of theater builds comprehension, fluency, and collaboration within the context of an authentic narrative (e.g., Boal, 1985, 2002; Spolin, 1986).

In the manner that characterizes critical educators, Angy brought the current political, racial, economic, and social issues of immigrant rights into the classroom as a subject of exploration, debate, discussion, and inquiry. Angy designed a PowerPoint presentation which integrated the picture story methodology, using pictures from newspapers and Internet news sources, clip art, and simple sentences to illustrate the struggle for immigrant rights.

Angy presented the PowerPoint presentation of sixteen slides starting on May Day, the International Labor Rights Day, which occurred at the same time as the immigrant protests and boycotts in the United States during the spring of 2006 (see figure 12.1). The picture story begins, "It's December 2005. [Wisconsin Republican U.S.] Representative [James] Sensenbrenner says, 'Being undocumented is a felony (big crime).'" Underneath the text is a picture of the representative speaking at a podium. The next slide focuses on the state-level issues. It reads, "It's 2006. Missouri lawmakers say, 'It's illegal for the undocumented to go to college in Missouri.'" This slide has clip art of a diploma, a graduation cap, and a stack of books. The picture story continues at the city level and includes a picture of a demonstration in front of the Arch in St. Louis. The text reads, "It's April 2006. Six thousand march in St. Louis for immigrant rights." The next slide continues, "It's May 2006. Today, millions of immigrants and their friends don't go to work or school." Clip art of a bus and a worker is included in this slide. When Angy introduces the story, she reads through each slide first as her students listen and follow along as she points to each of the words. They may have a short discussion about each of the slides to evoke background knowledge. The slides continue, "They don't go shopping." "This is the largest boycott and labor stoppage in the United States." "This is history." Next, the picture story moves into actions that were taken on behalf of immigrant rights. "In California, millions protest in the streets with signs. They shout, 'Sí se puede' ('Yes I can!')." As they discussed this slide, the Spanish speakers in the class taught the non-Spanish speakers what the phrase "Sí se puede" means in English. On the

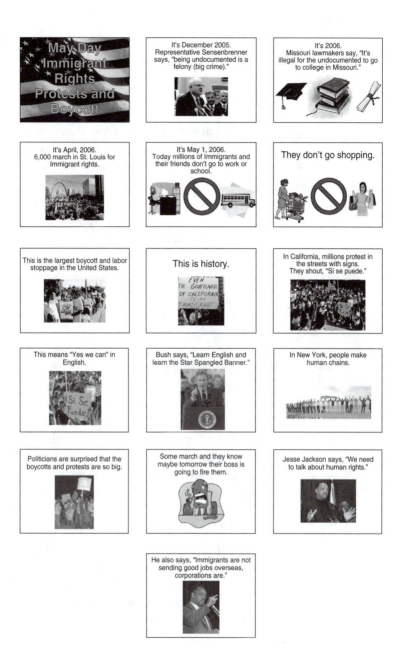

Figure 12.1 Angy Folkes's PowerPoint Presentation of Worker's Rights

next slide is a picture of President Bush. The text reads, "Bush says, 'Learn English and learn "The Star Spangled Banner."'" Angy has written the text in simple sentences using the illustrations on each of the slides to support the text. As the class becomes familiar with the picture story, the learners connect the spoken language with the written language and learn to problem solve unknown words using the support of the pictures and the structure of the sentences. "In New York, people make human chains," the next slide reads. "Politicians are surprised that the boycotts and protests are so big." "Some march and they know maybe tomorrow their boss is going to fire them." Each slide opens up the possibility of dialogue and discussion. Angy pauses and waits for the reactions and thoughts of the adults in the room. She assesses their comprehension and comfort with the picture story based on their participation and the nonverbal cues they give during the exercise. She watches for smiles, body language, and disengagement to determine the effectiveness of the discussion. The picture story ends with two slides featuring photos of Jesse Jackson and a call for bridging coalitions between oppressed groups in society. The text reads, "Jesse Jackson says, 'We need to talk about human rights.' He also says, 'Immigrants are not sending good jobs overseas; corporations are.'"

Angy used the picture story represented through PowerPoint for four days. She designed literacy activities to accompany the picture story, including word scrambles, true-false questions, multilevel dictations, and "wh" questions (where, when, who, and what). Each of these activities integrated the theme of immigrant rights.

During this time, her intermediate class read a newspaper article about three hundred Somali workers at a Tyson plant in Norfolk, Nebraska, who walked off the line because the company broke its promise to acknowledge prayer breaks for workers. At this plant, workers were followed into the restrooms to make sure they were not praying in there. In this case, the union and the community organizers won back the jobs of the ten employees who were fired. Angy has plans to turn the story into a picture story on PowerPoint for beginning and advanced students, visit the plant, contact the union, and ask for photographs of the event.

Dialogue partners are another common language and literacy method used in Angy's classroom. Angy generates dialogues based on real-life experiences that are typical occurrences for the adults in her classroom. Angy described how they dialogued about housing discrimination:

My students told me, "They told me this housing was available and now they are saying it isn't. I am going to call the Equal Housing Authority." So I've made up different dialogues of examples of discrimination and how they should respond to discrimination in housing as well as to the typical and equally important things like calling the landlord for maintenance. We practice saying expressions, such as "Will you come to the apartment at 5:00? My toilet is stopped up."

Angy uses dialogue partners not only to develop language proficiency but also to teach her students how to respond and act in their worlds, to become active citizens. As they are talking, Angy practices the art of listening to her students, so she can take them from where they are to another place. Rockhill (1990) states, "Unless students can bring their experiences into the classrooms and we can truly learn to listen—to hear their stories—to learn what they know, that they know, and how they have come to know what they know, I don't see how we can talk of critical literacy" (p. 23). Many of the books that Angy uses are also topically related to her students' lives. Angy is able to choose these books, again, because of the ways in which she listens to the issues and concerns that are important in her students' lives. Angy explained,

There is a book called The Working Experience *(New Readers Press, 1991), which has a short little reading written by a woman who is talking about her job: "I came to the U.S. from Puerto Rico. I clean houses for a lady and she pays me every two weeks." As they read and discuss the story, they identify with the themes of the workplace experience.*

She also used multiple forms of literacy, such as songs to teach language, again within a social justice framework. Angy described the song "What a Wonderful World," the song popularized by Louis Armstrong, to teach about antiracism. She will take a keyword from each line of Armstrong's song (e.g., "I see trees of green, red roses too") and connect it to a picture (e.g., trees and roses). She will display the picture and the word on the PowerPoint screen as the song is playing. The students also have a copy of the song. After the song plays, they talk about the song and what it means to them and their lives. Angy described that for her students, the song often generates a feeling of connectedness, especially when they talk about it in the context of Armstrong's life. That is, he wrote the song during the time of segregation and while he could have been an angry and bitter person, he was not. Angy's integration of language instruction within an antiracist framework is particularly salient given the context of her ESOL classroom. The classroom is located in the southern part of the city, a part of the city that sits on the racial divide. Part of this neighborhood is primarily populated by African Americans. Another part is populated by an increasingly integrated group of people but had been historically populated by European American people. Angy's instruction anticipates that the international learners will, at some point, become caught in this racial divide. Angy notes that many of her students comment on the racial tensions they experience in their life—at school or at work, and on public transportation. Her students will ask her, "Teacher Angy, why are most of the poor Americans black?" "Angy, why is there poverty in America?" "Why are most of the crimes in St. Louis committed by black people?" "Why are there so many black people on death row?" Such questions are fueled by public debates about immigrant rights and the economy. Through addressing these questions and unpacking the assumptions underlying such questions, Angy promotes an expanded critical consciousness about the intersecting oppressions of racism, classism, and sexism while, at the same time, respecting the diverse cultural worlds the adults bring with them into the classroom. As she does this, Angy is forging possible bridges between the historically oppressed groups in the city: African Americans and the more recently oppressed immigrant and refugee groups. Her literacy and language lessons are taught from the perspective that in a capitalist society, both groups are kept oppressed and separated from one another to keep the workforce divided.

Action, in these examples, is embedded in the critical consciousness raising of her students in class and may or may not transfer into their lives outside of the classroom. The point that Angy makes clear is that as her students are becoming more proficient with language and literacy, they are also learning more about their social world and how to be agents in their world. Unlike some of the teachers who are hesitant to do so, Angy also advocates for action that extends outside the classroom. Angy explained:

Today I told my students, "Monday, no class, go downtown and march for Martin Luther King!" I am restrained from directly giving my political opinions, because I am paid with federal funds, and I would be taking advantage of my position. I can teach them how to vote and participate, but can't tell them who to vote for or which side of the picket line to stand on. I do tell them about my personal experiences of being on strike and facing sexual discrimination on the job.

As Angy explained, teaching for social justice is not unproblematic. She gave several examples where there were unintended consequences of teaching from a social justice framework, particularly in an ESOL classroom. Often, her students come to the United States as political refugees from warring nations. Angy explained an emotional experience in her classroom that reflected the often tumultuous nature of teaching for social justice:

We were practicing formal pronouns and I was pulling out famous people, people whose faces were in the news, such as Nelson Mandela, Madonna, Tina Turner, President Bush, and the Dalai Lama. This was also during the time when [former Serbian President Slobodan] Miloševic was in the news. I had a picture of Miloševic. I did not say he was good, or he was bad; I just asked, "What is his name? What language does he speak?" Upon seeing the picture, one of my students broke out in tears. You never know what issues will trigger something.

Angy explained that it is not unusual to have two students sitting next to each other from warring countries, and so it becomes difficult to connect personally with her students' experiences from their home countries. Oftentimes, culturally relevant instruction and critical literacy or social justice education are assumed to work toward justice and democracy in the classroom, but, as Angy points out, this may impede rather than facilitate relations in her classroom, both between her students and her and between other students in the classroom. The goal, of course, would be to create a classroom community in which such difficult conversations could occur and people could agree to disagree. However, because attendance is voluntary, rather than mandatory, she often does not have the same group of students, which makes building the trust that is necessary to sustain these conversations difficult. At other times, the students are hesitant to engage in conversing about politics or critiquing policy and practices in the United States because they are not U.S. citizens and are not protected by the First Amendment, but want to be. Although Angy realizes that the personal is political/political is personal, she hesitates to make personal examples or issues a part of the whole-group dialogue (such as when a student brings in an electric bill and asks her to help interpret it) because, as she notes, "Even the electric bill is personal." On this issue, Auerbach (2001) writes,

Addressing social issues is no more political than teaching language or sur-
vival vocabulary. Every pedagogical approach is political in that it prepares
students for particular life roles. (p. 272)

For Angy, there is no separation between the personal and the political, between teaching and activism. Angy consistently reflected on her practices as a teacher and activist.

My instruction as a teacher comes less from my formal education, my master's
degree, than it does from my workplace experience. All of my teaching experi-
ences [before becoming a formal teacher] were with adults. I've worked in oil
fields with adults. I've worked on factory floors with adults. And these are the
experiences I bring into the classroom.

This ongoing process of acting and reflecting is what is referred to as "praxis." On praxis, Auerbach writes,

Praxis evolves through an ongoing process of embracing certain aspects of the
approach on one level, attempting to apply this preliminary understanding in
practice, bumping into problems that trigger further reflection, then applying
this new understanding, bumping into new problems (or the same ones) and
so on. (p. 269)

Conversations and actions around justice demand a democratic class-room community. Angy is committed to building the community of her classroom, which is a difficult feat given that she has a multina-tional classroom. She discussed the dilemmas of a student-centered classroom without students or the teacher dominating the content or the flow of the discussion. Angy was aware of the process as well as the content in her classroom. Auerbach (2001) writes about the com-plexity of teaching from a participatory framework and raises yet another issue. She writes, "Putting participatory ESOL into practice isn't easy. ESOL learners have their own ideas about what counts as language learning, and having a democratic classroom may not be one of them. They may want traditional, teacher directed, grammar focused instruction and rote learning" (p. 267).

Similarly, Auerbach (2001) stated,

Clearly teachers have their own goals and their own understandings of effec-
tive second language pedagogy, and, most important, they have power. To
deny this is both irresponsible and disingenuous: students know it and teach-
ers act on it whether or not they acknowledge it. At the same time, part of hav-
ing power is making space for students to exert their power and to participate

in decision making. The dance of teachers and students as they negotiate their respective goals, expectations, and understandings is central to participatory ESL. (p. 278)

As her students are learning language and literacy, they are also becoming politicized, or, rather, she encourages the political aspects of her students to enter into the discussion. Social justice, for Angy, is defined in terms of working for systemic change. She pivots between the issues of workers' rights, economic justice, antiracism, multiculturalism, multilingualism, antisexism, antiheterosexism, and antihomophobia. Angy's instruction is characterized by risk taking. For example, Angy described how she had an unusually advanced language group and so she decided to use a discussion starter on gay and lesbian rights that she read in the book *Speaking Fluency Activities for Advanced ESL/EFL Students* (Folse, 1996). Angy described how she started the discussion with her class: "I had handed out the text and I was standing in front of the class. I wondered, 'How do I start this one?' The students started it for me with their reactions of 'Oohhh, aahhh—what a topic!' Many of the students were smiling." Angy explained the mixture of reactions in the classroom:

I took this as a positive sign and relaxed. The discussion was sometimes heated as there were many opinions and perspectives. One man from Brazil noted that his uncle hires gay men in his hotel because they are polite. Another adult noted that being gay is not natural and it is wrong. An adult from Colombia noted that gay people have been around for centuries. A learner from Russia stated that gay people get an operation and end up one sex or the other. Many of the learners thought that gay and lesbian couples should have the right to make medical decisions for their partners.

Moving fluidly in and out of a critical literacy framework, Angy brought up several points that were missing in the text. She noted that in the United States, there is a long history of violating the rights of people who are gay and lesbian. She also brought up that in the United States, there have been many attacks, beatings, and murders of people who are gay or lesbian. Reflecting on this classroom discussion, Angy stated, "I felt I could have facilitated the discussion better, but if the point was to get them discussing, I accomplished that goal."

While some teachers drew on one or two critical frameworks, Angy (and Holiday) seemed to move between frameworks, depending on the issue at hand. Indeed, activism is embedded in the core of

Angy's teaching philosophy. As she said, the social justice aspect of her work is important because it makes her feel as though she has a "purpose for teaching, social justice, versus just teaching English."

Angy has been involved with many different organizations, including the Coalition of Labor Union Women, the International Association of Machinist and Aerospace Workers' Union, and the Toledo Area Anti-Apartheid Committee. Currently, she is a member of TESOL, MidAmerica Teachers of English to Speakers of Other Languages (MIDTESOL), and the TESOLers for Social Responsibility Caucus. She is also involved with the American-Arab Anti-discrimination Committee, Missourians against the Death Penalty, the Instead of War Coalition, the U.S. Campaign to End Israeli Occupation, various picket lines as they arise, and the St. Louis Literacy for Social Justice Teacher Research Group. She has also served as a volunteer tutor for the St. Louis Literacy Council and at an ESL school. She continued to be very active in her own professional development as an adult education teacher and has been recognized for leadership roles in her professional community. Angy was a presenter at the Educating for Change Curriculum Fair, which was a community fair of educators and activists who shared their work relating to education and social justice. Angy presented a table display on teaching about breast cancer and conducted a workshop session with several of her students on using PowerPoint in the ESOL classroom. She brought several of her students and collaborated with them on both presentations. The following year, Angy brought three of her students to the Chicago Teachers for Social Justice Curriculum Fair so they could learn about how their actions in the classroom were connected to a larger movement. She has also presented at the Acting for a Better Community Regional Conference (ABC's of Literacy) and at the Missouri Association for Adult, Community, and Continuing Education conference. She was on the planning committee for the Second Annual Educating for Change Curriculum Fair and has advocated to have the curriculum fair at the International Institute and focus on immigrant rights issues. She is also participating in the development of ESOL tutor training. Angy was one of less than twenty people across the state of Missouri who was asked to serve on a steering committee for developing state content standards for adult education and advocated for a unique culture strand, hoping to bring social justice topics into the adult ESOL content standards.

13

Disrupting Cultural Models of Education

SARAJANE CAMPBELL

Each adult deserves to be educated. — Sarajane Campbell, Interview

Sarajane, a European American teacher, was formally educated to become a teacher and has a master's degree in reading. Sarajane has been working in adult education since 1980 and has worked at several different sites such as the Southside Women's Center and the Salvation Army Women's Shelter. She also worked at a family literacy program in a St. Louis suburb. Sarajane most recently taught an adult education class located at the Urban League, a community-based program located in the city of St. Louis. Sarajane's class meets twice a week for a half a day at a time. Her greatest level of impact is at level 1, according to the Test of Adult Basic Education (TABE). At this level, 50 percent of her students progress to level 2. On average, she has forty-one students enrolled with twelve hours or more, which means she has a 62 percent retention rate. The programs and staff are funded through the Urban League. Her current students are men and women, the majority of whom are low income. However, historically, the majority of Sarajane's students have been low-income women. All of the adult learners in her classes are working toward their General Educational Development (GED) diploma and, at the same time, struggling to overcome problems of poverty, family violence, child care, unemployment, language barriers, and housing.

Sarajane has an undergraduate degree in elementary education and taught elementary education for six years, and then she returned to earn a master's degree in reading. Sarajane claimed that getting her master's in reading caused her to go into adult education part-time because of her "interest in adult literacy." Sarajane is the only teacher in our study who holds a degree in literacy. She is a tireless advocate of adult literacy education, in her role as a teacher in her classroom and as a tutor educator. Sarajane was trained as a Laubach tutor in 1980 and continues to train adult literacy tutors in the Laubach methods. She also works with the Literacy Council to develop the trainings for tutors. As she stated, "We trained a lot of tutors in the [Laubach] methods."

Sarajane comes from a long history of professionals who were college educated. Her sisters, parents, and grandparents all earned college degrees at the state university in Illinois. Sarajane's great-great-grandfather started a small college in Illinois, which her great-grandmother attended in the late 1800s. Sarajane stated,

I have a great-grandmother who graduated from college. She lived to be one hundred, and she was a suffragist and an activist.... Over the years I heard my mother talk about her, and she protested in Washington, D.C., for women's rights. She also went to England with her daughter and protested there for women's rights and was involved in the amendment that granted women the right to vote.

Reflecting on her family's history with education, Sarajane commented,

It makes me stop and think about the opportunities that Euro-American women and men have had and the experiences that we take for granted. On the other hand, so many minorities have had to struggle and fight to get the opportunities that we take for granted. It really bothers me when I think about how the institutions have not served all of society very well.

Similar to all of the exemplary teachers in this book, Sarajane is a committed teacher who sees adult education as a vocation. She stated,

I think about not teaching and I think, "What would I do with my life?" I love to teach and I love the interactions with my students, an adult to an adult. There are so many things I have learned from my students that you can't learn from teaching children. You are teaching adults who have real problems that you can relate to.

The Southside Women's Center, the center where Sarajane's adult education class was located, was housed in a five-room apartment over the gymnasium of a Catholic school/parish. Rooms were furnished based on their primary use for other programs offered at the center. For example, one room included a long table with chairs and had several sewing machines along each wall; another was a kitchen; and others were used for group meetings, prayer, and small-group activities. There was a screened-in porch off of the long hallway that ran alongside all of the rooms. Students were able to study in the room of their choice except in the kitchen, which was considered a "break" space with coffee and tea available during class time.

Sarajane used a table in the middle "group meeting" room as a substitute desk, with textbooks stored in the two large closets in this room. A file cabinet held the numerous handouts on various subjects that Sarajane brought with her to the center. Tutors and students worked together throughout the center. Sarajane circulated throughout the center, or students sought her assistance in this central location. Group instruction was offered in the "sewing/craft room," as it was most conducive to group instruction and held a large portable blackboard. The center itself was filled with positive and diverse women-centered images and messages. Books, pamphlets, announcements of upcoming events, and magazines were numerous and available throughout the center. Bulletin boards displaying information and resources on various issues relevant to women's lives were located in every room.

At the time when Sarajane was teaching at the women's center in south St. Louis, the community was starting to become more racially integrated. One of the goals of the center was to promote diversity and multiculturalism. At the site, there were pictures of multicultural women in diverse roles and quotes to reflect the importance of inclusion and diversity.

Sarajane has an authentic voice in the classroom. She dressed as someone her age and generation would dress, and she talked mutually with people. She was consistent with diverse groups of people and did not change based on who she was talking with (in terms of demeanor, tone of voice, and laughter). She assumed her authority when needed. For example, if people weren't really working, she would remind them about the purpose of the classroom, redirecting them to the purpose and goal of their education. She is accepting of other people's differences without having to take on the differences or change their differences. Students notice and appreciate her authenticity as a person. On authentic relationships, Freire (1973) stated, "To be human is to engage in relationships with others and with the world. It is to experience that world as an objective reality, as independent of oneself, capable of being known" (p. 1).

Sarajane recognized that there are many different reasons why adults may come back to adult education, such as to read the Bible, for enjoyment, to further their own education, or to read with their children. She stated, "A GED can open doors to higher education, a job, increases in self-esteem." She also stated, "People want that GED, because they can say, 'I got it!'" Sarajane explained that often adults come to the community center where she teaches in search of services such as food, housing, and clothing. Then, they will see that there is an adult education class and it will pique their interest. Sarajane is aware of the myriad of factors that either impede or facilitate adults' acquisition of (formal) education. Indeed, Sarajane was very aware of her students' needs that extended beyond academics (e.g., domestic violence and health care). When the women brought up an issue in class, Sarajane would listen to their issues and then provide them with resources so they could follow up with a trained professional in depth. Able to attend to their academic learning once the imminent social issues were off their minds, Sarajane's students progressed academically, and consequently, Sarajane continually had high retention rates in her classroom.

In her class, Sarajane uses a combination of individual work and group lessons. Sarajane discussed how she attends to individualized instruction within the context of group lessons. She stated,

Students come to class ready for academics. They are busy adults with jobs and families and often feel compelled to "catch up." I have found that becoming personally involved in each student's instructional plan helps with retention. I make the assignments, the students assess their own work, and with good record keeping, there is continual dialogue between the students and I about their progress. In addition, I try to tie their individual lessons with a group lesson or discussion. These group lessons involve the whole class, regardless of literacy level.

The whole-group lessons may involve reading and discussing articles and commentaries on the city of St. Louis, usually taken from the *St. Louis Post-Dispatch.* Sarajane integrates readings that are timely and newsworthy into the group lessons. Another focus of the group lessons has been reading and understanding local maps, where together, as a group, they locate institutions and places of interest and problem solve directions and distances based on these points of interest. Sarajane conducts whole-group mini-lessons in the areas of writing and math as well. She will involve the whole class in a mini-lesson on capitalization, punctuation, sentence structure, or grammar. Or, after students have written something, she will ask them to read and revise their own writing. In terms of math, Sarajane explained:

Including math in group activities was a good means to introduce and teach basic math skills to adults who have poor math fundamentals or a "math phobia." Incorporating real-life materials pertaining to math allowed the participation of many levels of students. All adults encounter math in their daily lives in a variety of ways. They deal with concepts in money matters (checkbooks, giving and receiving change, etc.), understanding taxes and sales on consumer items, comprehending labels on supermarket products, and competently dealing with measurement skills in sewing and cooking. In using ads or coupons that promote sales on consumer items, decimals and percents come alive.

Sarajane described how often the role of the adult education teacher is to disrupt the learners' cultural models of education. She stated:

Students who come in often think that the teacher is going to stand up in front of the class and she is going to lecture on the Declaration of Independence or something. But it is hard to do that in an adult education classroom because of the wide range of abilities.

Sarajane recognizes that adults have histories of participation with education and schools that they bring with them into their adult education classrooms. These histories of participation may be in either conflict or alignment with their current adult education classrooms (Rogers, 2004; Rogers & Fuller, in press). For example, many adults come back to adult education with a history of participation with schools and teachers that reflects a transmission model of education where the teacher deposits knowledge or content into empty students. Adult educators face the challenge of meeting their students where they are and, at the same time, urging them to move beyond their comfort zones. Sarajane's philosophy is that adults are not "blank slates" but, rather, come into the learning community with rich cultural, linguistic, and racial histories that can be used as a resource for learning in and out of the classroom. In terms of the purpose of education, Sarajane stated:

I think that each adult deserves to be educated, especially in the United States. Too many adults today do not have an education. I taught for many years and most of my students were adult women, and their biggest reason for furthering their education was setting an example for their kids. Many of my students were struggling in helping their children with homework because many could not read and understand their children's elementary materials. They didn't want to reach the age of twenty-five or thirty and still not be adequately educated. For many of the adults, setting a good example for their child is the main purpose in their pursuing adult education programs.

"Literacy education," Sarajane explained, "gives them confidence that is a part of empowerment. They begin to feel as if 'I can do that!' whether it is help their kids or get a job. They start to do things that before people told them they couldn't do." Sarajane further explained,

Becoming more proficient in reading, writing, and math enables adults to feel more confident and secure in their place in today's society. They feel more like a participant, rather than one on the outside looking in. This is empowering on many levels.

Sarajane was trained as an adult literacy tutor and then became a "trainer of tutors" in the Laubach method, which was created by Frank Laubach as a method of teaching reading and writing with a set of workbooks that could be used to teach adults. Because the format is very structured, the Laubach series is very "tutor friendly." Additionally, it is "student friendly," as there are no surprises from lesson to lesson because the format is so predictable.

The Laubach method emphasizes teaching the names and sounds of the English language (phonics) in conjunction with introducing sight words, underlying the principles that reading should be taught with a combination of phonics and sight approaches. Each lesson incorporates a chart (decoding activity) and a story (comprehension activity), plus a writing lesson, reinforcement exercises, and suggested supplementary materials. Comprehension, grammar, and punctuation instruction are included in each lesson.

Sarajane explained, in depth, the philosophy and practice of the Laubach series.

The Laubach series has been used extensively with those adults who have minimal literacy skills. There are four books in the series beginning with Book 1, which introduces beginning consonant sounds; this book lays the foundation

for the rest of the series. The vocabulary is highly controlled and true to what an adult hears and speaks.

Through his research, Frank Laubach developed this system of introducing sounds of vowels and consonants determined by their regularity in our language. The lessons progress with much repetition to ensure that words that initially may have had to be sounded out soon become sight words. After completion of Book 4, the student has been presented with all of the basic reading skills to move toward becoming an independent reader.

Sarajane puts her knowledge and skills as a reading teacher to work within the Laubach approach to teach adult literacy students. She teaches reading and writing within a personally relevant framework. While she is very familiar with traditional adult education materials (e.g., the Challenger and Steck Vaughn series), she supplements these books with articles and readings that relate to students' interests. She has a wide collection of readings that relate to various topics that she has collected over the years. Sometimes, she uses language experience approaches with her basic literacy students. She also uses the method of partner reading. Sarajane also uses multiple literacies to supplement their work in the workbooks. Her students may read articles from the newspaper, read and write a poem, read a phone bill, or figure out finances. Books in the classroom are often biographies of famous Americans that increase the students' knowledge in social studies or science fields.

In terms of writing, she stays fairly close to the writing demands of the GED. She often teaches essay writing and the concomitant steps of writing an essay, such as writing solid paragraphs, revising, sticking to the topic, editing for punctuation and spelling, and the like. She tends to emphasize the structure of writing by making sure that students have an outline, beginning, middle, and end and that each topic sentence supports the paragraph. She stated that writing is difficult for her students and they need to like the topic that they are writing about. Sarajane does not see herself as a writer, and she says that she needs much more professional development in teaching writing.

Sarajane described the importance of teaching literacy to all of her students, regardless of whether they were considered to be "literacy students" (reading below a sixth grade level) or close to getting their GED. She stated:

If a student comes in and if they test less than a sixth grade level, they are considered literacy students. And, they are also eligible to have a tutor, a one-on-one teacher, which is nice because at that level, that student who is reading below a sixth grade level needs to learn those basic skills in reading that they may have missed in early grades. The one-on-one tutoring really benefits that student. Even students who have come in and sa[id], "I'm dyslexic," or "I'm learning disabled," and "I haven't been able to learn to read," have probably been passed over in the classroom when they were kids. But when they come as an adult, there is a huge benefit for them to be able to sit across the table from an adult tutor and go through those skills. In most cases, an adult won't take three years to learn those basic skills that first, second, and third graders know. The adult comes in with experiences and vocabulary and some understanding of the written language.

As she talked about the one-on-one reading and writing support that literacy students in her classroom receive, we hear Sarajane's philosophy about adult learners. As seen above, she stated that adults come in "with experiences and vocabulary and some understanding of the written language." In other words, adults have an active listening and speaking vocabulary from critically reading and participating in their social worlds. Sarajane explained, "To enhance their reading vocabulary, the tutor can help them apply those experiences to the decoding and encoding of texts."

Sarajane continued to discuss the students in her classroom, who are working at the "middle level between fifth and eighth grade level." She continued,

In order for the folks in the middle levels who already know how to read to become better readers, they need to strengthen their vocabulary in all areas. In order to appreciate social studies and science, they need to understand the vocabulary. I provide materials that are probably written at upper elementary level; and in particular, with social studies and science materials, I give them relatively short passages that help familiarize the reader with new vocabulary. I think that helps to have some sort of a background. Often students come away with a better appreciation of those subjects they found so difficult. At this midlevel, students are reading to learn.

Sarajane would agree that learners who are at the most basic levels of literacy are also reading to learn. Importantly, she points out that students at the "middle level," students who technically already know how to read, still need literacy instruction that focuses on vocabulary, content knowledge, and learning how to read informational texts. Sarajane explained that as a teacher, she provides them with background information as they are reading a text—what Clay (1993) would refer to as a book introduction which helps the readers to debug the text. She also discussed contextualizing vocabulary instruction within authentic reading and writing contexts.

Recognizing that 90 percent of the students in the program are reading below an eighth grade level, Sarajane started group instruction for literacy students at the Southside Women's Center. She knew that these students were not getting the literacy support they needed to accelerate as readers and writers, so she started small-group instruction. These small groups were flexibly grouped; sometimes there were multileveled groups, and at other times learners at the same level would work in a group. For the multileveled group, Sarajane would pull a passage that seemed relevant to them, perhaps something that came out of a discussion, and they would read and discuss the passage together. She would pick a passage that was at the midlevel of the learners in this group. It would be too difficult for some, which demands more support in terms of shared reading, and too easy for others. It allowed some students to practice their fluency and comprehension, and others to work on problem solving, see models of fluency, and engage in a dialogue around the issues. She would also group similarly leveled students and ask a tutor to guide their reading.

Recognizing that the GED is fundamentally a reading test, Sarajane continues to emphasize the importance of literacy instruction for students who are what she calls the "upper-level, high school–level readers." She stated,

Those folks at the upper level are independent readers. They should be able to be given an assignment, in reading, social studies, science, or literature, and be able to handle that on their own.... At the upper level they are reading to learn, also, but they are also working towards that GED or high school diploma.

We hear Sarajane as she described her strategy for teaching literacy with different levels of students. She stressed the importance of providing materials that were within the range of difficulty for the students. Clay (1993) writes about the importance of instructional- and independent-level texts for students. Instructional-level texts are those texts that can be read independently, but students are still problem solving on a percentage of the words, which will help them to generalize their problem solving from one text to another. Sarajane stated that if she has a student reading at an eighth or ninth grade level, she would most likely give the student materials that are at a sixth or seventh grade level to "boost his confidence and then work up a level." She also described using texts that have higher content but are written at a lower level and why this is important for adults who have had many life experiences. Providing texts that are at an instructional level for learners is a vital aspect of teaching for literacy acceleration. An instructional-level text is one in which the reader can read within his or her zone of proximal development— one that is neither too hard nor too easy.

Sarajane's teaching of reading and writing is rooted in a theory of andragogy—teaching and learning specific to adults. "Andragogy" refers to the theory and practice of educating adults, or the art and science of helping adults learn (Knowles, 1989). Andragogy is based on two central ideas. First is the conception of learners as directed (either individually or socially). Second is the idea that the teacher is a critical facilitator rather than a provider or transmitter of knowledge. Sarajane stated,

This is not like teaching a first or second grader. An adult, even though he may read at the first grade level, brings experiences that a child doesn't have. He has opinions and attitudes about things that lend to the reading process that children don't have. But he also has things that may interfere with the reading process.

Sarajane goes on to say more about the differences between children and adult readers, a theme that resurfaced as she talked about her tutor trainings.

Adults come in with a good listening vocabulary. They may not be able to read, but they have watched television and conversed with people around them. They have heard words, so they know what they mean and that gives them a big jump on the reading process right there. So we talk about what adults bring to the reading process.

While Sarajane was trained in the Laubach method of literacy instruction and is a trainer of tutors, she is flexible in her approach to teaching. She emphasizes to new tutors that they should plan on spending about one and a half hours with the student; however, they should spend only 30–45 minutes for each lesson in the skill books. More time than that can sometimes become tedious for both the student and the tutor. The remainder of the time should be spent with reinforcement activities or materials that will enable the student to reach his or her goals. Tutors are encouraged to use language experience to promote vocabulary building, reinforce decoding skills, and provide an opportunity for the student to see that what he or she says can be written. "Tutors," explained Sarajane, "need to be aware of students' goals and use this information to formulate lessons outside the skill books. In their trainings, tutors are given information on the use of supplementary materials, but it takes time and experience for a new tutor to become competent in diverting from the script in the workbooks." Sarajane encourages tutors and adult education teachers to work closely together to design a learning program that is relevant and engaging and that progresses the student toward his or her personal and academic goals.

"Facilitated by a tutor, students can progress quickly through the material," Sarajane explained. She deeply appreciates and recognizes the hard work of the dedicated volunteer tutors. Indeed, she participates in training many of the volunteers who will become tutors at various adult education centers. As a literacy teacher, she recognizes the strengths and constraints of these well-intentioned but underprepared tutors in the classroom. Sarajane expressed the dilemma in this way:

In our system today, the people who need the help the most are being taught by tutors. Not that tutors don't have the expertise, but we are expecting them to work with the group that needs the most and needs a teacher or someone who is trained.

She went on to say,

Those students at the lowest literacy levels have historically been neglected throughout their lives; assigning them a volunteer tutor is a first step in helping them gain independence in reading. However, they need and deserve the full attention of an experienced teacher to guide them in their educational pursuits.

Sarajane explained that tutors tend to overrely on phonics and on the workbooks because they feel more comfortable with the script than with engaging the learners in a dialogue which would reinforce the sight words or decoding strategies in context.

Sarajane talked in depth and with passion about her work training adult education tutors. She pointed out that she is often quick to dispel the literacy mystique, that is, that people just learn to read naturally. She talked about this in relation to her work in training tutors. She said, "They have taken on this job because this sounds wonderful because they want to teach someone to read but they don't know anything about teaching reading."

Sarajane educates the tutors on the components of the reading process and on how adults learn. She explains that adults have experiences they bring with them which make them ready for the reading experience in different ways than children. She also teaches the components of reading, decoding, and comprehension. She states,

We talk about how a person figures out what a word is that they don't know. I often ask them, "What do you do when you come to a word you don't know as an adult reader?" And, you know, they respond that "they sound it out, get a dictionary; they will look for the root word," and then I ask them, "How would you teach this to an adult?"

She dispels the myth with her adult tutors that reading is a magical process that "just happens." Similar to Vivian Jett, Sarajane talked specifically about strategies that support students' problem solving when they get to an unknown word. Her strategy instruction focuses on determining the grapho-phonic level (sounding the word out), finding a word pattern within the word, using structural analysis (compound words, prefixes, and suffixes), or using context.

In addition to being confident as a literacy teacher, Sarajane is aware of who she is as a woman and a teacher and aims to treat her students with dignity and respect. One of Sarajane's classes was located in a women's center, where one of the underlying missions was building community, inside and outside the center, through democratic processes. The director of the center at the time (also the coauthor of this book) actively tried to connect women's support groups with education and education with women's support groups. This sense of community extended into the classroom because oftentimes the women knew each other from participating in other services provided at the center. One year, for example, Sarajane had a number of women who enrolled in adult basic education (ABE) classes who studied and prepared to take their GED test. This group of women supported each other's achievements and goals in and out of the class. Several of their members later became participants of the first Women in Leadership Development (WILD) Program at the center. The responses from students indicated that they loved Sarajane as a teacher and were very upset when she left. Sarajane provided her students with a caring classroom, where she actively attended to their learning. She is constantly engaged as a teacher, working with people one-on-one or in small groups (rather than handing out workbooks and sitting behind her desk).

The students appreciate Sarajane because she is consistently herself. She does not try to falsely adopt the culture and language of her students to "fit in." Sarajane attends to the women in her classes as whole people, not simply as students or learners. For example, one of her students, Jackie (a pseudonym), had been pushed out of school because she had her first child at sixteen years of age, and was raising three young sons during her time as a student at the center. After earning her GED, Jackie invited Sarajane and Mary Ann (coauthor of the book) to a celebration at her home. Sarajane went and brought her husband and son to celebrate with Jackie's friends and relatives. Sarajane's commitment to her students characterizes her as an exemplary teacher.

While Sarajane recognizes that some of her students are activists in their own lives and says that people have come into her classroom to register students to vote, she does not consciously bring politics into her classroom. She did recognize that one of her students was an activist. She stated, "After obtaining his GED, he became actively involved in his community and he came in and spoke with our group. He is a real activist and model for others." She is politically active in her own life in political campaigns—at both the local and national levels. She doesn't, however, bring her political activism into the classroom discussions; but, regardless, she stated, "They probably have an idea of where I stand," which suggests that she is not value neutral in her classroom. She is careful to say that when they do discuss political events in class, they don't "necessarily formulate opinions" but, rather, discuss the issues and examine multiple sides and perspectives. She does let students who are activists talk to other students about how they can get involved in their communities. Similar to Janet Omurtag, Sarajane allows activism in her classroom but as it comes from other people, not herself.

Sarajane provides tutor trainings for the Literacy Council and Adult Education and Literacy in Missouri and Illinois. She also is a board member of the Montessori School in St. Charles, Missouri. She is a member of various social justice groups in the community. She has also been actively involved in past presidential campaigns through door-to-door canvassing, get-out-the-vote canvassing, and voter registration.

14

Inquiry and Perspective

SISTER MARTHA JAEGERS

If this is a democracy, and I have a voice, then I have a right and deserve to be heard.

— Sister Martha Jaegers, Interview

"I started teaching in 1958, and it has been almost nonstop ever since." A member of a Catholic religious order, Sister Martha speaks with a soft tone and a ready laugh. Certified as a teacher, Sister Martha has a master's degree in education and taught for 20 years in K–12; she has taught almost every grade and every subject. She entered the teaching profession because that was a viable option for women in the 1950s. She has been an adult education teacher for 19 years. Her entry into adult education was through volunteering as a tutor. Sister Martha works at two different adult education sites, the YMCA Literacy Council and a probation and parole site.

The YMCA Literacy Council, where Sister Martha spends most of her teaching time, is located in the South Side of the city of St. Louis. Historically a European American working-class neighborhood, residents are now more racially diverse and predominantly working class or working poor. The Literacy Council is housed in a social service center that is a resource for utility, food, and clothing assistance to local families. Students are referred to the class from various other service providers, churches, and employment agencies in the area. The class is composed of American- and foreign-born students focused on basic skill development, preparation for the General Educational Development (GED) test, and learning English.

Sister Martha, like many other adult education teachers, believes that her work is more than a job—it is a vocation. She has a vision with a humanist philosophy, one that has meant, for Sister

Martha, committing to the community where she teaches. A European American woman with short, pepper-gray hair, Sister Martha is very humble about her accomplishments as an educator. She is deeply guided by her spiritual beliefs, and perhaps, as a result, Sister Martha structures her class to honor relationships, caring, and compassion, rather than hierarchies and power structures. Sister Martha uses a combination of approaches, methods, and materials in her classroom. Sister Martha often has fifteen to twenty students in her classroom daily. On average, three to five people from Sister Martha's class obtain a GED each year. She has a 67 percent retention rate, and her greatest levels of impact are levels 2 and 4, indicating that 31 percent and 33 percent of her students, respectively, progress into levels 3 and 5. She has a combination of adult literacy students and ESOL students. Her students range from basic to advanced levels. She has a large number of tutors who volunteer in her classroom on a daily basis. While Sister Martha is deeply guided in her own life by social justice values and principles, she struggles with teaching about social justice in the classroom.

This class, like most adult education classes in this district, has open enrollment, which means that students can come and go as their schedule or interests dictate. Therefore, it is not unusual to have a different group of students on any given day. Sister Martha tries to provide a sense of stability and predictability in her classroom through how she structures the day. Similarly, she is very conscious of the use of space and time in her classroom. Sister Martha positions her desk to the side of the class (rather than in the front of the class), which signifies the way in which she tries to disrupt hierarchies in her classroom. The long tables, where the adults sit, are arranged in short rows. The tables will hold three or four adults and their reading and writing materials comfortably. The tables are arranged in a way to promote the students talking with each other, rather than talking only to the teacher. She designs the classroom to encourage community, and she intentionally arranges space and furniture in ways that encourage a safe learning environment for her students.

The classroom is a print-rich environment. Sister Martha has reading materials throughout the room, including a shelf of multileveled books ranging from children's books to adult literature to poetry. The reading workbooks are kept behind Sister Martha's desk.

She also has current magazines and newspapers throughout the room on the tops of bookcases and tables. There are bulletin boards around the room with flyers for current events, lists of resources, announcements for social justice activities, and pictures. Her bulletin boards are constantly changing as she brings in community announcements, a peace calendar, and a bake sale poster ("It will be a great day when our schools have all of the money they need and the Air Force has to hold a bake sale to buy a bomber"). The environmental print in the classroom is an active representation of Sister Martha's values as a teacher and citizen. Sister Martha laughed as she said that one of her students even brought a selection of reading materials into the bathroom.

The class meets from 8:00 a.m. to 12:00 p.m. each day. Each day, the students review their assignment sheets from their folder. They may review these independently or with the support of a tutor. This provides a framework for them to make decisions about where they should start each day. As students get settled into class and check in with each other and with Sister Martha about news events, happenings with their children (e.g., sicknesses, celebrations, and reports on school), or other news, they also get their folders and materials they need before sitting down at a table where they will work for the next four hours. During this time Sister Martha will orient new students to the classroom, talk with them about their goals and experiences, and begin to administer the Test of Adult Basic Education (TABE). If there are no new students, she may help tutors to organize their materials, consult with tutors about teaching techniques or reading strategies, or sit down to work one-on-one with a student. Most of the work in Sister Martha's classroom is one-on-one because of the high number of tutors and because of the wide range of students, both in terms of American-born and foreign-born students and in terms of ability levels.

During this time, the room is filled with the quiet hum of learning—students "whisper reading" to themselves and the sound of tutors coaching students to try the word again, to look more closely at the word parts, or to retell what the passage meant to them. Learners walk around the classroom as they need to, sharpen pencils, get new reading materials, put work in their folders, or talk with a fellow classmate. A discussion may come up in a small group or between a tutor and a student that becomes the focus of a whole-group discussion. Such discussions are generally focused on important themes in the adults' lives. There are four PLATO computers in the classroom, and her younger students, in particular, tend to like working on the computers. On Fridays, Sister Martha sometimes incorporates group work, such as "fraction Fridays" or a writers' workshop.

Upon entering Sister Martha's classroom, it is easy to read how the design of the space, time, and physical layout of the classroom combined with the emotional and physical energy in the classroom contribute to a high-energy classroom. Sister Martha is constantly circulating throughout the classroom and encouraging students to ask her questions. As she stated, "Don't be afraid. Questions are good." During this time, she informally assesses students' progress, checks on tutors' methods and techniques, and gives teaching suggestions. As she moves around the classroom, sitting down next to a student to help him or her with a difficult word, listening to a tutor-student dyad, or helping a student make a book choice, Sister Martha is able to assess the emotional dynamics of the classroom, the tenor of the dialogue, and the relationships between the tutors and the students and between the students. This movement reflects a whole perspective that is symbolic of the importance of not only reading and writing in the classroom but also reading the world. Sister Martha knows that when her students come into the classroom, they are reading the entire classroom, their fellow students, the teacher, and the use of space and time. Sister Martha knows that her task is to design a learning environment, where her students can continue to feel engaged.

Sister Martha had difficulty calling on the names of educational theorists who informed her practice, and instead called on her tacit wisdom or what she referred to as "common sense." She stated,

I myself am a huge idealist, and [my philosophy] would probably be lumped under the umbrella of humanist philosophies, where the students' needs, the students' ambitions and goals, are seen as rich and important. If we can tap into those things, the students tend to connect and to remember. I would dearly love to work with someone who is experienced in Paulo Freire's work.

Just like several other teachers, Sister Martha is intuitively drawn to the theory and practice of Freire. Freire (1993) advocated for an education whose purpose was to set up the conditions so people could liberate themselves and achieve their true humanity. Freire started with the assumptions that the world is characterized by many inequities (e.g., social, political, economic, and educational) and that education can either function to sustain inequities or work toward liberation. Humanistic educational processes construct opportunities for men and women to perceive themselves as active, reflective beings—as creators and transformers of the world. Freire (1985) writes,

The educator who makes a humanistic choice must correctly perceive the relationship between consciousness and world.... A liberating form of educational practice by definition proposes an "archaeology" of consciousness. Through their own efforts people can remake the natural path where consciousness emerges as the capacity for self perception. (p. 115)

Sister Martha designs educational experiences in her classroom that are based on joint inquiry and exploration, criticism and self-criticism, and relevant content materials. She designs classroom experiences that make connections inside and outside of the classroom, and make the classroom a student-centered place, all aspects of a humanistic educational process. She stated,

It made so much sense to me to use things that the students already know but they just don't know what it looks like in print. As far as reading is concerned, they learn when you have that emotional connection. That is what they want to know, and so I think they learn faster than with other methods.

In terms of the purpose of education, Sister Martha noted the importance of personal empowerment that is gained in the process of participating in adult education, empowerment that extends beyond the classroom.

I think that education gives them both the confidence to go out and do the things that other people do. Not that they don't do those things, but it often feels like that way to them. So it gives them the inner energy, and that enables them to face what they need to do with much more confidence.

Sister Martha's understanding about how personal empowerment in the classroom creates a sense of confidence and empowerment out of the classroom is similar to what Scott and Schmitt-Boshnick (2001) write about in a community-based adult education program:

The notion of empowerment is inherent in everything they do. As people find power within the collective, they can overcome the lack of self-confidence that may have been holding them back from confronting difficulties that they face.... This type of empowerment, though, is not promoted from a standpoint of individualism, because it has its roots in community. Instead, it is a notion of independence through interdependence. (p. 135)

Sister Martha described her literacy instruction within the context of the community of her classroom, the diversity of her students, and the importance of student-centered and individualized instruction. Sister Martha sets up the conditions for her students to accelerate as readers, writers, and thinkers. When Sister Martha described how she teaches literacy, she stated that she thinks whole language and phonics are both important.

We go through processes of phonics methods and the whole language method. I really think a person needs to use both of those, especially with adults who have so much experience already. It is not the same with a fifth grader or sixth or seventh grader, who has experience but mostly secondhand experience and open to a lot of misinterpretation. Adults have lived long enough and seen enough that the phonics can help them a lot because that may be the missing thing that they didn't pick up when they were in school. Someone comes along and tells them the simplest thing, and you watch their eyes light up, and they say, "I did not know that." That sometimes happens—not everyday, of course. On the other hand, the more holistic approach to reading includes approaches such as partner reading. I find that it is a wonderful thing to read along with the student. Just read and pace yourself to the students' tempo, but I try to guide them with the pencil for not reading single words. Strategies like that give them a sense of what it feels like to read. Even though they will go very hesitantly and they may stumble over or miss a word here or there, it gives them a sense of "I am moving along," and it gives them a sense of what it is like to read. I think that is very helpful.

Sister Martha uses a combination of part-to-whole and whole-to-part methods to accelerate students' literacy development. She generally uses traditional, commercially prepared materials that come from Laubach but supplements these materials with real-life materials and literature. She expressed that she is fortunate to have five to ten tutors on any given day (several of whom are also members of a religious order) working in her classroom. To capitalize on the extra help in her classroom, she pairs the volunteers with individual students (usually reading below a fifth grade level) and helps the tutors to find appropriate materials to work on with their students. The match between student and workbook is determined by the results of the TABE. The workbooks are scripted and sequential, and while they may have content that is relevant to adults' experiences (rather than children's experiences), they do not necessarily include texts, questions, and exercises that have relevance in the lives of the adults using the workbooks. Her use of Laubach in the classroom is related to the fact that she has so many tutors and the tutors are trained in the Laubach method. She stated,

We use the Laubach method, primarily because the tutors think the manuals are detailed enough and the script is right there and the tutor working with them is following the script, and they usually do very well.

Even though she uses the Laubach reading materials, she and the tutors give the learners a choice of which series they want to work in. She stated, "Sometimes I give them two or three books and I say, 'Pick the one you think will help you because I am not sure.'... Sometimes they like the format of one book over another."

Sister Martha supplements the workbooks with authentic reading materials. There are many different literacy materials at the Literacy Council: books, magazines, newspapers, and newsletters. Sometimes social issues come up in these stories in the traditional reading materials, which "lend themselves to questions such as 'What would you do if you came home and your house had been broken into?'" She discussed how they would talk about women-centered problems, such as the unpaid labor of parenting, violence, wages, and the associated social actions. She recalled a time when they were reading a story about people who lived in a neighborhood where there were many vacant lots, and in the story, the people got together and started to clean up their neighborhood. She talked with her students about if they would be willing to do that, if they had the time to do that, and if they knew people like that.

Sister Martha brings in newspaper articles that she wants to read with her class. She chooses newspaper articles based on familiar and relevant content or content that may be completely unfamiliar to her students because she wants to expand their experiences and vocabulary. She also encouraged her students to read with their children and, when they did, to read not just the words in books but also multiple sign systems embedded in texts. She stated,

It is wonderful, even if they just look at the pictures, because we read more than words. You need to read body language, signs, pictures, and what is going on in the picture. What do you think these people are talking about even before you start to read the story?

She also introduces new genres that come out of familiar reading materials. Sister Martha explains how she conducted a small-group mini-lesson on the genre of obituaries in the newspaper.

I had been saving up some of the more interesting obituaries, and I had about eight or nine of them on a piece of paper. I said to my students, "I am introducing a part of the paper that you may have never even looked at. I just want you to see what it [the obituaries] is like. Just scan the obituaries and pick out one of these people that you wished you had known at some point in your life, as a child growing up, as a coworker, as a neighbor." And they did some pretty fun stuff.

Sister Martha explicitly taught the genre of obituaries in the paper (how they were written, what information was included, and what information was excluded). This is an example of how Sister Martha explicitly teaches a genre of writing. She connects with what is already familiar to students, and asks them to think critically and extend beyond what they already know. Sister Martha also chooses newspaper articles for her class to read in small groups.

I try to pick short newspaper articles. I try different things. I might try something from the local St. Louis area that I think they should be aware of. That can range from police reports to school board issues to neighborhood happenings. Or if there is an [music] entertainment group in town, they know this just like this [snaps fingers]. Sometimes I bring in something that I know they would never know or read about simply because I want them to be aware that there is a whole big world out there.

She realizes that not every article they read together will connect to the interests and imagination of all of the students in her classroom. She makes an effort to get to know her students (their wants, desires, concerns, aspirations, interests, and fears) and keeps her eyes open for materials that may connect to them personally. She will bring in something she has seen in a magazine or a newspaper, give it to the student, and note that she thought he or she would like it. Or, she may point students in the direction of an author or piece of literature she thinks they might like.

Sister Martha stated that she tends to stay focused on academics (versus explicitly teaching for reading and writing acceleration within a social justice framework) unless something comes up in her students' lives. She stated,

Maybe it is an assumption that the students come here primarily for academic background. When they bring up another situation or issue, we would deal with it. The majority of the students are very willing to do their work in here, so I guess I am not terribly aware of their other needs unless they are comfortable bringing it up.

Sister Martha balances the competing demands of attending to her students' social and personal needs (which are political) and academics. Her working philosophy is that when her students accelerate toward more traditional academic goals (e.g., passing the GED test or obtaining their citizenship), they are also accelerating personal and social empowerment, which is connected to issues of social justice.

Sister Martha incorporated a range of writing practices into her class—from essays, to letters, to personal journals, to submitting articles they have written to the St. Louis Schools Adult Education and Literacy *Newsletter.* She taught writing in a variety of formats from whole class, to small group, to one-on-one. Sister Martha spoke about how she has incorporated journal writing or "freewriting," inspired by writer and author Peter Elbow (1981), into her class.

I have gotten notebooks, and each student has a notebook to write in. We started with two minutes and are building this a little bit. I tell them, "Keep pushing that pencil and keep writing and I do not care if all you say is 'I hate writing, I hate writing, I don't know what to say' —write for two minutes." And then we have extended the time and we are up to ten minutes. I will extend that to fifteen. And I tell them they can write their own stuff if they want to, if that is something they need to explore. On the other hand, we brainstormed one day on possible topics and I have a little Tupperware container full of their topics on pieces of paper, and so each day I have a student pull one of those out. And I will put it on the board as an option. If their mind is blank or they do not want to write about what is going on in their lives, I will say, "Try this." One writing prompt was as general as "What's my next step?" And they can take this anyplace they want to. And I tell them up-front, "I am not going to read your notebooks, unless you want me to and ask me to look at it." That is turning into a very interesting new thing.

Sister Martha's approach to teaching writers using the "freewriting" process has been written about by Peter Elbow. Elbow (1981) writes about freewriting in this way:

The open-ended writing process is ideal for the situation where you have a sense you have something to write about but you do not quite know what. Just start writing about anything at all. If you have special trouble with the first moment of writing, that confrontation with the blank page, ask yourself what you do not want to write about and start writing about it before you have a chance to resist. First thoughts. They are likely to lead you to what you are needing to write. (p. 51)

Sister Martha advocates for freewriting as a means of getting ideas down on paper and helping people to see themselves as writers. She is clear, however, that all writing (both the production and the consumption) has a purpose and an audience, and consequently is social and political. Sister Martha is implicitly teaching that literacy is a set of social practices. Writing is also embedded with power relationships in terms of what types of writing get valued, who writes about what, and for whom. Clark and Ivanic (1997) write,

Vast numbers of people as individuals, but more importantly, as powerless social groups, are excluded from contributing to the collective store of knowledge, cultural and ideological activity; from the production and projection of ideas that fundamentally shape society ... their experiences unrecorded and their right to contribute to the shaping of society virtually denied. (p. 55)

During an observation of her class, Sister Martha led a writers' workshop with a small group of her students. In this workshop, Sister Martha taught the various stages of writing. She started with brainstorming a topic, then generated a list of topics, and then settled on one that was of interest to the students in the group, hip-hop as a cultural practice. Seated around a table, seven students (five African American and two European American) could clearly see and hear each other. Sister Martha stood next to a flipchart and recorded the adults' ideas as they brainstormed ideas for writing. After they had time to cultivate their own ideas, they wrote. Sister Martha wrote during this time, too. The adults had a chance to share their writing with each other, to get and give feedback, and to revise their writing. In this case, Sister Martha modeled the writing of a personal essay as a way to integrate their funds of cultural and social knowledge into the classroom. She also models other genres of writing such as letters, poems, and diaries.

Sister Martha shares her life as a writer and activist with her students. She told her students about how when she was younger, she was an avid member of the Sierra Club and was very passionate about the environment. A policy was being reviewed at the federal level that dealt with environmental issues, and she wanted her voice to be heard, so she wrote a letter to Congress.

I remember nervously writing those first letters to congresspeople and I thought, "Oh my gosh, I do not know how to do this." I felt just like a student. I really, really did. But many social action groups are very good about providing sample letters, and so I took a phrase here and a phrase there to write my letter. And I got a response from Congress.

After sharing this experience with her students, she reported that there were a few instances that came up in class that related to the adult learning community, and they decided to make their voices heard through letter writing. Sister Martha explained,

And that is another thing we have done a few times in class. I have asked the students when it comes to the budget time in the state to write to their congresspeople and their state representatives and tell them, "Look, I am a student and I have an interest in this issue. Adult education is important to me, and I do not want to see it go down the tubes." So occasionally they have done that and have gotten a response back, and they get so pleased. Well, I know the feeling. Now, that was a long time ago when I started doing that.

Sister Martha is modeling a form of civic engagement for the learners in her classroom. As a strong woman teacher, she serves as a public figure for the students in her classroom. Sister Martha continued to talk about her own activism:

And then my own religious community has been very encouraging in pursuing social justice activities, so in a whole variety of ways, I have joined interest groups—for women's issues, environmental issues, and antiwar issues. There are just so many issues out there. If we do not speak up, then we don't have a leg to stand on when something else happens. Over the years I have become more and more involved with social justice until sometimes I feel like I am drowning in it, but I will not quit. I have held banners over Highway 40 against the war. I have marched on Washington, D.C., against the war. I also do simple stuff. It is not hard, or I would never be able to do it. But I firmly believe that if this is a democracy, and I have a voice, then I have a right and deserve to be heard. And even though certain senators, in particular, are not going to agree with me and they are going to do what they see is right, they are still going to hear from me.

While she is adamant about fighting for social justice in her own life, she expresses concern about her role as a teacher in terms of teaching for social justice. A tension arose for Sister Martha, which was between acknowledging the oppressive social structures which shape the reality of life in adult education and the lives of those in adult education, including teachers, and yet not wanting to force her critical consciousness on the adults in her class.

I try to carry that over without being blatant about it because I don't believe in politicking or proselytizing in this situation. Now, if a student brings up an issue and has a question, I will deal with it. And I leave stuff around the room with regard to political issues, environmental issues, and things like that. If they see it, wonderful; if they do not, there it goes. That is OK.... If anyone ever came in with that sense of organization (and wanted to act), I would follow that. And we do have things around like community resource groups [and] phone numbers.... The local politicians' numbers we have and are available. If you are having housing problems or sewer problems, all of that information is available. Would I devote class time? Certainly. If they were that interested, I would go to the blackboard and say, "What do you want to say?" and write it down and let them go with it.

Hearing Sister Martha wrestle with these big issues of how and when teachers should teach for social justice captures her exemplariness as a teacher. That is, she is highly reflective about her practices and thinks deeply about her responsibilities as a teacher to her students. The following example illustrates how Sister Martha reconciles this tension when a student approached her with an issue that she wanted to act on. The student reported to Sister Martha that she was being treated unfairly by her daughter's school every time she went into the school to conference about her daughter. Sister Martha listened to her concerns and then showed the woman how to write a letter to the superintendent. She described the process this way:

I am reminded of a student who a little while back was having a terrific struggle with her local school. Her daughter was in special education, and there was a big problem. She had visited the school several times and had not gotten a very welcome reception from the administration. As a result, she wanted to write a letter to the superintendent. We worked on that letter for days before we got it right. And then I didn't see her for a little while. When she did come back, I did ask her how that had turned out, and if anything had happened, and she said that the next time she went to visit that school to visit her child's class that there was no hassle, that she was able to go and see what was happening in the room. I didn't follow up after that because she found a job. I was very impressed with her tenacity and the determination of how she tackled that task, and she was determined for her child's sake that she was going to do this, even if it was difficult for her.... She believed in what she was doing, and she knew she had a right as a parent to be listened to and to have the problem addressed. And it wasn't just her because apparently she had talked with other parents and there were many who were dissatisfied, so she was going to take some action.

Sister Martha consistently talked about her students with a deep sense of respect and dignity. She also has a repertoire of organizing and activist strategies from her own activism that she can draw on when her students ask for her support. At the same time, she is deliberately conscious about her role as a teacher and authority in the classroom. Sister Martha is aware of the "dynamics of position" (Maher & Thompson Tetreault, 1994, p. 165) in her classroom, the multiple positions she occupies as a racialized, gendered, classed, politicized human being. "A positional perspective," Maher and Thompson Tetreault (1994) write, "also illuminates the constantly shifting context of professional authority and the relational aspects of authority among professors and students.... Feminist teachers tend to make their authority positional, rather than externally imposed, by grounding it in personal experience, knowledge, and situation" (p. 165).

As Sister Martha talks, we hear the tension she has between being an activist in her own life and not wanting to impose her views on her students. When we asked her if the classroom could be a place to address important social issues, Sister Martha responded,

I hope that it can. I know it can be. One of the difficulties with having curricular materials that bring up social issues is that I do not feel it is my place to design curricula around things that only I think are important. The classroom population is varied enough that I do not know that there will ever be an issue that everyone would feel interested enough in to make it a group project of some kind. I do not want to impose my biases, if you will, on a group of people. Because I feel like they are really coming here for their academics and they are coming here for their credentials, they want their GED certificate, and with others they are coming here for their citizenship and just to be able to read. But most definitely, there is a lot going on. In this neighborhood, there are multiple social difficulties of housing, health care, employment. All of those things are very real in this community, and yet I do not feel that I am in a position to say this is something we are going to get involved in as a group. I do not know enough people out there. I do not live in this neighborhood. It is a little sticky.

Sister Martha models social justice, morality, and compassion with the way she interacts with her students and the examples that she brings to life in her classroom.

These moments are rarely planned. Rather, she follows her students' leads, whether it is during the whole-group, small-group, or one-on-one instruction. Often, critical social issues arise during discussions that occur during breaks from the formal class time. Sister Martha recounted an example:

Just recently, one of the men in class told me that he was thinking about possibilities for his own future. I said, "What would you like to do?" and he said, "I want to contribute to world peace." I said, "Wow!" And then, he contradicted it and said, "It will probably never happen." I said to him, "But you can do that right now. You can do that where you are right now. If you can make just your little world better, then the whole world is a better place." Later on, I asked the group that was leaving, "Is the world a better place because you are in it?" They said, "No, not really," I said, "Well, I am in it—it's better." I joked around about it, but I meant it.

This example is another reflection of Sister Martha's rejection of violence at the personal, institutional, and global levels. Along with being conscious about her role as a teacher, she also positions herself as a learner in the classroom. She retold the following incident, which she labeled "her latest faux pas."

In class, one of the stories we read recently was about an eagle, a young eagle that had attacked a child on a beach in North Carolina. I used a set of guided questions to guide the discussion when we were done reading the story. I remember that when I read it and picked my own answers, there was one question where the wording wasn't so straightforward. It said, "All of the following are reasons why eagles are afraid of humans except which one?" That took a lot of mental maneuvering to understand. We had a good discussion about the wording of that question, but they got it. For another question, I thought the answer was B, but from a different point of view it might be C, and I didn't have the answer key right there. That evening, I checked their answers with mine. When I returned them next day, there was a student who had not been present, so I gave him my copy. When we got to the question in question, he quickly pointed out where it said, "Circle A or B." Of course, he announced it to the whole group, so I said, "Well, I did not know. I was not sure." I think it is good for students to know that nobody has all the answers and that everybody needs help sometimes.

Sister Martha models for her students that she, too, is a learner, and encourages them to read all texts critically and search for evidence to support their theories. She believes in the importance of connecting with her students on a human level, which then opens a space for compassion, humility, and risk taking. She does this through modeling for her students her love of learning, her passion for inquiry, and the way in which she finds wonder in her world.

I stumbled across a film on the TV, and I taped it and brought it into the class. It was a Nova film about the universe, which is something that just fascinates me. I really hesitated to show it to them because it was so theoretical, but they really watched it. It was amazing to me how well they took to it. It had to do with Einstein's theory of relativity and how that conflicts with the laws that govern the tiny stuff, and of course the physicists' dream is to get this unified field theory so that everything from the universe to subatomic is in one big scheme. I talked about it before I showed the movie and explained what we were watching and that it was not really pictures but created photography and artwork and not the real thing. The movie explored string theory, which is a total mystery to me. They really liked the movie, and I think it was because of the novelty and it really challenged their imaginations as well as their vocabulary. It covered some of the scientific history from the 1930s and how there has always been conflicting evidence.

As Sister Martha models her inquisitiveness, she breaks down the traditional barriers between herself as a teacher and the adults in her classroom as students. She demonstrates that she, too, is a learner, filled with wonder and many more big questions than answers. On the role of knowledge construction in the educative process, Freire (1985) writes,

In a humanistic form of education, once we verify our inquisitive nature as researchers and investigators of reflexive consciousness, and once we make that knowledge accessible, we automatically ascertain our capacity to recognize or to remake existing knowledge.... Instead of being an alienating transference of knowledge, education or cultural action for freedom is the authentication of knowledge by which learners and educators as "consciousness" or as ones filled with "intention" join in the quest for new knowledge as a consequence of their apprehending existing knowledge. (pp. 114–115)

Sister Martha views her students' progress in a wholistic manner and consciously looks for their stated and implied reasons for coming to adult education classes. Students may benefit as much from the process of participating in adult education as from the specific outcomes (Fingeret & Drennon, 1997). She shared that some students will come in after they have a child and say, "I want to learn to read by the time my son is three years old. He is now eight months old. I want to be able to read to him." Other students have had a hard time finding a job, because they do not have a high school diploma or GED, and so they enroll in her class. She recognizes that there are different "turning points" for each and every one of her students. Her role is to acknowledge and respect these turning points and to provide students with ongoing instructional opportunities and feedback, so they can see their progress. However, also in a wholistic manner, she recognizes the indicators of progress may not always be connected to traditional measures of assessment, such as the TABE or the Comprehensive Adult Student Assessment System. She stated,

Everyone who comes in wants to pass the GED test, and sometimes I would like to take those letters out of the alphabet. But they do have that expectation somehow. So it is a little crushing when I go over the test results and they are at a 4.7 in an area. I hope that they will experience enough satisfaction, enough progress, not to quit. One of the things that I frequently say is "There's always more." When we finish this book, there's another one. When you finish this chapter, there is another chapter. If you are interested in astronomy, every day there are new developments in that area. I hope they will continue to value learning and value the time they spend here and see that it is not a waste of time for them in any sense.

She continued:

There are a couple of students who come to me depressed to some degree, and if they will stay and work—it does not have to be every day—but if they will keep on coming in and chipping away at it, as I say, then they will feel better about themselves so they are not as depressed. It is very nice when their test scores show their progress. Then they are very pleased.

It is important to accept them where they are from the beginning. I make it a point to congratulate them for every step they take. Even coming in and registering for class can be a huge step for them. The testing is also a big deal for them because they feel like they cannot do it and they are going to fail. When they come in to test, I tell them, "This test is just a tool for me to get some input, so I know what to help you with." I tell them, "Your time is precious and you aren't coming here to do the same thing that someone else is doing. We are going to cover the skills you need." I give them an example I think they can relate to. I say, "When you are writing your shopping list, you open the pantry door and see that you have plenty of macaroni, then you do not add macaroni to your list. That's what we are doing. We are only working on what you need."

She also stated:

I guess that I am coming more and more to see the value of little things. I don't have to be on the evening news, but as I said to my student before, "If you are making your world better, then you are making the whole world better." If I can help a student, I know there are several right now who came in very tentative and very hesitant because they did not think they could do it. I have a student who I know could have passed that GED test yesterday. She is only beginning to see that herself, but I can see that change. Another student came in at a very low level at reading and barely functioning. She has been working with a tutor for three or four months; you should see the smile she comes in with. These are the things that keep me going now. I can see change and development in all of the learners. Now, if they ever reach the point where they can see beyond the limitations that they are living, then there is the hope that keeps them going.

Sister Martha sets up the conditions in her classroom that unveil the possibility of hope for her students. She recognizes the universal drive of her students who come into her class and are struggling for a better life. Sister Martha recently brought students from her classroom to a Voices of Adult Literacy United for Education / Acting for a Better Community forum held at the public library, where adult education students shared the process and results of their leadership training. This displays Sister Martha's commitment to making links between community and classroom literacy practices, another characteristic of exemplary teachers.

15

The Struggle for
Critical Literacy

ANGELA, SARAJANE,
AND SISTER MARTHA

Critical literacy is the ability not only to read and write, but also to assess texts in order to understand the relationships between power and domination that underlie and inform these texts. The struggle over and for critical literacy looks and feels different in each of the classrooms presented in the last section, and indeed in each of the teachers' cases throughout the book, but is woven through reading, writing, listening, and speaking. Literacy in each of the classrooms extends beyond print-based literacy to reading images, body language, environmental print, and other social semiotics to participate in the community of the classroom. In each of the teachers' classrooms, participants (both teachers and students) are expected to be active, rather than passive, consumers and producers of texts (spoken and written). The teachers consciously design the conditions where learners are active in the process of becoming literate. Critical literacy designs include attention to both content and process.

Underlying or supporting critical literacy practices is the development of a "critical frame" (New London Group, 1996). Each of the teachers brings a critical framing with her into the classroom. The teachers were all conscious of their various positionalities and fight to overcome various inequalities in their everyday lives.

Angy, for example, recognizes that adult education teachers are paid low wages and are offered mainly part-time jobs with little or no benefits; Sister Martha recognizes the limited choices that she had as a woman when she made a career choice; and Sarajane has consciously chosen to work with women at various adult education centers. Angy has worked side by side in factories with African Americans and with people who speak English as a second language and has seen how a classist, racist society works to keep people separated. Arguably, as women who do the gendered work of teaching, they each are operating from the lens of feminist perspectives (e.g., Maher & Thompson Tetreault, 1994; Weiler, 1988).

The teachers in this section (and throughout the book) diverge in their awareness and integration of these critical frames across various facets of their lives. We can clearly see the different levels of comfort in bringing critical social issues into the classroom. Therein lies the distinction embedded within the emergent framework; a teacher who consciously adopts a critical frame or stance consistently will most likely be found in the field where critical teaching occurs. Angy, for example, believes that she is really mining out the social issues that already exist in the classroom and then using classroom space and time as a way to dialogue around these issues. Sister Martha will address these issues when they are brought up by the learners and then will integrate them into the curriculum, where she can. Sarajane focused on teaching academics, a stance she believes leads to social and personal empowerment, a form of social justice. She does not, however, explicitly seek out or weave social justice issues into the curriculum.

All three teachers are cognizant of the various positionalities they bring with them into the classroom. Sister Martha hesitates to fully address social issues because she is afraid that it is really her agenda and she is not part of her students' community. Sarajane is committed to democracy and yet does not see her role as actively teaching about or for social justice. Angy's teaching practices seem to linger in the critical and accelerative field most consistently. She seems to see herself in solidarity with her students, a position that comes from working the boundaries of class, race, and gender alongside marginalized people throughout her life. Clearly, Sister Martha and Sarajane are less confident about their position in the classroom around accelerating students as readers and writers within a social justice framework. Both educated as teachers, they do not take on the authority that we see with Angy, Carolyn, Vivian, or Holiday, an authority that comes, in part, from taking a stance and recognizing that teaching is always value laden. What Sister Martha, Sarajane, and many other teachers who are afraid of taking a stance may not realize is that every curricular choice, every lesson plan, and every choice to assess a student one day and not the next is driven by values that are not neutral. In a sense, the reluctance to discuss and address critical social issues, whether they are generated from the student or the teacher, is separating the teacher from the student and reiterating a power difference. Only those with privilege (granted through race, class, gender, or another privileged status in society) can choose not to discuss and act on critical social issues. As Baym (1990) remarks, "I take it that whenever there is teaching, there is a power relationship. The question is what is produced by and through that relation" (p. 66). Sister Martha and Sarajane clearly work toward justice in their everyday out-of-school lives but also clearly struggle with the space and place of critical literacy in the classroom. Such a struggle is not uncommon for teachers. On this, Maher and Thompson Tetreault (1994) write,

As the process of personal development and the construction of multiple identities of gender, sexuality, ethnicity, and culture came into contact, teachers and students were engaged in shaping each other's voice. To the extent that the classrooms became communities of discourse, dialogues (and the identities that fed and grew out of them) were shaped by permissible and/or impressible topics, concerns and experiences; they evolved by negation as well as by affirmation, by means of silence as well as by expression. (p. 92)

The struggle for critical literacy represents constant inquiry and reflection about the intersections of theory, practice, and action in and out of the classroom. Designing literacy practices that seek to identify and disrupt the working of power and language can feel more of less liberating (Ellsworth, 1989). With teachers having more than enough to do during teaching hours (e.g., assess students, work with tutors, and construct lesson plans), the hard work of setting up the conditions necessary for critical inquiry into language and literacy practices to occur in a sustained fashion can easily get cut. Teachers struggle with balancing the time needed for the dialogue and community building necessary in a critical literacy classroom with the time needed for sustained reading, writing, math, and other academic practices. On this, Angy stated, "I see teaching life skills as really important. I don't want to spend too much time teaching the civil rights movement because they need to know how to go to the doctor." Designing space for critical awareness into the workings of language also means a commitment to social change at the classroom and the community-societal level. Once students are encouraged to think critically about language and power, the question often becomes, what can be done about the unjust structuring of society?

The teachers in this section also recognize, to varying degrees, the extent to which language and literacy can be tools of both empowerment and oppression. Sarajane is a certified reading specialist and could be teaching in a number of academic settings but consciously chooses to teach in adult education because she sees how literacy can be used to solve problems. Sister Martha suggests that adult literacy education is a fundamental right in the United States. She recognizes the myriads of social structures that maintain the status quo. On this, she said, "There are so many struggles that adults deal with. The school system is one of the structures that keep people in their place." All of the teachers recognize that the majority of people who cannot read and who live in poverty globally are women and children. They move in and out of various critical frameworks (antisexism, anticlassism, antiracism, and antiheterosexism) and are able to use these frameworks as a pivot point when issues come up in their own lives or in their classrooms.

In Sister Martha's case, we saw how she provided models and explicit teaching in a number of genres of writing that her students could choose from (freewriting, letters to their school board, letters to Congress, and essays). In each genre of writing, Sister Martha encourages her students to consider the audience and purpose of their writing. She makes it clear that as students write for real purposes, they develop a sense of agency which encourages democratic decision making and participation. Through this process, they learn that they have a voice and can use literacy to accomplish important social goals. We heard how one of her students wrote a letter to the superintendent of her daughter's school to improve the conditions of her daughter's education. We see, in this example, the process of becoming critically literate by starting to understand the socially constructed meanings in texts as well as the political and economic contexts in which the texts are produced, consumed, and reproduced.

Angy admits the majority of her teaching time is often teaching basic life skills in English (teaching the difference between "chicken" and "kitchen"); nonetheless, she sees teaching even basic vocabulary as value laden. Even when she is teaching basic vocabulary, she is trying to make links that are relevant to the adults' lives. Angy stated,

I like to know what kinds of jobs they are in and then I bring that into the classroom. If I get a group of landscapers, I will pull out the picture dictionary

and teach the word "yard."... The next week, we might do the word "painting"
if there is someone who paints in the room.

Angy's teaching comes to life when she is able to spend time teaching language and literacy skills through workers' rights, civil rights, or women's rights. She also designs a technology-rich classroom by modeling how she, as the teacher, is using language and literacy critically and for a purpose. She pulls together pictures, clip art, and quotations from various sources including magazines, newspapers, books, and the Internet to create multimodal pictures stories represented through PowerPoint. She is also modeling how to use the computer for a purpose. Reflecting on the importance of integrating technology into the classroom, Angy stated, "Even in industrial jobs, you have to look up an order on the computer and you have to punch the right buttons that program the machines." There are computers available at the International Institute for students to work on. This is not the case at many adult education classrooms.

Sarajane views language and literacy as means of solving important social problems. Her literacy teaching subtly disrupts her learners' expectations for traditional banking models of education where the teacher stands at the front of the room and lectures. Instead, she invites her students into dialogue with each other and with her—and in the process of participating in a dialogue, students hear multiple voices and viewpoints. Sarajane encourages her students to question each other, the texts they are reading and listening to, and her, as the teacher. Invitations to question are the heart of critical literacy. We hear this questioning disposition in Sister Martha and Angy as well. Sister Martha adopts a quizzical stance in her life and in her classroom. Indeed, a closer look at the discourse structure of her talk demonstrates that she adopts questioning as a rhetorical strategy when she is in a discussion.

Angy, too, lives a life full of questions. She constantly seeks out new professional and personal development opportunities related to language and literacy education, social justice, and workers' rights. Her questions and desire for more information often guide her teaching experiments in the classroom. However, even Angy, a teacher who describes her teaching as avowedly critical, was nervous when she began a discussion on gay and lesbian rights in her classroom. Each of the teachers shared her teacher blunders and reflected on how they became teachable moments in the classroom. We heard Sister Martha reflect on her latest "faux pas" where she did not know the answers to a problem her students were working on. Sarajane reflected on her stance as a European American woman and the educational benefits she has received at the expense of people of color. Angy reflected on what happened when she invited her students to dialogue about gay and lesbian rights—a socially sensitive issue in the state of Missouri, where an amendment was passed declaring gay marriage unconstitutional. She talked about how the discussion did not go quite as she would have hoped but the students were engaged, and there were multiple voices and opinions in the discussion.

Such risk taking is characteristic of some exemplary teachers and demonstrates their openness to being vulnerable in the classroom. We heard how Angy, Sister Martha, and Sarajane continually move in and out of their comfort zones and demonstrate their risk taking and stance of inquiry. Angy stated, "I am more confident because I have hit bumps in the road and found out what did not work. When you start out you are nervous, and then you realize after some months that nothing really bizarre will happen." Indeed, the struggle over critical literacy often means learning to live with discomfort in the classroom.

Critical literacy resides in both the content and the processes of classroom practices. Sister Martha invites her students to search for evidence—whether it is in a workbook passage, in a movie they see on television, or in a newspaper article they read. She models how to search out evidence in the text and multiple viewpoints, and how to think about what might be missing in the texts. She models this for her students. In doing so, her students realize that she, too, is a learner and that becoming critically literate is a lifelong process. Each of the teachers invites her students to examine their knowledge and lived experiences and uses these experiences as the basis for accelerating language and literacy development. The process of inviting students' voices and experiences into the classroom challenges traditional power structures.

When a teacher or learner becomes an active participant in the literacy education process, as we saw in all three cases, he or she begins to accelerate the transformation of literacy and social relations. Literacy education is a space where the revolutionary potential of education and the educational potential of revolution can be linked. Liberatory education cannot be separated from the struggles for a more liberated society.

Sister Martha, Sarajane, and Angy are each engaging in the struggle for critical literacy in more subtle ways, too. They each ground their teaching in a deep respect for the cultural and human values their learners bring with them into the classroom. They encourage criticism and self-criticism of themselves and their students. They all consider the content of their teaching as well as the way in which they are teaching, including their role as a teacher and who their students perceive them to be. Similarly, they model a form of civic engagement for the learners in the classroom. They consider ways of challenging their students' stereotypical views. They each choose to address women's issues in a variety of ways including in the texts they choose to teach, in the topics they emphasize, and in the examples provided on a daily basis. They intuitively model critical literacy as teachers in the sense that they are conscious that every topic, book, and discussion can be "read" according to race, class, and gender issues. In doing so, they invite learners into a process of participation and engagement in their educational process. In many ways, critical literacy can disrupt the power relationships based on knowledge through the collaborative deconstruction and construction of texts (oral, written, and media) (Comber, 2001; Luke, 2000).

Opening up spaces for critical literacy is not unproblematic. Critical interrogation into language and literacy raises larger questions, such as, what happens when controversial topics are raised and the conversation leads in oppressive directions? For example, when Angy begins a lesson to teach language and literacy with a focus on racial justice using the civil rights movement or Louis Armstrong's songs, the adults in her class ask well-intentioned but sometimes racially stereotypic questions or statements, such as "Why are all of the crimes in St. Louis committed by blacks?" If this question were left alone, it could reinforce racial stereotypes and deepen the historical segregation between immigrant and refugee groups and African Americans in the city. However, Angy's intention, operating from a larger critical framework, is to build alliances between oppressed groups in the city, and so the discussion would move to question why the assumption that African Americans commit all of the crimes in St. Louis is so pervasive and the ways in which biases in media coverage contribute to this assumption.

Angy, Sister Martha, and Sarajane put into practice what Sister Martha so eloquently stated, "If this is a democracy, and I have a voice, then I have a right and deserve to be heard." Each of them actively works from this belief in her classroom. Each teacher believes in the importance of voice in the democratic space of the classroom. On this, Freire (1973) writes,

Radicalization involves increased commitment to the position one has chosen. It is predominantly critical, loving, humble, and communicative and therefore a positive stance. The person who has made a radical option does not deny another person's right to choose, nor does he try to impose his own choice. They can discuss their respective positions.... The radical does, however, have the duty, imposed by love itself, to react against the violence of those who try to silence him—of those who, in the name of freedom, kill his freedom and their own.... Radicals cannot passively accept a situation in which the excessive power of a few leads to the dehumanization of all. (pp. 10–11)

Using the adults' voices as the substance of the discussion and adding their own voice and perspective to address socially sensitive issues facilitate an authentic understanding of the complexity of the issues. This happens as the individual chooses to hear and consider multiple perspectives, which is a longer lasting transformation than being told what the "right" answer is.

The striking difference between the three teachers—the difference that epitomizes the constantly shifting quadrants of the emergent framework—is the extent to which they internalize the social justice aspects of their own identity and bring it with them into the classroom. This choice reflects an aspect of the teachers' voice. Angy is comfortable teaching for social justice. Sister Martha is comfortable modeling social justice and, through her teaching practices, sets up a democratic and just classroom. Sarajane is concerned with personal and social empowerment as a means toward social equity but does not see her role to explicitly teach for social justice. She separates her personal life from the curriculum of her classroom and walks a fine line between her concern for personal and social empowerment and overtly teaching for social justice.

We hear how Angy uses her voice to recommend that her students join the public march on Martin Luther King Jr. Day. Angy revoiced what she will say to her students, "Monday, no class, go downtown and march for Martin Luther King!" Sister Martha's voice comes through more subtly—in the processes and design of her classroom. She consciously designs a social justice frame in the classroom space—through the social justice posters on the wall; the brochures and flyers advertising meetings, protests, rallies, and the like; and magazines and newspapers that reflect a variety of viewpoints. Whereas Sister Martha says that she would not deliberately bring up a social justice issue unless her students did, she makes it clear through the design of the space that this classroom is a space where students can feel comfortable bringing up important social issues. Indeed, one of Sister Martha's voices is social justice. Sister Martha's students might perceive her as less authentic if she completely stifled this voice in her classroom. In the debriefing conversations we had with the teachers, we really heard the struggle for teaching for literacy acceleration within a critical framework. Sarajane is not as transparent about her political or social views on a personal level. She is not as assertive about her social justice perspectives. Yet her social justice perspectives and values drive her as well as anyone else's but are more centered on the literacy focus and how literacy can address these problems.

These teachers see teaching and learning in terms of places where consciousness is raised, where meanings are questioned, and where a critical analysis of the textual and social worlds is encouraged. They do not define learning solely in terms of standardized test results or mastery of facts. They do, however, recognize that their students sometimes come into their classrooms with a deep-rooted belief that learning does equal test results.

In a small-group discussion where Angy, Sister Martha, and Sarajane debriefed about each of their chapters with Mary Ann and I (Rebecca), they reflected on the issue of teacher voice and the complexity of teaching for social justice. Reflecting on a time when the state was deliberating over budget cuts that would have crippled adult education and literacy services, Angy stated, "You had to be careful how you brought up this issue in the classroom because you are paid by the government." Sister Martha responded, "You can't tell them how to vote."

Angy responded, "And you don't want to tell your students what to do because that would be using your position for the wrong reason, but at the same time, when things are so obvious and it will affect their lives because they may not have a classroom to come to ..."

Sister Martha described a situation in which a representative from the governor's office came to their classroom and the students told her how important adult education was to them and why the budget should not be cut. Sister Martha described the visit this way: "A representative came to the classroom at 4:00 p.m. and we asked the students to come back so their voices could be heard. They came back and brought other people with them, and they said in no uncertain terms how important the classroom was for them." Sarajane, listening intently, stated, "Great!"

I was trying to reconcile why it is acceptable for some values—those of the mainstream and status quo—to enter the classroom, but when voices and perspectives of social justice are brought into the classroom they are questioned as violating students' rights. I ask, "Why can someone from the governor's office come to the classroom and talk with the students, but Angy feels silenced about talking about some of the same issues but from a different perspective?"

Mary Ann stated, "You can tell your students what the situation is and what is happening, and you can teach about the budget cuts and what is being proposed. If the students ask, what can we do? Then you can say that there are people you can write to."

Sister Martha agreed, "We made all of the information available, and they wrote follow-up letters to the governor's office."

I asked, "I am wondering if you can engage in critical literacy without the politics."

To this, Sister Martha responded, "Everything is political."

Angy, continuing the discussion around politics, stated, "Even when I teach beginning learners and students who speak English as their first language, you are empowering them, because you are teaching them to read. I see that as political because I think we get so used to the word 'political' as connected to politics when it should be used in the more social sense."

This conversation is an example of teacher-led professional development that is reflective and aimed at making classrooms more democratic places. We did not resolve any of the big issues surrounding the complexity of teaching for social justice, but through sustained dialogue, action, and reflection we contribute to a more just society.

RETHINKING PRACTICE

1. Why is it legitimate to raise social justice issues in the classroom? What do you see as the differences between raising social justice issues in the classroom and having a politician or elected official come into the classroom?

2. If one of the primary purposes of literacy education is to eliminate poverty (which goes hand in hand with redistributing power), then how can literacy programs design curricula that critically examine and challenge the various sources of poverty?

3. Ask the adults in your class, what do you like about your community? What would you like to change about your

community? How would you work with others to make these changes? Brainstorm individually and then as a group. Make a list of all of the ways that the adults might change their community. Vote on one of the projects to start working on as a class.

4. In reading each of the teachers' cases, you have seen the complexity of teaching for literacy acceleration within critical frameworks. Indeed, there is a wide diversity of approaches that characterizes the emergent framework. Reflect on the emergent framework we presented in chapter 2. Where do you position yourself in this emergent framework?

FURTHER READING:

Boal, A. (2002). *Games for actors and non-actors* (2nd ed.). New York: Routledge.

Shannon, P. (1998). *Reading poverty*. Westport, CT: Heinemann.

Shor, I. (1996). *When students have power*. Chicago: University of Chicago Press.

Part 5

Conclusions

16

Conclusions
Lessons Learned

"THE DANCE WE DO"

Inquiring into best teaching practices is a reiterative process. In the spirit of participatory research, we shared a draft of the book with the teachers and invited them to a celebration-meeting to talk about their teaching practices, learn from other teachers, and provide us with feedback. We were heartened to learn that our writing and representation of their teaching practices resonated with them. During the whole-group discussion, Sister Martha stated, "You used the idea of constantly shifting continua and I thought, 'You got it!!' It said so much to me about the reality of adult education. I mean, if you think you got it, uh-uh, the next day it will shift again." Angy, one of the English for Speakers of Other Languages (ESOL) teachers, responded, "I like the part about the dance that we do of constantly reading our students and going back to the drawing board and recreating to have our practices better fit our students. We are always doing that."

They also reflected on their participation in the project. Angy stated, "Reading the book made me reflect on my own teaching because sometimes you are so busy with the routines and it brings more meaning to my teaching to reflect on it." Carolyn, an Adult Education and Literacy (AEL) teacher at a full-service community center, stated,

You've given us the language. I do things in my classroom because I just thought they made sense. I do not come from an educational background, but you gave us the language to connect our practice to the theory. Most of the

time you get the theory and apply it to practice. Here, I put the practice in place and you gave it the language.

They pointed out many of the themes that resonated through the book. Sister Martha made an astute observation of our research design and methodology when she stated,

Our students are doing a lot of good things, too, but they don't see them or don't have the language to talk about these things. I feel very honored to be in this book, but what you have done is take some pretty ordinary stuff and put some names on it and that is very hopeful.

Sister Martha's comment points to the parallel teaching and learning practices of teachers and students and also notes the importance of a strengths framework when talking about these practices. Commenting on the tacit theories that teachers operate from, Angy stated,

I felt honored because when I was working on my master's degree, I read articles about Freire and Auerbach and critical literacy, and then when I started teaching, I was busy doing what I was doing and nervous before class and didn't have time to think about theory and philosophy. When I read this, I was reminded, "Oh yeah, I really do have a philosophy."

Vivian, an AEL teacher, shared during the small-group debriefing session that reading her chapter "made me do things a little differently because I forgot all of the good things I do!"

Dorothy, drawing on fifty years of teaching experience, commented in her usual sage manner, "No matter where I am, I find myself practicing literacy and teaching strategies and it is a part of us and the more you work on it, the better you get."

"I felt very privileged to be in this group. You all are wonderful teachers," Sarajane stated. Angy said she "felt connected to GED teachers" after she read this book.

They also saw connections between their teaching styles. Vivian stated, "I thought it was interesting to see all of the different styles that teachers have. Basically, we are all doing the same thing with different styles." Her comment points to the need for more teacher-led professional development. They discussed how a piece of literature or a discussion topic may work well in one classroom but not in another because the context of each classroom is different. Janet stated, "I realized what a complex group of teachers we are, and that is really important." Angy pointed out that the book was an example of teacher-focused research, a type of research that had been advocated for in professional development circles.

Throughout the discussion, the teachers challenged and inspired each other (and us) with questions such as the following: how can we, as adult literacy teachers and researchers, advocate for adult literacy education? What is the purpose of adult literacy education? What are our responsibilities as adult literacy teachers? How do we balance the demands of teaching for literacy acceleration within critical frameworks? How do we productively use students' resistance in the classroom? What should the future of adult literacy education look like? Who will decide? Over and over again, they came back to the needs and dilemmas faced by their students. They discussed the dilemma they sometimes faced with more traditional colleagues who were not open to hearing about new practices. "Sometimes," Carolyn admitted, "I just mind my own business and do what works for me." Angy commented, "When I was reading this book, I was thinking about my other colleagues who are not as critical but who are doing a good job and their students are learning. Other times, I think 'You are not doing it right!'"

We left these debriefing meetings reinspired about the importance of case-based professional development and the importance of teachers sharing their "best practices." In some instances, the teachers were unaware of their exemplary practices. They explained that "it just came natural to us" and "it just made sense." These comments reminded us of the importance of this book—adult education teachers sharing their "wisdom of practice." As we listen to and visualize the practices and theories of these nine teachers, we are reminded of their connection to adult educators throughout history who have managed to do the intellectual work of teaching, organizing, activism, and making their voices heard—to make significant contributions in the lives of their students and in society.

In this final section, we provide a summary of our conclusions and suggest possible implications for our work. We believe that the conclusions drawn from this study are significant to the following audiences: (1) policy makers who influence the design, funding, and evaluation of adult education programs; (2) researchers who are interested in adult literacy education; (3) educators who prepare teachers to work with adults; (4) the adult education and literacy teachers; and, most importantly, (5) the adult education students, who are at the basis of all of our teaching and research.

THE EMERGENT FRAMEWORK

Day after day, adult education teachers without professional background experiences in education engage classes of fifteen to twenty students with little more than the books provided in the classroom and the desire to make the world a better place. Without formal preparation, a wide array of materials, or curriculum guides, the teachers listen to the guides in the classroom—the adult students. As a result, they design creative and flexible curricula that respond to the needs, hopes, and desires of the adults in their classroom. As teachers, they are willing to try new approaches, are committed to their own lifelong learning, and are willing to share authority with their students.

All of the teachers were successful at accelerating their students toward their goals. Many of the teachers had high rates of students moving from level to level in the Test of Adult Basic Education (TABE) and obtaining their GED certificate. They also had high attendance and retention rates. In addition to more traditional measures of achievement, the teachers also demonstrated a commitment to their students' reaching more nontraditional life goals, including active citizenship, democratic participation in the communities in which they work and live, and a critical understanding of the world.

Because there is more flexibility in the design of adult literacy classrooms than there is in many K–12 classrooms under the present regime of testing, standardized curricula, and accountability measures, adult literacy education could lead the way in informing educators across the life span with models for implementing New Literacy Studies.

We saw the teachers presented throughout the pages of this book managing to coexist with federal and state policies that insist on a functional literacy paradigm while at the same time struggling to create literacy education in their local contexts that is relevant and authentic to their students' lives. They are each teaching literacy within the context of critical frameworks. In each of the teachers' cases, we witnessed how they move in and out of each of the four fields of critical literacy education (e.g., critical, noncritical, functional, and emancipatory) depending on their students, the context in which teachers are teaching, the materials that they have designed and are available, and their backgrounds and interests.

To review, the emergent framework can be imagined as two constantly shifting continua which intersect. One continuum represents literacy practices. The other continuum represents critical frameworks. At one end of the literacy continuum are practices that might be considered accelerative and emancipatory. At the other end of the continuum are literacy practices that would be considered functional and traditional, that rely on commercially scripted materials and are less student focused.

The other intersecting continuum in this emergent framework is that of critical practices. At one end of this continuum are educators who explicitly see education as value laden and ideological and explicitly construct critical literacy practices in their classrooms. At the other end of the critical frameworks continuum are teachers who see education as value "free" or "noncritical." They do not see their place as a teacher to educate for or about social justice. This position in the framework does not exclude them from designing accelerative literacy practices. Indeed, one could imagine a noncritical teacher who teaches for literacy acceleration. One can also imagine an accelerative literacy teacher who is, at the same time, critical in her stances toward the social world and embeds this into her practices.

Both continua—literacy education and critical frameworks— intersect in the middle of each continuum. Surrounding the two continua are four fields (A, B, C, and D), which represent the infinite points of intersection between the two continua. We invite you to reread our description of the emergent framework in chapter 2 and also see figure 2.1 for a visual of this heuristic. It is important to stress that there are an infinite number of positions and places that a teacher may teach from within this framework. What follows is a review of each of the potential fields within the emergent framework:

Field A: accelerative/critical. This field represents the intersection of the accelerative and critical parts of the continua. When a teacher was located in this field, she would be teaching for literacy acceleration within a critical framework. She may be either high or low in each of these dimensions.

Field B: traditional/critical. This field represents the intersection of the traditional literacy teaching and the critical parts of the continua. When a teacher was located in this field, she would be traditional in her approaches to literacy education and would also be critical in her approach to teaching and learning. She may be high or low in each of these dimensions.

Field C: traditional/noncritical. This field represents the inter-section of the traditional literacy teaching and the noncriti-cal parts of the continua. When a teacher was located in this field, she would be traditional in her approaches to literacy education and would be noncritical in the frameworks in her classroom. She may be either high or low in each of these dimensions.

Field D: accelerative/noncritical. This field represents the intersection of the accelerative and noncritical parts of the continua. When a teacher was located in this quadrant, she would be teaching for literacy acceleration (either extensively or minimally) but would be noncritical in her framework (either extensively noncritical or minimally noncritical).

Much like exemplary adult educators across the nation, the teachers in this book did not fall into one field or another—with regard to literacy instruction or critical frameworks. Rather, they move in and out of instruction that might be characterized as on a continuum from emancipatory to traditional literacy instruction and from critical to noncritical practices. We learned that depending on the stance the teachers brought into the classroom—informed by all of their social positionalities (e.g., gender, class, race, linguistic and geographic backgrounds, and political affiliations)—they dif-fered in terms of their location on the two continua (literacy and critical practices). Their location in the intersecting fields of criti-cal and accelerative literacy practices shifts, depending on their stu-dents, their materials, the reading and writing strategies and designs at their disposal, and the location of their classroom, to name a few factors. For instance, Dorothy Walker's stance on Black English (as we heard in chapter 8) was informed by her experiences as a black woman growing up during the civil rights era, which influenced her choice to emphasize Standard English in her classroom. Her empha-sis on the dominant code (in pronouncing words "correctly" and talking and writing in Standard English), whether in talking or in writing, reflects her values in social context. It is this same set of positionalities, though, that also influences Dorothy's decision to use relevant and authentic materials. We heard this as she discussed teaching the preacher how to design sermons (both in writing and in talking). Such stances come out of the multiple and intersecting positionalities that teachers bring with them into their classroom.

It is easier to see and hear the ways in which teachers' multiple positions (e.g., race, class, gender, sexuality, and religion) inform their stance with regard to critical teaching. It is less clear to imagine the ways in which these positionalities shape their stance in terms of literacy teaching. We have tried to demonstrate the ways in which these are interconnected. Ultimately, we would strive for instructional practices that are fully integrated—thus the essence of teaching for literacy acceleration within critical frameworks. This model recognizes the social and political nature of literacy education—in theory as well as in practice. Within this model, every instructional move in literacy education, whether it is word study, comprehension, or a writers' workshop, would operate within a larger purpose and goal that seek not just to learn isolated skills but also to put literacy to use to make the world a better place. Attention would be given to the areas where critical and accelerative frameworks overlap and intersect, such as the following:

- Using multiple forms of evidence
- Making self-corrections
- Noticing differences in perspectives and positions
- Noticing and naming how language works
- Flexible problem-solving processes
- Offering counter-interpretations
- Theorizing about the ways in which texts are put together

The teachers have shown us where we are in the process of moving toward this integration. Sister Martha Jaegers tends to use more traditional literacy materials, such as workbooks, but supplements the workbooks with relevant materials. She is also skilled in teaching writers' workshop and setting up purposeful conditions for her students to write. Here, we saw how a teacher can be more comfortable teaching one aspect of literacy (writing) than another (reading). Less likely to explicitly bring social justice issues into the classroom, Sister Martha speaks to her personal commitment to justice and peace education through the environment of her classroom. Similarly, Vivian Jett uses a combination of literacy materials and is proficient with strategy instruction and flexible grouping. She also uses multiple modalities in the classroom: songs, speeches, and theater. She is less comfortable with teaching writers. As an African American woman, she readily integrates black history into the curriculum but does not explicitly teach about or for social justice. On the other hand, Carolyn, Holiday, and Angy position themselves as explicitly teaching for social justice and move in and out of traditional and accelerative literacy practices. Further, we learned from the teachers that the field of "critical frameworks" can be further broken into multiple literacies, culturally relevant instruction, and critical literacy. We have structured the cross-case chapters at the end of each section with these critical threads that can be seen as pivot points or points of departure for any literacy lesson in the adult education classroom.

It seems relevant to turn this emergent framework back on our own practices as adult education teachers. As a teacher educator primarily charged with the preparation of literacy teachers, I (Rebecca) often find myself moving in and out of the fields that constitute the emergent framework. I model integrating critical and accelerative approaches to literacy instruction as often as I can in my classes. For example, when I conduct a leveling texts workshop, the teachers level multicultural books or books that contained critical social issues (e.g., poverty, homelessness, gender roles, and environmental racism). When I teach a session on word study, I provide examples of word work that were developmentally appropriate *and* come from the students' life experiences. While I am concerned that all of the teachers in my classes have foundational knowledge and practice of teaching for literacy acceleration I struggle with when, how, and how much time to spend within critical frameworks (Dozier, Johnston, & Rogers, 2005; Rogers, 2007).

As literacy coordinator, teaching for literacy acceleration within a critical framework seems, to borrow a phrase from Carolyn, to "just make sense." I (Mary Ann) recognize that the purpose for learning and then teaching determines the strategy or approach selected similarly as with identifying the purpose and strategy for reading. In doing so, I consider who the student is, investigate what they want to learn and why they want to learn a particular subject or skill, and determine the context within which we will be situated. This, along with my own positions and stance that I bring to the classroom, influences the direction in which we will move and ultimately, where on the fields of the emergent framework my teaching will be located. For example, when a student only wanted to learn how to complete a money order, that is what I taught him without going into a thorough analysis of our economic system. However, when teaching a series called "Real World Reading," the content was only identified after students and I collectively brainstormed all topics of interest, decided on a process for narrowing the topics, and then democratically made a final selection. Throughout the classes, I selected appropriate materials, and students sometimes brought in relevant items as well. Our sources were newspapers, magazines, government publications, and the Internet and included articles, laws, editorials, political cartoons, tables, graphs, and charts. Giving explicit instruction in how to "read" the various genres, ensuring selections were level appropriate, providing essential text introductions, using graphic organizers, and engaging in group oral reading and discussion positively impacted reading progress even as we developed our critical analysis of Social Security proposals, budget cuts, and the consequences of the war in Iraq. At the end of each session, we reflected on our learning and determined our continuing direction and process. Many of these same students became actively involved with student leadership and advocacy activities on a broader community level during this period.

As we reflected on our positions within the emergent framework, it validated for us the idea that our stance and position as critical educators are always changing and shifting depending on our students, the context, our materials, and a range of other factors. Indeed, while we would like to locate ourselves in the critical and accelerative field all of the time, we recognize that we sometimes fall short of this goal. We can use the emergent framework as a reminder of the intersections of our hopes and realities. We believe that the emergent framework provides an analytic frame for envisioning the complexity of adult education teachers' practices. We do not think it is useful to explicitly categorize the teachers in this book, or teachers anywhere, squarely in one field or another. That is against the concept of the emergent framework, which leans on the assumption that because teaching and learning are social practices, they are constantly shifting and changing. We also believe there is value in reading the teachers' cases with the emergent framework in mind and discussing with colleagues where each of the teachers falls within the fields and continua and why. This is likely to lead to the type of reflection and dialogue amongst adult education professionals that is at the heart of quality professional development. The framework can also provide a set of guideposts for professional development and teacher change because it allows us to talk, with more detail, about the nature of literacy practices. Weiner (2005/2006) writes, "Adult literacy education is an enormously complex social project and the more complex a map we have of the field, the better prepared we will be to meet the needs of those in the U.S. who often need it the most" (p. 300). Our intention is that the framework can be used as an analytic tool for teachers to analyze their own practices.

Amidst the complexities and differences, there were similarities amongst the teachers. The teachers were united in their stance that adult education can lead to a more just and equitable society. Indeed, these teachers recognize that adult education is inherently about facing the realities of broken school systems, social issues that get in the way of people attending school, and instruction that does not meet the intellectual, social, political, or emotional needs of students who attend school. In the sense that all teachers are actively working on providing the best educational contexts for their students, they are contributing to a more just world as they move students into a power base. Indeed, we would argue that the realities of adult education predispose adult education teachers to view literacy as a social practice—one that is connected to systems of power to which, historically, their students have not had access. Whether the resources and tools that the teachers have access to—the books and reading materials, the classroom space, the professional development, their testing regime, and so on—will support or constrain the development of critical literacy practices is another matter.

The exemplary teachers are in different places in both the literacy and critical practices continua and as they move around. They seem to be drawing on practices that are performance based and emancipatory. That is the "dance we do." As we have seen, the adult education teachers taught students how to construct business letters and organize to stop the closing of their adult education center; they taught students how to read passages in the GED and political speeches also. The emergent framework provides suggestions for the education of adult education teachers, whether it is in an in-service professional development or professional development in the university classroom for recognizing the complexity of adult education practices. It also points to the importance of applying the learning theories commonly advocated for application in teaching adult education students to the education of adult educators themselves.

Oftentimes in adult education, the radical theoretical conceptualizations of adult education fall short of the practice of adult education. We believe part of the rationale for this is because we assume that critical literacy is an all-or-nothing proposition. The cases of teachers' literacy practices indicate that it is more productive to think about the *emergence of critical literacy*. The contribution of this book and the adult educators represented in its pages are to show a reconciliation of theory and practice. The extent to which the literacy education was considered critical depended on the *stance* that each of the teachers brought with her into the classroom and the extent to which they fostered a critical stance with their students. This reminds us that no practice is inherently liberatory or oppressive; rather, it is how the practice is negotiated and mediated.

PROFESSIONALIZATION VERSUS PROFESSIONAL DEVELOPMENT

Increasingly, programs are held accountable to outside performance standards, which creates a dilemma. On the one hand, the standards create a structure of accountability for the teachers and programs and also for the programs to hold funding agencies accountable to provide the resources and professional development necessary to teach for those standards. On the other hand, teachers spend more and more of their time administering practice tests and recording their students' assessments and less time on instruction and curriculum development. The standards and top-down model of reform could potentially exclude the "wisdom of practice" of adult education teachers who design curricula responsive to the needs of their students. The movement to standardize adult education runs counter to the best practices we have seen in the teachers in this study. That is, the teachers are effective because they have flexible and creatively designed curricula and experiences that uniquely responded to the needs of the adults in their classes. Even worse, the move to standardize threatens to place a veil between the real conditions adults experience and respond to in society and their adult education classrooms. Indeed, there is the real fear that as adult education becomes increasingly professionalized, it will lose its radical edges and cease to function in emancipatory ways.

It is important to point out that only half of the teachers in this book were ever certified as classroom teachers or had any experience in education before teaching in an adult education classroom. It has been argued that the presence of nontraditional teachers, including individuals who have not completed a four-year degree, or individuals with a college degree but without experience as a formal educator, is a strength of the current adult literacy education system because it increases local community participation, innovation, and diversity.

Indeed, throughout history, there have been exemplary teachers like Bernice Robinson, who was part of the Citizenship Schools teaching African American people to read and write so they could register to vote, which formed the basis of the civil rights movement; and Vivian Jett, presented in this book, who when asked to teach said, "I've never taught before." Once they go into the classroom, however, they rely on their wisdom of practice and their connection with the lived realities of the adults in the classroom to attend to the dual goals of accelerating students' literacy development and doing so within a framework that respects the importance of community building, participation, and democracy.

While nontraditional teachers bring many strengths to the adult education classroom, they are less likely to have the best working conditions because they are often part-time, which leaves little time for organizing. Smith (2006) has argued for the importance of adult education teachers unionizing for better pay, better working conditions, and benefits that will keep and attract highly qualified professionals to adult education. Indeed, we can find evidence of this increasing professionalization in the existence of professional organizations, degree programs at universities, listservs, research centers, and conferences.

While adult education has, historically, distinguished itself from K–12 education by relying on the development of adult education theories and practices, increasingly, the field has moved closer to the K–12 education system through its professionalization, reliance on accountability measures, narrowed curriculum, increased testing, and insistence on research that comes from increasingly narrow paradigms of thought (Wilson, 1993). As we have tried to demonstrate throughout this book, we can look to research and practice in K–12 education to provide examples of best literacy practices. We do not necessarily advocate for a hard-and-fast separation between adult education and K–12 education, nor do we believe that advancement of adult education is dependent on the K–12 system. Instead, we believe there is synergy in a life span approach to literacy development and would advocate for using aspects of adult literacy education as a model for K–12 education. Quigley (2005) puts the life span idea this way:

If we are seriously concerned about almost half of the adult population across North America and the thousands of children and youth dropping out of school systems that sustain these numbers, not to mention issues of recidivism in literacy skills, we need to ask: Can we not make an effort to build a more coherent

path of informal learning and formal education that focuses on the common
foundation of lifelong learning—literacy across the lifespan? (p. 323)

K–12 teachers could surely benefit from reflecting on the characteristics of the exemplary teachers illustrated in this book. Moreover, there is a greater likelihood that adult education and literacy teachers (regardless of whether they are teaching an adult who is an emergent reader or who needs comprehension strategies to process college-level texts) are encouraged to see themselves as literacy teachers. They understand that all of their students need support with various aspects of literacy learning. Students in the K–12 system would benefit from teachers who similarly saw themselves as their students' primary literacy teachers

The emergent framework and the associated (and intersecting) fields of literacy instruction and critical practices cause us to think about the following question: how do we want to prepare adult education and literacy teachers? The emergent framework allows teachers to locate their own practices, and then professional development can proceed from what teachers already know. Do we want to continue to prepare teachers to move in and out of the fields of the framework? Or, do we want to locate teachers squarely in any one field? How might the five components of reading instruction being legislated—phonemic awareness, phonics, fluency, vocabulary, and comprehension—be embedded within a critical framework?

These big issues around teacher preparation raise a larger question about the purpose of adult literacy education. There has long been debate about the purpose and function of adult education—classical versus practical—that was played out in the debates between the "Bookerites and the Talented Tenth faction" and had its roots in the Greek civilization of Socrates, Plato, and Aristotle (Denton, 1993, p. 196). These debates continue to characterize adult literacy education and teacher development.

We are at a point in the profession in deciding between returning to radical roots or increasing the professionalization—which will, in turn, move the profession further and further from the radical roots. As Giroux (1987) reminds us,

*To be literate is not to be free. It is to be present and active in the struggle for
reclaiming one's voice, history, and future. Just as illiteracy does not explain
the cause of massive unemployment, bureaucracy, or the growing racism in
major cities in the United States, South Africa, and elsewhere, literacy neither*

automatically reveals nor automatically guarantees social, political, and economic freedom. (p. 11)

We are reminded that critical literacy practices cannot address the material conditions underlying low literacy. Teachers who know how to teach literacy but who do not attend to the reasons why people need to become literate are bound to reproduce the existing social strata. On the other hand, teachers who are critical but who do not know how to accelerate adults as readers and writers are likely to do the same. As we have tried to demonstrate throughout the book, attention to one without the other will not do. We see this split between radical roots and functional leanings in the voices of the teachers. Indeed, the larger conversations appearing on listservs, in journals, and at conferences are echoed in the themes and voices of the adult education teachers. It would serve us well to listen more closely to what they have to say.

In reality, the debate of professionalization versus professional development is not an either/or scenario. Opportunities for teacher development that are responsive and supportive of teachers' needs are crucial. Adult education teachers are learners, classroom teachers, program members, community members, and members of the larger field of adult education. Professional development should be relevant and meaningful to situated contexts and mirror what we know are effective practices in adult education. Teacher-led professional development, including teacher research, case-based professional development, book discussion groups, and study groups, is ideal for meeting the complex demands of adult education teachers. Supporting and encouraging adult education and literacy teachers to become researchers of their own practice will promote and strengthen leadership, enhance practice, and inform research (Quigley, 1997, 2006). Adult education teachers rarely get the opportunity to collaborate together, and consequently, teachers find themselves missing what Angy Folkes called "the camaraderie of the coworkers."

Examining literacy education through the lens of the emergent framework allows those involved in adult education a chance to reflect on best practices that feature aspects of teaching for literacy acceleration within critical frameworks. It also allows us to identify areas where teachers are in need of professional support and development. Indeed, we wrote the case studies from a strengths framework by highlighting the teachers' best practices—but we also recognize there are areas in which each teacher needs more support and development. Such a framework allows us to resocialize our attention and language to focus on what teachers are doing well, what they can do independently, and the areas in which they need more support. Table 16.1 displays some of the places for professional development that came from the teachers' recommendations and also from the "rough edges" in their case studies.

Table 16.1   Rough Edges: Places for Professional Development

Forums for Professional Development

Teachers sharing their best practices

Opportunities for teachers to observe each other's practices and dialogue

Study groups

Dialogue groups

Action research

Case-based professional development

Teacher research methodologies

Weblogs, chat rooms, voice e-mails, and other online discussion forums

Literacy

Critical reflection on the question "Literacy for what?"

Writer's workshops

Leveling books; becoming familiar with the characteristics of texts

Assessing oral reading and designing strategy instruction based on problem solving

Designing flexible reading groups

Spelling instruction and word study that are appropriate for the adult's level of reading and writing development

Multiple forms of assessment that are teacher rather than instrument dependent (e g., Informal Reading Inventories, running records, and qualitative analyses of writing and reading)

Moving from language experience stories to developing strategic reading

More education in online technologies and digital literacies

Book clubs

Critical Practices

Examples of critical literacy practices (e.g., videos and observations)

Encouragement and invitations that value critical literacy practices

Trade books and magazines which include critical social issues

Coteachers to support inquiry around problems in the community

Forums to share problem-posing/problem-solving models of education

Mini-courses or small-group instruction

"Coaching" model where teachers observe each other and give each other feedback

Self-evaluation based on the emergent framework

FUTURE DIRECTIONS
CASE-BASED PROFESSIONAL DEVELOPMENT
IN ADULT LITERACY EDUCATION

The heart of this book has been the case studies developed through a series of interviews, observations, and focus-group conversations with the adult education teachers. Cases provide teachers with the complexity of instructional philosophies, practices, materials, and choices as well as problems, tensions, and issues that arise during the teaching-learning process. Case studies can provide a model for professional development in adult literacy education for beginning and experienced AEL teachers. Cases allow teachers to showcase exemplary practices and, at the same time, recognize the complexities that are part and parcel of teaching literacy. Oftentimes, adult education teachers are isolated from other teachers, and this isolation prevents teachers from sharing practices, and asking for and sharing feedback and teaching suggestions. Encouraging the use of cases, whether they are written by the adult education teachers or by researchers or directors, can lead to an enhanced connection between and amongst teachers.

When we asked the teachers what they saw as important in the future of adult education, they had much to say. Table 16.2 represents some of the frequently cited themes.

Continued struggle in adult education means building solidarity between adult education classrooms—where adults are struggling with the same basic issues of apartheid systems of education and housing, draconian cuts in social services, discrimination in employment, and violence in their communities. The continued struggle in adult education also points to the necessity of building alliances across groups that have, historically, been disconnected from each other. Bringing together university students and adult education students, for example, could lead to dialogue and solidarity that are necessary for the historically separated groups to mobilize. The adult education centers in St. Louis, for example, are many times located within several miles of major universities. At the universities, students learn, in theory, about the practices and theories of adult education but often do not have the opportunity to build relationships and to experience the conditions of people who are living marginal existences in the city where they live and go to school. More connections should be made between foreign-born and American-born students and historically oppressed groups within adult education programs. Indeed, these groups are generally pitted against

Table 16.2 Future Directions for Adult Literacy Education

- Move toward full-time, full-service centers.
- Literacy coaching.
- Paid preparation and planning time.
- Ongoing professional development that is topic based rather than time based. Presently, teachers pick in-service professional development based on convenient dates rather than on topics and themes that are of interest to them.
- Standards that reflect the authentic and diverse needs of adults (versus standardization).
- Professional development should come out of and be responsive to the needs of local sites and contexts.
- Teacher-led professional development.
- Teacher-initiated curriculum development.
- More research into effective teaching practices.
- Career paths in adult education so people can see adult education as a viable career opportunity.
- Policy development.
- Dissemination of research (federal funding for the National Center for the Study of Adult Learning and Literacy [NSCALL] has been cut as of March 31, 2007).
- New teachers should be provided with an overview of the reading process, more time in strategies for accelerating middle-level readers, using group methods while recognizing individual needs, and thematic approaches to tying subjects together.
- Encourage creativity and innovation at the local level.

one another in the workforce and would benefit from adult education programming that supports building bridges between groups. More attention needs to be paid to the relationships and interactions between community-based organizations and institutionalized programs.

We worry about the narrowing of the field of adult literacy education through teacher certification programs, standards, and tighter testing regimes. We would argue for more dialogue and theorizing about the boundaries, history, and future of adult literacy education. If we limit who we consider to be a part of adult literacy education, we also narrow the power base for organizing and advocating for education and other vital social issues that impact the adults enrolled in adult education programs. We also need to look to groups that are not formally considered to be adult education but are working toward accomplishing important social goals, such as increasing voter registration, increasing the minimum wage, and advocating for best practices by parents for their children in public schools. In the process of working toward these social goals, adults are involved in a type of informal adult literacy education that involves critically and strategically motivated literacy practices, literacy practices that are multimodal, digital, and often more complicated than the types of literacy practices found in classrooms. Adult educators need to more thoroughly look to these out-of-school literacy practices (and the teachers of these practices and activities) in which the adults in their classrooms are already involved and use them as guides for best practices. Often, there are communities of practices that include theories of learning which are effective for adults. In the same vein, it is important that we turn this reflexive lens on ourselves and on this book project and recognize that the teachers foregrounded in this book are all adult literacy education teachers who are involved with grant-funded, institutionalized systems. In providing their cases, we have excluded many different types of adult education and literacy teachers from the sample.

The organizing around adult literacy education that has been occurring in St. Louis over the past five years can provide a potential model for other programs. We have witnessed and participated in organizing that includes building alliances across groups, institutions, and people across the life span. The Literacy Roundtable (described in chapter 2) serves as a hub for literacy providers, activists, and educators to share resources, network, and plan programs. The Literacy Roundtable is composed of diverse organizations, such as LIFT-Missouri (Literacy Investment for Tomorrow), Pro-Literacy, the Literacy Council, the University of Missouri–St. Louis, community colleges, community-based adult education programs, faith-based adult education programs, St. Louis Public Libraries, and others. People who do not traditionally see themselves as working in adult education are joining efforts for increasing awareness around adult literacy education issues. This helps to broaden the base of support around adult literacy education and the ways in which literacy education is connected to broader social issues. This broader base allows us to speak about literacy education without continuous reference to one particular institution (Cowan, 2006). This is hopeful because it means people can dream about the ways in which literacy education can be linked with larger social struggles over health care and workers' rights and quality public education and the ways in which such struggles can be used as the basis for literacy education.

During the 2005–2006 academic year, the ABC's (Acting for a Better Community) group met six times for forums held at public libraries. At these forums, student leadership groups from adult education sites met to share their leadership projects, plan and organize with others at their sites, listen to speakers, and attend workshops. The ABC's conference was held in May 2006. A documentary video was produced called "Organizing for Change" on the ABC's process.* In 2007, three graduates of adult education and literacy programs were hired as interns to move the student leadership and organizing forward. Additionally, a blog was created to encourage dialogue and information sharing about the organizing around adult literacy education. The address of the blog is: http:// abcsofliteracy.blogspot.com/

The Educating for Change Curriculum Fair, sponsored by the Literacy for Social Justice Teacher Research Group, the Literacy Roundtable, and the International Institute, focused on immigrant and refugee rights in the context of racial justice. This fair brought together members from across the educational community, including ESOL and Adult Basic Education (ABE) groups. Each of these forums brings together people from across the literacy continuum (educators from early childhood, K–12, adult education, and higher education; students from adult education sites and universities; program coordinators; folks from community organizations, public libraries, and the business sectors; interns; and so forth). This fair was offered to adult education teachers in the city of St. Louis as a choice for their professional development credits (four credits). This movement to provide teachers with choice in their professional development as opposed to state-authorized professional development only, which tended not to meet the needs of teachers at all sites, is a positive move. There has been discussion of using a video we prepared in connection with this book for professional development at the state level. This would constitute an important move toward teacher-led professional development, a model that relies on the expertise and professional wisdom of teachers. There are

---

* The documentary video is called "Organizing for Change: Adult Literacy Education in St. Louis" and information about the video, including how to order a copy of the video can be found at the following website: http:// abcsofliteracy.blogspot.com/

other examples of local innovation in St. Louis. At the Adult Learning Center, a critical literacy lab was started (Kramer & Jones, in progress), which integrates the values identified with feminist teaching methodology, critical literacy, liberation theology, and popular education within a comprehensive approach to literacy instruction which includes the primary reading components of phonemic awareness/phonics, vocabulary, fluency, and comprehension.

The organizing that is occurring around adult literacy education in St. Louis arises out of the specific needs of the people and organizations in this area. It is dependent on local people finding local solutions to problems and challenges. Each city, around the country and around the world, will need to find its own problem-posing/problem-solving model of organizing. However, we can also look to each other for ideas, energy, inspiration, and hope.

While we recognize the limits of education and social change, the teachers represented in this book help us to focus on stories of strength and achievement while we agitate and prepare for the next movement. Adult literacy education constantly reminds us of the fragility of our democracy; it forces us to ask difficult questions about why some people in society are visible and marked as deserving, and others are seen as undeserving. Adult literacy teachers everywhere provide hope that education, combined with changes in other social systems, can lead to a better world. Studying the beliefs and practices of adult education teachers provides new knowledge on the significance of the complexity of the work they do. As Angy Folkes noted, "If adult education teachers don't speak up, who will?"

Appendix 1

Research Design and Methodology
Eliciting the "Wisdom of Practice"

Our research methods have been an example of research that intimately involves practitioners in research. Throughout the process, we have foregrounded teachers' voices, experiences, and ideas for adult education and literacy. Each of the phases of the research design—the interviews, classroom observations, and member-checking and debriefing meetings—afforded the teachers the opportunity to talk, think, and reflect on their teaching practices.

In selecting the teachers to participate in this project, we used what Foster (1997) has referred to as the process of "community nomination" where we asked members of the adult education community to nominate exemplary teachers. We designed an "exemplary teacher nomination" form that consisted of basic program information, the name of the person submitting the nomination, and a checklist of possible criteria for nominating a teacher as exemplary. Some of the criteria that we included on this form came from the literature in adult education that suggests that in addition to professional background and degree, adult educators call on dispositions or on interpersonal strategies and skills that may be important to student achievement and retention (Cantor, 2001; Johnson, 1998; Knowles, Holton, & Swanson, 1998; Shanahan, Meehan, & Mogge, 1994). These criteria were as follows:

- Actively engage all students at every level.
- Demonstrate commitment to students and their goals.
- Integrate relevant content into classroom instruction.
- Demonstrate use of creative and inclusive instructional strategies.

- Engage in professional development.
- Facilitate a high rate of student achievement (multilevels and objectives).
- Contribute to the positive development of their students and community.

In addition, there was a space for additional comments. The nomination forms were mailed with a cover letter to sixty-one contact persons of adult education and literacy class sites served by the school district. In addition, five nomination letters were given to administrative staff supervising adult education teachers. They were asked to respond within seven days. We received a total of nineteen nominations for exemplary teachers. Two teachers were nominated twice. One teacher left the program. One teacher declined our invitation to be interviewed. We scheduled interviews with the remaining fourteen teachers. We ultimately included nine of the fourteen teachers from this sample in our analysis and in this book because they discussed their literacy practices in depth, whereas the other teachers discussed math or other content areas more in depth.

INTERVIEWS

We used an interview protocol designed for exemplary elementary teachers (Allington & Johnston, 2001) but modified for adult education teachers (see appendix 3, "Interview Protocol"). Our purpose was to get the adult education teachers describing and theorizing about their practices. We interviewed the teachers wherever it was most convenient for them. The interviews took place at either their adult education site or the main adult education center in the district. The interviews were semistructured. We followed the interview protocol but allowed the participants to expand on their answers and lead into other questions. Each of the interviews was audio- and video-recorded using digital video and audio recorders. Both of the researchers were generally present for the interview—we rotated roles: one of us would conduct the interview and the other would run the video camera and take notes. Each of the interviews lasted from 60 to 180 minutes. The tapes were logged into a video and audio log. We received signed permission slips from each of the participants prior to conducting the interview.

We modified the interview protocol after the first few interviews to delete repetitive questions and to reorganize the protocol to flow more smoothly. We debriefed after the first few interviews to get a sense of what else we could be doing. We consulted with each of the participants about the color gain and setup level of the videotape to make sure that they were satisfied with the way their skin color was represented in camera. We also videotaped examples of what the teachers defined as "best practices" in their classrooms and have selectively included some of these data in each of their cases. We conducted follow-up and debriefing interviews with each of the teachers that lasted from two to five hours.

CLASSROOM OBSERVATIONS

During the interviews, we asked all of the teachers when a good time would be to come into their classroom to videotape what they thought of as their best practices in reading and writing instruction. We then scheduled appointments to observe and videotape in their classrooms during this time. We observed in each classroom at least once. Mary Ann's role as the literacy coordinator afforded her the opportunity to visit the classroom on a semiregular basis. Thus, in addition to our formal classroom observations, we have an understanding of how the classrooms function on a day-to-day basis as well as a deeper understanding of the culture of the site and other contextual information. We found this "big picture" information invaluable in helping to create contextualized portraits of the classrooms and of the teachers' literacy teaching.

DOCUMENTS

We collected supporting documents that would help us to understand aspects of the teachers' teaching performance such as students' achievement rates, retention rates, and the level (according to the National Reporting System) in which there was the most student progress (level of impact). The level of impact is determined by the number of students who started at a particular level and the number of those students who progressed to the next level. We conducted historical research on adult literacy education in St. Louis, consulting primary records associated with John Meachum and the Freedom Schools and the archives of several adult literacy programs. The National Adult Literacy Survey was consulted for national literacy rates, and the Missouri State Assessment of Adult Literacy for local rates.

We rotated between "watching," "asking," and "reviewing" in a holistic manner. We rely primarily on the interviews and the observations in our development of the case studies. We did call on document analysis, including the surveys that were returned and each teacher's student achievement record. Patton (1990) points out that "multiple sources of information are sought and used because no single source of information can be trusted to provide a comprehensive perspective.... By using a combination of observations, interviews, and document analysis the fieldworker is able to use different data sources to validate and cross check findings" (p. 244).

ANALYSIS

Our analysis was inductive and aimed at uncovering the adult educators' tacit theories about literacy practices. Our analysis was ongoing. We took notes during the videotaped interview—either we took them by hand or a research assistant typed notes on the computer as the interview progressed. The researchers transcribed the interviews and noted themes, surprises, and follow-up questions as they transcribed. These notes were shared amongst the researchers. We also met once a month during data collection to debrief on changes in the interview protocol, emerging themes, and observations across the interviews.

Throughout the analysis, we turned to social theory and literature in adult literacy education and teacher preparation in a hermeneutical manner. That is, we sought to understand how these adult education teachers bring meaning to their literacy teaching. Patricia Collins's (1998) concept of "visionary pragmatism" has made a great deal of sense to us in our research. Visionary pragmatism links "caring, theoretical vision with informed, practical struggle" (p. 188). As with other feminist research, visionary pragmatism starts with the interests of the participants and seeks to build understandings in reciprocal, dialogic ways.

ANALYTIC PROCEDURES

When we had finished all of the transcriptions of the interviews, we read through each interview multiple times and developed open codes that answered our research questions. Our research questions were as follows: what instructional beliefs and practices, specific to literacy instruction, do exemplary adult education teachers hold? How do adult education teachers understand literacy learning and development? What can the "wisdom of practice" garnered from adult education teachers tell us about teacher preparation and professional development?

We each took one interview and wrote our broad open codes in the margins of the transcript. Each open code was given a broad descriptive title (e.g., "philosophy of education," "literacy teaching," and "description of class") and was supported with an example and page number. We compared our notes and generated a set of initial codes that we then used to analyze an additional two interviews. After our discussion, we generated a list of broad-level categories that we then used with the rest of the interviews.

We recursively moved back and forth between our development of codes and themes and the literature in literacy research. We tried to keep as close as possible to the teachers' descriptions of their literacy practices. Sometimes, a teacher would describe a practice without "naming it" as a particular approach to literacy pedagogy (e.g., language experience stories, or critical literacy). After open codes were generated by both researchers for all participants, we then went through the process of eliminating overlap between the codes.

We then went about category construction, where we collapsed our descriptive codes into themes or categories. We started first with literacy practices. We developed themes that reflected the literacy practices that the teachers reported on. Next, we sorted and categorized by reading and writing. Next, we looked at the purpose of each of the literacy practices. In our next stage of analysis, we grouped the literacy practices by "type" of practice and the different functions embedded under each type of practice or the different ways in which each of the teachers used the particular literacy practice. At each stage in this process, we would either meet in person or talk over the phone to talk through our categories, recontextualizing the categories within the context of the big picture of the teachers—their histories as teachers, the site where they teach, and so on.

What we noticed at this stage of the analysis was that each of the teachers described teaching literacy in the context of culturally relevant, multicultural, antiracist, or feminist frameworks. That is, a strong theme that emerged at this point was that the teachers were not just teaching reading and writing—they were teaching reading and writing for social purposes. In typical ethnographic fashion, we decided to focus our next level of analysis on the ways in which the teachers defined, talked about, and taught using various critical or social justice frameworks. Thus, we repeated the process of developing open codes, constructing categories, and defining categories, moving back and forth from the data to the literature in participatory adult education in an iterative manner.

We used constant comparative method, which developed conceptual links between categories, properties, and hypotheses in the data (Glaser & Strauss, 1967). Comparing the interviews, one against another, led us to tentative categories that we then compared again to each other. Comparisons are made within and between levels of concepts until a theory (in our case, of exemplary practice) can be ascertained from the teachers' practices and theories. During this process, we developed visual heuristics to help us organize the themes we were noticing in the data. For example, we developed a Venn diagram of three broad categories that seemed to reflect the different clusters of teachers in the study—in terms of their purposes of teaching literacy education—as revolutionaries, reformers, or stabilizers. We also developed a set of Venn diagrams to represent the diversity in literacy practices from participatory, to balanced, to functional in approach. These heuristics helped us to see that we needed to be more specific with regard to the similarities and differences in their literacy practices and that the Venn diagram did not account for the movement between categories that occurred for each of the teachers. That is, it was not easy to place the teachers at one point in the diagram because their position often changed based on the context. Thus, the idea of an emergent framework with four fields and two constantly shifting continua (accelerative and critical) arose (see figure 2.1).

In our continued analysis, we brought a feminist framework to bear on our analysis. This analysis was inductive in the sense that we let the teachers' thoughts and descriptions of their practice guide our analysis. However, we also turned to literature in feminism (e.g., Belenky, Clinchy, Goldberger, & Tarule, 1986; Collins, 2000; Maher & Thompson Tetreault, 1994) to help us theorize the teachers' descriptions. This stage of our analysis was pivotal for three reasons. First, it helped to deepen our analysis of all of the teachers—but particularly the teachers who were less "critical" than the others. That is, while some of the teachers were not directly teaching literacy within a social justice framework, they all respected and nurtured students' voices, built community in their classrooms, and attended to women's personal and social empowerment. Second, it was during this stage (after much discussion and feminist analysis) that we aimed for more fluidity in our descriptions of the teachers.

We started to shy away from the hierarchies that the Venn diagrams brought to the surface and sought to describe and illustrate what each teacher was doing that was exemplary, rather than comparing the teachers to one another. Third, the explicit feminist analysis also brought to the surface the way in which our process of conducting the study—from design, to data collection, to analysis and writing—was itself part of adult education and professional development and could be characterized as feminist in process.

CASE STUDIES

Our writing of the case studies was done in an interactive manner with the analysis and, indeed, served as another layer of analysis. We developed two- to three-page case summaries of each of the teachers. We analyzed the data with the guiding research questions both on a case-by-case manner and also across the cases, using constant comparative analysis (Miles & Huberman, 1994).

After we developed cases of each of the teachers, drawing on the interview data, the observational data, and supporting documents, we compared them with another interview. After we had broad groupings, we analyzed the interviews within the groupings for differences and then looked across the groupings for similarities and differences (Merriam, 1998). We also looked across the cases to develop our cross-case analysis that is located at the end of each section of the book. We decided to represent each of the teachers in a case study to foreground the complexity of their practices, their students, and their contexts as much as possible.

MEMBER CHECKING AND DEBRIEFING

We sent each teacher a draft of the book and asked her to read chapter 1, her chapter, and the chapters included in her section. We also sent a copy of Septima Clark's book *Ready from Within* (2001) and a Borders book card to thank them for their participation in the project. Over dinner at the adult learning center, the teachers (some of whom had never met each other) shared their thoughts, reactions, questions, and insights about the book. The purpose of this meeting was twofold: to member-check and debrief with the teachers to see if we captured a trustworthy portrait of who they are as adult education teachers, and also to celebrate and share exemplary adult literacy education practices. Two of the teachers could not attend because they had moved to another location. We also scheduled two-hour follow-up meetings with the three teachers in each section. The follow-up meetings gave the teachers more time to reflect on their practices and to look across the teaching practices presented in their section to notice themes and discontinuities.

We started each of the follow-up meetings with a similar set of questions:

What themes and/or threads do you see across the chapters?
What specific places do you recommend we revise?
Where do you see accelerative literacy instruction and critical literacy in each of the chapters?
Have we represented who you are as a teacher in a trustworthy manner?

During the whole group celebration and reflection, Carolyn, one of the teachers, had suggested that we ask all of the teachers what their own backgrounds with education were because it was important to understand how this influenced their teaching practices. We included this as one of the questions we asked each of the teachers, and revised the chapters accordingly. We also developed questions that were specific to each of the teachers' cases—to expand on or give examples of aspects of their cases. We tape recorded, transcribed, and read the transcripts from each of these meetings—looking for places that confirmed or poked holes in our representation of the teachers. We were (pleasantly) surprised at how authentically we seemed to present each of the teachers. Much of our writing resonated with the teachers, which we discuss in chapter 16.

While all of the teachers have examples of critical literacy embedded in their practice, a few of the teachers had not heard of the term "critical literacy" before. This again points to our premise that teachers are drawing on their tacit theories of what works in the classroom and may not be aware of the literature and research base of effective practices. Janet, for example, stated that "as a teacher I am familiar with critical reading and critical writing, but I have a feeling that this critical literacy has a whole richness and depth that is different from critical reading and writing." This wondering caused a rich discussion about definitions and examples of critical literacy. Carolyn responded that:

Critical literacy means reading beyond the stated and really analyzing what someone is saying. I give them literacy that relates to their everyday life. If we introduce a book that is relevant to them, it is critical to them and they find it relevant ... and then the social consciousness comes when they take what they learn and apply it to change things.

Janet replied that "on this level, then, it is the ability to rip someone's thought processes apart (focus group interview, April 2001)." This discussion illustrates the process of critical literacy itself. Paulo Freire reminds us that "critical educational practice is not a specific methodology to be applied blindly but rather one that emerges when teachers can practice teaching from a critical perspective and have time to reflect on their practice."

The follow-up meetings left us with many good ideas for revision—including a glossary of terms, places to clarify or delete because they were repetitious, and photos for each of the teachers' chapters. The teachers gave us copies of their chapters where they had revised, added, or deleted sections. Several teachers sent us sections to add to their chapter via e-mail. Holiday (chapter 9) has moved to another city and sent us her feedback through the mail. One of her comments for revision was to be "careful not to put all of my methods in the feminist basket; a theory that has been elitist and rooted in white supremacy. My methods also root from Pan Africanism, anti-oppression and womanism." This comment reminded us of her thoughtful and reflective practices as a teacher, moving easily between critical theory and practice.

In addition to debriefing with the teachers, we also shared a copy of the book with the current director of adult education in St. Louis. He provided us with feedback on the book. We also conducted an interview with a former director of adult literacy education, and she provided us with important historical information about adult literacy education in St. Louis that is included in chapter 3.

REFLEXIVITY

Our analysis was an interactive process which made us very much aware of our own positionalities and more readily able to take into account ambiguities and differences in our interpretations. We both have past and present connections in the adult education community and with some of the students who were in classrooms of the teachers included in this study. Further, we had worked on other projects together and cofounded a voluntary professional development group called the Literacy for Social Justice Teacher Research Group (LSJTRG). This group includes educators across the life span, and several of the teachers included in this study were members of

LSJTRG. This interconnectedness—both between the researchers and sometimes between the researchers and the participants—challenges the traditional conceptions of objectivity and distance in the research process. We believe this is a strength of our research—that is, through these interconnected relationships, we are more likely to capture a well-developed portrait of the adult education teachers.

We are also very conscious of the time we have spent poring over the interview transcripts and classroom observations as we have analyzed the data and written this book. Because our positions include time spent for the reflective work of research and writing, we ourselves have benefited from this study in terms of our own professional development. Our participants, by contrast, are constantly engaged in teaching and the material realities of their adult education classrooms on a day-to-day basis, and often do not have the luxury of reflective time to think and write about their practices. We believe this project has been mutually beneficial for the teachers. In a very authentic way, they were nominated as exemplary, and they were given the opportunity to reflect on and describe their practices; furthermore, their insight into their practices is being used to educate other adult education teachers. We gave all of the teachers a copy of their videotaped interview and classroom observations. Several of the teachers responded with comments like "I never realized that what I was doing fit into a bigger picture"; "I didn't see what I was doing as exemplary—I was just meeting my students' needs"; and "The video really helped me to see my purpose for teaching in adult education." As we have noted elsewhere, this type of authentic professional development is important for teachers to share their best practices. We see this at the heart of the dilemma in adult education, and the best we could offer was to give voice to the adult education teachers' practices through the study and the book. Our intention is that this book will help to elicit the voices of other adult educators as they read and come together to discuss the cases represented in this book. We also recognize that the portraits we have crafted of their beliefs and practices with regard to literacy education are snapshots of a moment in time—they do not reflect the entirety of their experiences or their practices.

We see a layered process of knowledge construction in the adult education teachers' classrooms and how we as researchers are constructing knowledge. That is, both are done through relational knowing, by listening, and by foregrounding the voices of the participants (either the teachers for us or the students for the teachers).

Our awareness of differences with regard to ourselves between each other and between our participants has shaped our understandings. At one point, Mary Ann said, "What right do I have to analyze their practices?" This question served to highlight the tension we felt as researchers analyzing and representing the teachers' practices.

We kept reflective journals where we recorded our hunches, intuitions, and the like. We also sent e-mail correspondences to each other testing out hypothesis, wonderings, and intuitions in the data. We were constantly moving back and forth between the literature and the data. At one point in our analysis, we were visualizing the teachers' literacy practices embedded within a social justice framework as a linear continuum with "participatory literacy education" and "radical" frameworks on one side of the continuum and "functional literacy education" and "stabilizer" frameworks on the other side of the continuum. Mary Ann sent me a note asking, "Should we consider the Venn diagram a visual rather than a linear continuum especially if we are discussing teachers in the context of three overlapping groups?" Our constant reflective practice incorporated research in adult literacy education, the teachers' voices, and our own stances as critical educators.

LIMITATIONS

As the project nears a close, we are very aware of all of the adult education teachers who might have been represented as exemplary adult literacy education teachers. The research we have presented in this book is not representative or generalizable to all adult education teachers. Indeed, the teachers have illustrated throughout this book that there is no "one-size-fits-all approach" to literacy education. Rather, we have presented cases as a way for adult education teachers to see and hear other adult education teachers talk about their practices—to provide inspiration and ongoing professional development.

Appendix 2

Nomination Letter

May 23, 2003

Dear Contact Person:

In our efforts to ensure quality improvement in the delivery of our instruction to our AEL students, we are developing resources to facilitate the professional development of our instructors. Toward this end, we are planning to create a compilation of best practices and video demonstrating exemplary teaching among our instructional staff.

As a first step in this endeavor, we are seeking nominations of exemplary teachers from which we will select those to include in our final product. As the contact person at one of our centers, we would appreciate your assistance. If you think the AEL instructor regularly assigned to your site provides exemplary teaching or should be considered for inclusion because of her/his creative classroom practices, please complete and return the enclosed nomination form.

Regarding criteria, we consider exemplary teachers to be those that:

- Actively engage all students at every level
- Demonstrate commitment to students and their goals
- Integrate relevant content into classroom instruction
- Demonstrate use of creative and inclusive instructional strategies
- Engage in professional development
- Facilitate a high rate of student achievement (multilevels and objectives)
- Contribute to the positive development of their students and community

You are welcome to nominate more than one teacher if preferred—simply duplicate the nomination form. **Please return the nomination form no later than June 13** in the enclosed self-addressed envelope included for your convenience.

Please contact me at 367-5000 or MaryAnn.Kramer@slps. org if you have any questions or would like additional information. Thank you for your assistance.

Sincerely,

Mary Ann Kramer
Literacy Coordinator

cc: Bob Weng

Enclosure

ADULT EDUCATION AND LITERACY
ST. LOUIS PUBLIC SCHOOLS

EXEMPLARY TEACHER NOMINATION

Nominated Teacher's Name: _____

Program Info:
- Program Name:_____
- Address: _____
- Phone: _____
- Number of Students (approx.): _____
- Briefly Describe Program (e.g., family literacy, ESOL, etc.):
  _____

Name of Person Submitting Nomination: _____
- Relationship to Teacher or Program: _____

Please check any of the criteria listed below that are the basis for your nomination of the teacher listed above as exemplary:

Nominated Teacher:
_____ Actively engages all students
_____ Demonstrates commitment to students and their goals
_____ Integrates relevant content into classroom instruction
_____ Demonstrates use of creative and inclusive instructional strategies
_____ Engages in professional development
_____ Facilitates a high rate of student achievement (multilevels and objectives)
_____ Contributes to the positive development of their students and community
_____ Other: _____

Please add any additional comments on the back of this form and sign.

Additional Comments: _____
_____
_____

Signature: _____
Date: _____

Appendix 3

Interview Protocol

Everybody thinks differently about teaching and for lots of different reasons. We would like to know more about how you think about your teaching. This interview will take approximately two hours. We are going to audiotape and videotape it.

Name?

School where you teach?

Level?

Why did you become an adult education teacher?

What is your educational and professional background?

How did you learn to teach?

Are there key people, readings, and theories that influence your teaching? In what ways? Be specific.

How long have you been teaching?

Explain to a new adult education teacher the structure of your day, including the amount of time spent on different activities.

Talk about your classroom this year.

PRIMARY GOALS

When your students finish their adult education program, what do you most hope to have accomplished?

(If goals do not particularly include literacy and communication arts, prompt with "What about specifically in literacy and communication arts?")

How can you tell when they have achieved this?

LITERACY INSTRUCTION

How do you teach reading and writing? Give specific examples.

How do you know what to teach?

How did you learn how to teach people to read and write?

What kinds of writing do your students do? How do you decide on topics and genres?

What kinds of reading do your students do? (Ask for specific examples.)

One of the adult education teachers in this project said that she tries to connect the literacy materials to her students' lives. What are your thoughts about this?

How do you choose the books your students read?

When talking about a book in class, do you ever find that some students have a very different understanding of the book than you do? What do you do about that?

How do you keep track of the students' development as readers and writers?

LEARNING

How do the students learn in your classroom? How do you know?

Pick a student in your classroom who is struggling. What obstacles does this student face in learning? What strengths does this student have as a learner?

I've heard some teachers say that they think students learn best when they are told what to do and the teacher directly teaches them. What are your thoughts about that?

ADULT EDUCATION AND SOCIAL JUSTICE

What do you see as the purpose of adult education?

Do you ever find that students try to bring in literacy practices from their daily lives (e.g., letters from social service, or notes from teachers) and it gets in the way of what you have to "get done"?

How do you integrate African American history and the history of other people of color into the curriculum?

What do you do in social studies or science when the students bring up controversial issues, or when there is ambiguity about the correct answer? What are some examples?

Can you think of other examples of activism or social change that you and your students engage with?

Some people believe that adult education teachers are the real revolutionaries and social change agents in our society because they are teaching people not only how to read and write but also how to participate in society in active and critical ways. How do you see yourself doing this? What are some examples?

Have you been involved in any community organizing or social change work in your own life? Please describe.

Some research has shown that ABE/GED students are active, engaged citizens who work for social change in their communities. Students are preachers, start community organizations, write petitions, and so forth. Can you give me some examples of students you have had who sound like this?

How do you manage to accelerate your lowest students?

What are some important directions for adult education?

What can a GED get you in society?

What are your views on parental involvement?

ASSESSMENT

How do you use the TABE results?

What assessments, other than the TABE, do you use?

What additional information would be helpful to inform your instructional practices (other than the TABE)? How would you get that information?

How many of your students have been classified as special education? What are your thoughts on this?

PROFESSIONAL DEVELOPMENT

What do you do well as a teacher?

What are some of the things that get in your way as an effective teacher?

What problems have you encountered in your teaching? Examples? How did you solve it (or them)?

What things do you want to do better as a teacher?

What sorts of professional development opportunities would you like to participate in?

What are the qualities and experiences that have served you best as a teacher?

Have you changed as a teacher over time? In what ways? Are there particular experiences that led to those changes?

How would you describe your teaching philosophy?

With your obviously busy life, do you find much time to read yourself? How would you describe yourself as a reader?

What about time to write? How would you describe yourself as a writer?

Does the way you view yourself as a reader and a writer affect the way you teach your students?

COMMUNITY OF PRACTICE

What would you tell a new adult education teacher is important for a classroom to run smoothly?

How did you decide to organize the desks (or tables) the way you have them? (Alternate question: how is your room organized?)

What would you tell a new teacher to do when a new student comes into the classroom?

One of the adult education teachers in this project commented that she likes her students to talk a lot during the school day. How do you feel about that?

VIDEOTAPING EXEMPLARY PRACTICES

If we were to come into your classroom to videotape your best instructional practices, which part of your day would you want us to videotape?

What would we be viewing?

Is it OK if we set up a time with you to do this?

Appendix 4

Glossary of Terms and People

TERMS AND ACRONYMS

AAL: African American Language

AAVE: African American Vernacular English

ABC's: Acting for a Better Community

ABC's of Literacy: Acting for a Better Community forums and conferences—grassroots organizing around literacy education occurring in St. Louis, Missouri

ABE: Adult Basic Education

AEL: Adult Education and Literacy

BSE: Black Stylized English

BTW: Beginning Teachers' Workshop

CASAS: Comprehensive Adult Student Assessment System

CLL: Critical Literacy Lab

COABE: Commission on Adult Basic Education

DEAR time: Drop Everything and Read time

EEOC: U.S. Equal Employment Opportunity Commission

EOC: Educational Opportunity Center

ERA: Equal Rights Amendment

ESOL: English for Speakers of Other Languages

GED: General Educational Development; can refer to either the GED test or the diploma earned from passing this test

IRI: Informal Reading Inventories

LIFT—Missouri: Literacy Investment for Tomorrow

Literacy Roundtable: a coalition of literacy providers throughout the St. Louis–metro East area that advocates for literacy education at the local, state, and national levels

LSJTRG: Literacy for Social Justice Teacher Research Group

NAAL: The National Assessment of Adult Literacy (NAAL) provides nationally representative and continuing assessment of English language literacy skills of American adults. A sample of adults was assessed in 2003, providing an indication of the nation's progress in adult literacy since 1992

NALS: National Adult Literacy Survey

NCLB: No Child Left Behind Act

NPR: National Public Radio

NRS: National Reporting System; the NRS includes the adult education performance measures baseline standards. There are six standards for adult literacy and secondary education, and six standards for ESOL

Performance measures:

Beginning ABE Literacy (0–1.9): the percentage of adult learners enrolled in beginning literacy who completed that level

Beginning Basic Education (2.0–3.9): the percentage of adult learners enrolled in beginning ABE who completed that level

Low Intermediate Basic Education (4.0–5.9): the percentage of adult learners enrolled in low intermediate basic education who completed that level

High Intermediate Basic Education (6.0–8.9): the percentage of adult learners enrolled in high intermediate basic education who completed that level

Low Adult Secondary Education (9.0–10.9): the percentage of adult learners enrolled in low adult secondary education who completed that level

High Adult Secondary Education (11.0–12.9): the percentage of adult learners enrolled in high adult secondary education who completed that level

Beginning ESL Literacy: The percentage of adult learners enrolled in Beginning ESL who completed that level

Beginning ESL: The percentage of adult learners enrolled in Beginning ESL who completed that level

Low Intermediate ESL: The percentage of adult learners enrolled in Low Intermediate ESL who completed that level

High Intermediate ESL: The percentage of adult learners enrolled in High Intermediate ESL who completed that level

Low Advanced ESL: The percentage of adult learners enrolled in Low Advanced ESL who completed that level

High Advanced ESL: The percentage of adult learners enrolled in High Advanced ESL who completed that level

PACT: Parent and Child Together time

PLATO computer: a computerized instructional system

SALS: State Assessment of Adult Literacy

SFL: Systemic Functional Linguistics

SLPS AEL: St. Louis Public Schools Adult Education and Literacy

TABE: Test of Adult Basic Education

TESOL: Teaching English for Speakers of Other Languages

ZPD: Zone of Proximal Development

FAMOUS ADULT EDUCATORS AND INSTITUTIONS

THEODORE BRAMELD (1904–1987)

Born in Neillsville, Wisconsin, Theodore Brameld is best known for his theory of reconstructionism. After he completed his PhD at the University of Chicago in 1931, he taught at Long Island University. Much of his time was spent at New York University and at Boston University. Brameld believed that education is an agent for social change. He stated that "education is the only power capable of controlling the other powers that man has gained and [man] will use it either for his annihilation or for his transformation." He lamented the illness of America's virtues and argued this was a loss of equilibrium. He believed learning occurs through a cultural context that involves cooperation and democracy. He focused on the scientific method and research as key components for education. Reconstructionism further holds that the findings of behavioral scientists can bring about fundamental changes in the economic and social structures of society.

SEPTIMA POINSETTE CLARK (1898–1987)

Known as the "Queen Mother" of the civil rights movement in the United States, Septima Clark innovatively taught reading and writing to African Americans in order to free them from the oppression of those wanting to deny them full citizenship. After being fired from her teaching job for revealing her name on the list of NAACP members, Septima went to work at the Highlander School in Tennessee. There she worked with Myles Horton alongside other civil rights notables such as Rosa Parks and Martin Luther King Jr. As part of the Southern Christian Leadership Conference, she began Citizenship Schools that worked toward educating African Americans in the South in order to vote and to grow as people. Her methods included using "real-life" materials for teaching adults to read (Brown, 1990). Eventually, Clark's schools trained ten thousand teachers to teach literacy and led to the registration of seventy thousand African American voters in the South.

RUTH COLVIN (1916–)

Ruth Colvin received her BS from Syracuse University in New York. In 1962, she founded Literacy Volunteers after realizing the high prevalence of illiteracy in Syracuse. She began a tutor training program for English as a Second Language that used reading series she created. She helped to found the National Coalition for Literacy to increase public awareness and resources. She has produced many handbooks and videos documenting literacy teaching, which is student centered. In the 1990s she helped Swaziland set up a national literacy campaign. She also worked in Zambia, China, Papua New Guinea, Cambodia, and Madagascar, among other countries. Her focus is on the development of community networks to empower adult learners.

PAULO FREIRE (1921–1997)

Born in Recife, Brazil, Paulo Freire studied law, philosophy, and the psychology of language. Freire held leadership offices both at the University of Recife and in state politics. His first literacy project involved teaching three hundred sugarcane workers to read in forty-five days. The Brazilian government instituted thousands of culture circles across the country after Freire's success with the sugarcane workers. A military coup imprisoned Freire before exiling him to Bolivia. From there he moved to Chile, to Cambridge, to Harvard, to Geneva, and finally back to Brazil. The Paulo Freire Institute was established in São Paulo, Brazil. Freire's philosophy of education reacts against the banking model wherein students' minds are seen as receptacles for facts. As a founder of critical pedagogy, he supports a democratic, anticolonial model of education in which both the word and the world are linked in studies. Freire supports a teacher-student relationship that is equally reciprocal.

HAMPTON UNIVERSITY

The Hampton Institute, now known as Hampton University, is located in Hampton, Virginia. It was founded shortly after the end of the Civil War, when Mary Smith Peake first taught outdoor classes and two years later read the Emancipation Proclamation. Serving mostly Native American and African American students, the university received much of its early financial support from church groups and former officers and soldiers of the Union Army. Booker T. Washington was one of Hampton's early students and teachers.

HIGHLANDER CENTER

The Highlander Center was founded in 1932 as an adult education center for community workers. Up-and-coming as well as established leaders attend workshops and trainings to build the tools and skills necessary for movements for change. The founding principle is that the answers to problems facing society lie within the experiences of ordinary people. In the 1930s and 1940s, Highlander helped build a labor movement in the South among woodcutters, coal miners, government relief workers, textile workers, and farmers. In the 1950s, Highlander worked for civil rights. The Citizenship Schools were a notable achievement stemming from Highlander that helped many Southerners to register to vote. In the 1960s through the 1990s, Highlander moved away from civil rights toward Appalachian struggles and global issues.

BELL HOOKS (1952–)

Born Gloria Jean Watkins, bell hooks grew up in a working-class family. hooks has studied the intersections of race, class, and gender and their effects on oppression and domination through education, art, history, sexuality, mass media, and feminism. hooks experienced education in the empowering environment of an all-black school where she began her studies as well as in an integrated school where she experienced white supremacy. A prolific writer, hooks has written on many topics and has taught on many college campuses. Lately her topics of interest have included how love and communication can break through racism.

AIMEE HORTON (1922–)

Aimee Horton exhibited an early interest in social change which led her to a teacher's college in Milwaukee, Wisconsin. During her matriculation at Rockford College, she went abroad to work with refugees. Here, she found that she saw herself as a student just as much as the refugees were students. After almost completing her PhD, she became the director of the Illinois Commission on Human Relations. This took her to Southern Illinois University, where she helped black students to gain admittance to barbershops and other businesses. She met her future husband, Myles Horton, at an American Education Association Convention. They were married in less than a year, and Aimee and Myles worked together at Highlander Folk School. Aimee mainly oversaw the workshops, fundraised, and wrote reports at Highlander. She returned to Chicago to write her PhD dissertation on the history of Highlander. In 1983, she cofounded the Lindeman Center with Tom Heaney. Her ideas for adult education stem from Paulo Freire and the Citizenship Schools.

MYLES HORTON (1905–1990)

Horton was influenced by his studies in New York with Reinhold Niebuhr at the Union Theological Seminary. Along with Don West, Horton founded the Highlander Folk School (now Highlander Research and Education Center). During the 1930s and 1940s, the Highlander Folk School focused on labor education, whereas in the 1950s and 1960s its focus was on desegregation and the civil rights movement. In the 1970s, the school worked on health and safety in the coalfields of Appalachia, playing a role in the emergence of the region's environmental justice movement.

IVAN ILLICH (1926–2002)

Born in Vienna, Ivan Illich was an Austrian development critic. He critiqued modern cultures on all levels. He studied at the Pontifical Gregorian University in the Vatican. In 1956 he was appointed vice rector of the Catholic University of Puerto Rico. In 1961 he founded the Centro Intercultural de Documentacion at Cuernavaca (CIDC) in Mexico. Ostensibly a research center offering language courses to missionaries from North America, the CIDC was an attempt to counterfoil the Vatican's participation in Third World development. Illich saw Third World development by the First World as industrial hegemony and a war on subsistence. He taught missionaries to identify as tourists and guests. In 1976, after pressure from the Vatican, Illich closed CIDC, though several members continue their own language schools in Cuernavaca. In 1971 he wrote *Deschooling Society*, a critical discourse on education. The formality of education, Illich believed, was not helpful for the student. Rather, students should learn in informal arrangements, self-directed but supported by social relations. He refers to current institutionalized education as a funnel and calls for education to instead be the inverse, a web.

HARRIET A. JACOBS (1813–1897)

Born a slave, Harriet Jacobs was taught to read and write by her master's daughter, even though it was illegal at the time to teach blacks literacy. After sexual advances from her master, Harriet ran away, hiding for seven years in a garret between the ceiling and roof that was only seven feet wide, nine feet in length, and three feet high. Harriet was approached by an older black man looking to learn how to read and write. After informing him of the law forbidding it, Harriet worked with him three times a week. Later in life, after achieving her freedom, Harriet taught in the Freedmen's Schools. These schools were set up after the Civil War as part of the Freedmen's Aid Societies, under the jurisdiction of the U.S. Bureau of Refugees, Freedmen, and Abandoned Lands, and operated until disbanded in 1872.

MALCOLM KNOWLES (1913–1997)

Malcolm Knowles was born in Montana. An avid Boy Scout in his youth, he earned a scholarship to Harvard, where he received his BA in 1934. He then worked at the National Youth Administration in Massachusetts. In 1940 he became the director of adult education at the Boston YMCA. He worked there for three years until he was drafted into the U.S. Navy. In 1946 he became the director of adult education at the YMCA in Chicago. From 1951 to 1959, he served as the executive director of the Adult Education Association. He then worked at Boston University and at North Carolina State University. He invented the term "andragogy" in opposition to pedagogy. His theory of andragogy, education for adults, follows four postulates: (1) adults need to be involved in the planning and evaluation of their instruction, (2) experience provides the basis for learning activities, (3) adults are most interested in learning subjects that have immediate relevance to their life, and (4) adult learning is problem centered rather than content oriented.

EDUARD LINDEMAN (1885–1953)

Eduard Lindeman was orphaned at a young age. He subsequently worked many jobs while intermittently receiving some education. In 1907 he attended Michigan Agricultural College. Upon graduation he worked in various jobs, including a post of chair of the American Civil Liberties Union Commission of Academic Freedom. In 1926 he published his major work, *The Meaning of Adult Education*. As a friend and colleague of John Dewey, Lindeman's ideas were influenced by Dewey's pragmatism, Ralph Waldo Emerson, and Nikolai Grundtvig. His view of adult education placed the learner at the center, around whom the curriculum wrapped, rather than the learner wrapping around a set curriculum. Lindeman believed that adult education was about the life of the learner. Everyday experiences were central. He contrasted adult education with conventional education rather than youth education, suggesting that youths could be educated in the same way he suggested adults should be.

LINDEMAN CENTER

The Lindeman Center in Chicago was cofounded by Aimee Horton and Tom Heaney. The purpose of the center in the 1990s was to give new form to Lindeman's, Horton's, and Freire's education for democratic social change by nurturing grassroots educational initiatives and facilitating access to resources which promote and strengthen local struggles to solve community programs (Lindeman Center, n.d.). The center is a place for resource sharing, gathering, problem solving, and strategy building.

JAMES BERRY MEACHUM (1789–1854)

Born into slavery, John Meachum bought his freedom and that of over twenty other slaves, including his wife. Once free, he attended the First Baptist Church of St. Louis, where Reverend John Mason Peck taught him to read and write. Meachum became the reverend for the First African Baptist Church of St. Louis when it opened in 1825. As a reverend, Meachum used his pulpit and connections to encourage black adults to band together to bring about changes for their children, including education and a good moral upbringing. He established Candle Tallow School, which taught black St. Louisans, free and enslaved, to read and write. In 1847, Missouri passed a law that prohibited teaching blacks to read and write. Meachum moved onto a steamship on the Mississippi River under the name "the Freedom School." Hundreds of black students became literate at the Freedom School. Meachum also offered jobs to many recently freed blacks studying at his school. It is unknown what became of the Freedom School after Meachum's death.

ALEXANDER MEIKLEJOHN (1872–1964)

Alexander Meiklejohn was born in England and moved to Rhode Island at the age of eight. He earned his BA, MA, and PhD by the age of twenty-five. At twenty-nine, he was named the dean of Brown University. After twelve years in that position, he became president of Amherst College for ten years. From there he went to the University of Wisconsin–Madison to set up an experimental college. In 1938 he joined the School of Social Studies in San Francisco, where he involved himself with adult education. In his later years he became involved in national and international groups and earned many medals and awards. He was a strong advocate for First Amendment rights and peace.

JO ANN ROBINSON (1912–)

Born in Georgia, Jo Ann Robinson attended Fort Valley State College and then became a public school teacher in Macon. Five years later, she went to Atlanta for her MA and ended up teaching at Alabama State College in Montgomery. She joined the Women's Political Council in Montgomery. After being verbally attacked by a bus driver, Robinson focused the Women's Political Council on bus abuses. Five years later in 1955, Rosa Parks was arrested for refusing to move to the back of the bus. That night, Robinson mimeographed 35,000 fliers calling for a bus boycott. A few days later the Montgomery Improvement Association was formed to focus on the boycott, and Robinson was a member. Robinson personally provided transportation for blacks who were in need during the boycott. In 1961 she moved to Los Angeles to teach English. She stayed active in local women's organizations.

CORA WILSON STEWART (1875–1958)

Cora Wilson Stewart organized for educational rights for the mountain people of Kentucky. She was elected the first woman president of the Kentucky Education Association. Cora began her illiteracy movement by informing local parents of the need to get involved in the education of their children and of what good education could provide. She began using the public school buildings in the evening to educate adults. Her Moonlight Schools were so named because classes were only held on nights with enough moonlight to provide safety for adults traveling to the schools. By insisting that educated parents would support the county, the schools, and their children, the daytime teachers volunteered to stay some nights to teach the parents and neighbors of their day students. Cora published the first readers for adults, which contained simple sentences about rural life that inspired personal and civic responsibility. She even created the Moonlight School Teachers' Institute, which brought together teachers for discussions on best practices with adult students.

SUSIE BAKER KING TAYLOR (1848–1912)

Born a slave, Susie Baker King Taylor was educated by a free woman to whom her grandmother sent Susie and one of her brothers. Though illegally educated, Susie was enlisted to teach the African Americans in the Union Army during the Civil War; they were not allowed promotion and advancement without literacy. She was engaged by Colonel Thomas W. Higginson of the 33rd U.S. Colored Troops to teach the soldiers in Florida for four years and three months without pay. Susie was one of thousands of teachers who worked to educate the newly freed slaves who enlisted. Both children and adults were instructed. By the war's end, it was estimated some 20,000 African American troops had been taught to read.

BOOKER T. WASHINGTON (1856–1915)

Booker T. Washington worked toward the acculturation of former slaves through the educational process with the Hampton Institute, which later developed into the Tuskegee Institute in Alabama. After attending the Hampton Institute, Booker T. taught adult education classes there. He built up programs in academics, agriculture, industrial arts, health, religion, and music. For example, Farmers' Institutes were created to instruct black farmers on practical agricultural issues. Booker worked with George Washington Carver to create a wagon to travel to the poorest farmers to spread the knowledge to those who couldn't get to Tuskegee. These moveable schools expanded to include home, health, cooking, and horticulture, among other subjects; all teaching was done through demonstrations and hands-on learning. Many national and international programs of adult education grew out of his local initiative.

Appendix 5

Adult Literacy Education Resources

ONLINE INSTRUCTIONAL RESOURCES

California Distance Learning Project:

> http://www.cdlponline.org
>
> This site provides news stories for learners to read. There is also an audio component that accompanies the stories.

Center for Civic Education:

> http://www.civiced.org
>
> This website focuses on the U.S. Constitution and the Bill of Rights. It also explains U.S. institutions at the local, state, and federal levels.

Center for Literacy:

> http://www.centerforliteracy.org
>
> The Center for Literacy has developed a toolkit for serving out-of-school youth with low literacy levels. The toolkit includes standards, lesson plans, literature review, and professional development.

Conversation Café:

> http://www.conversationcafe.org
>
> Conversation cafés are hosted, drop-in conversations in public places about feelings, thoughts, and actions about current issues. The aim is to promote community and democracy through ongoing dialogue.

DiscoverySchool.com, "Puzzlemaker":

> http://www.puzzlemaker.school.discovery.com

> The puzzle maker site allows you to create and personalize your own puzzle based on the vocabulary words the learners are working on.

EdHelper:

> http://www.edhelper.com

Equipped for the Future—the standards-based reform initiative:

> http://www.nifl.gov/lines/collections/eff

Illinois Community College Board, "Preparing Technology-Proficient Educators in Illinois":

> http://www.iccb.state.il.us/PT3

Lincs:

> http://www.nifl.gov/lincs

> http://www.nifl.gov/lincs/collections

> Lincs is the online connection to adult literacy information.

Literacy Assistance Center—Resources:

> http://www.lacnyc.org/resources/adult/

> The website is part of the Literacy Assistance Center. This page includes professional development resources of adult education teachers and tutors, including frequently asked questions about the Test of Adult Basic Education (TABE), a definition of the NRS descriptors, learning disabilities organizations, and so on.

Literacy.org:

> http://www.literacyonline.org

> This site contains general information on literacy as well as information on international literacy rates and literacy campaigns.

Literacy Site:

> http://www.literacyconnections.com

> This website includes tutoring techniques and ESL literacy and adult literacy materials.

Migrant.org:

> http://www.migrant.org/esl

> This is a site that provides techniques for working with ESL students.

National Coalition for Dialogue and Deliberation:

http://www.thatway.org

NCDD is a coalition of organizations and individuals who are committed to strengthening a dialogic and deliberative community. The website serves as a hub for practitioners, activists, and scholars.

National Issues Forum:

http://www.nifi.org

National Issues Forum brings people together to talk about important issues in forums that range from small study circles to large community gatherings. Many resources are available on this website.

Public Conversations Project:

http://www.publicconversations.org

The Public Conversations Project (PCP) helps people with disagreements over divisive issues develop mutual understanding for ongoing action. The website has stories and articles about people who have participated in the dialogues as well as a free toolbox and dialogue guides packed with exercises.

Study Circles Resource Center:

http://www.studycircles.org

The Study Circles Resource Center helps communities develop their own ability to problem solve by bringing people together across boundaries to dialogue about important issues. Guides for facilitating study circles are available on the website.

TEACHER NETWORKS

Teachers for Social Justice—Chicago
www.teachersforjustice.org

Teachers for Social Justice (T4SJ)—San Francisco
www.t4sj.org

New York Collective of Radical Educators (NYCoRE)
www.nycore.org

Literacy for Social Justice Teacher Research Group:
www.umsl.edu/~/sjtrg/

Teachers for Social Justice:

http://www.teachersforjustice.org/database.html

The webpage is part of the Teachers for Social Justice main page and provides a curriculum database with resources.

RESOURCES BY GEOGRAPHIC AREA
AUSTRALIA

Adult Literacy and Numeracy Research Consortium (ALNARC):

http://www.staff.vu.edu.au/alnarc

National Center for English Language Teaching & Research (NCELTR):

http://www.nceltr.mq.edu.au/amep/index.html

CANADA

Adult Literacy Research in Ontario:

http://www.research.alphaplus.ca

Directory of Canadian Adult Literacy Research in English:

http://www.nald.ca/crd

Festival of Literacies, Ontario:

http://www.literaciesoise.ca

National Adult Literacy Database:

http://www.nald.ca

Research-in-Practice in Adult Literacy:

http://www.nald.ca/ripal

ENGLAND

Lancaster Literacy Research Centre:

http://www.literacy.lancaster.ac.uk/what/teachers.htm

Research & Practice in Adult Literacy:

http://www.literacy.lancs.ac.uk/rapal

UNITED STATES

Kentucky Practitioner Inquiry Projects:

http://www.workforce.ky.gov

National Center for the Study of Adult Learning and Literacy:

http://gseweb.harvard.edu/~ncsall/index.html

Pennsylvania Action Research Network (PAARN):

http://www.learningfrompractice/org/paarn/default.htm

Pennsylvania Adult Literacy Practitioner Inquiry Network (PALPIN):

http://www.learningfrompractice/org/palpin/default.htm

Project Idea, Texas:

http://slincs.coe.utk.edu/research.htm

Virginia Adult Education Research Network (VAERN):

http://www.aelweb.vcu.edu/resguide/resguide1

Women Expanding / Literacy Education Action Resource Network:

http://www.litwomen.org/welearn.html

CENTERS AND PROFESSIONAL ORGANIZATIONS

Association of Adult Literacy Professional Developers:

http://www.aalpd.org

Center for Literacy:

http://www.centerforliteracy.org

Center for Literacy Studies:

http://www.cls.utk.edu

Committee on Adult Basic Education:

http://www.coabe.org

International Reading Association:

http://www.reading.org

Literacy Assistance Center:

http://www.lacnyc.org

Literacy USA:

http://www.naulc.org

National Center for the Study of Adult Learning and Literacy (NCSALL):

http://www.ncsall.gse.harvard.edu

National Institute for Literacy:

http://www.nifl.gov

National Institute of Adult Continuing Education—England and Wales (NIACE):

http://www.niace.org.uk/Default.htm

ProLiteracy Worldwide:

http://www.literacyvolunteers.org

Rethinking Schools

www.rethinkingschools.org

United Nations Educational, Scientific and Cultural Organization (UNESCO):

http://portal.unesco.org/education/

Voices of Adult Literacy United for Education:

http://www.valueusa.org

World Education:

http://www.worlded.org/WEIInternet/

ADULT EDUCATION LISTSERVS / BLOGS

Daphne Greenberg, list moderator, Women and Literacy listserv,

http://www.nifl.gov/mailman/listinfo/nifl-pl

Mev Miller, director, We Learn, welearn@litwomen.org,

http://www.litwomen.org/welearn.html

Andy Nash, Change Agent, New England Literacy Resource Center, World Education,

http://www.nelrc.org/changeagent

David J. Rosen, adult literacy advocate, DJRosen@theworld.com

Gail Spangenberg, president, Council for Advancement of Adult Literacy, gspangenberg@caalusa.org

Jackie Taylor, list moderator, NIFL—AALPD, jataylor@utk.edu

Archie Willard,

http://www.readiowa.org/archiew.html

ABCs of Literacy Blog

www.abcsofliteracy.blogspot.com

Deborah W. Yoho, co-moderator, NIFL—Health Listserv, dwyoho@earthlink.net

AUDIO-VIDEO RESOURCES

Democracy Now:

http://www.democracynow.org

Digital History:

http://www.digitalhistory.uh.edu

Songs with a global conscience:

> http://www.rethinkingschools.org/publication/rg/
> RGResource01.shtml

Videos with a global conscience:

> http://www.rethinkingschools.org/publication/rg/
> RGResource02.shtml

NEWSLETTERS AND NEWSPAPERS

Change Agent:

> http://www.nelrc.org/changeagent/

CNN news site:

> http://literacynet.org/cnnsf/

Concern America Social Justice News:

> http://www.concernamerica.org/SocJusticeNews.html

Global Issues in Language Education Newsletter:

> http://www.jalt.org/global/index.html

The Key: A Newspaper for New Readers:

> http://www.keynews.org
>
> This website is a newspaper for low-level readers, ESL students, and students with learning disabilities

PBS news site:

> http://www.pbs.org/literacy/

PROFESSIONAL JOURNALS

Adult Education Quarterly:

> http://aeq.sagepub.com

Focus on Basics:

> http://www.ncsall.net/?id=31

Journal of Adolescent and Adult Literacy:

> http://www.reading.org/publications/journals/jaal/index.
> html

Literacy Harvest:

> http://www.lacnyc.org/resources/publications/harvest/
> harvest.htm

ADULT EDUCATION PUBLISHING COMPANIES

Alta ESL
14 Adrian Court
Burlingame, CA 94010
800-258-2375, fax 800-258-2329

Arte Publico Press
University of Houston
4800 Calhoun
Houston, TX 77204
800-633-2783, fax 713-743-2847

City Lore Culture Catalog
72 East First Avenue
New York, NY 10003
800-333.5982, fax 212-529-5062

Contemporary Books Order Services
P.O. Box 545
Blacklick, OH 43004-0545
800-621-1918, fax 800-998-3103

Creative Publications
19201 120th Avenue NW
Bothell, WA 98011
800-624-0822, fax 800-624-0821

Delta Systems
1400 Miller Parkway
McHenry, IL 60050-7030
800-323-8270, fax 800-909-9901

EAI/Eric Armin Inc.
567 Commerce Street
P.O. Box 664
Franklin Lakes, NJ 07417
800-770-8010, fax 201-891-5689

Educators for Social Responsibility
23 Garden Street
Cambridge, MA 02138
800-370-2515, fax 617-864-5164

Educators Publishing Service
31 Smith Place
Cambridge, MA 02138
800-225-5750, fax 617-547-0412

The Feminist Press
CUNY Graduate Center
365 Fifth Avenue
New York, NY 10016
212-817-7920, fax 212-987-4008

Globe Fearon (Pearson Learning)
135 S. Mount Zion Rd.
P.O. Box 2500
Lebanon, IN 46052
800-526-9907, fax 800-393-3156

Grass Roots Press
P.O. Box 52192
Edmonton, AB Canada T6G2T5
888-303-3213, fax 780-413-6582

Great Source
Harvard Education Publishing Group
8 Story Street
Cambridge, MA 02138
800-513-0763, fax 617-496-3584

Heinemann
88 Post Road West
P.O. Box 5007
Westport, CT 06881
800-793-2154, fax 800-847-0938

Heinle & Heinle
25 Thomson Place
Boston, MA 02210
800-354-9706, fax 800-487-8488

Interact
P.O. Box 900
Fort Atkinson, WI 53538
800-359-0961, fax 800-700-5093

Intercultural Press
P.O. Box 700
Yarmouth, ME 04096
800-370-2665, fax 207-846-5181

Jossey-Bass
989 Market Street
San Francisco, CA 94103
800-956-7739, fax 800-605-2665

Key Curriculum Press
1150 65th Street
Emeryville, CA 94608
800-995-6284, fax 800-541-2442

Longman
200 Old Tappan Road
Old Tappan, NJ 07675
877-202-4572, fax 800-445-6991

MindSparks
P.O. Box 800
Fort Atkinson, WI 53538
800-558-2110, fax 800-835-2329

National Council of Teachers of Mathematics
1906 Association Drive
Reston, VA 20191
800-235-7566, fax 800-220-8483

The New Press
450 West 41st Street
New York, NY 10036
800-233-4830, fax 212-629-8617

New Readers Press
P.O. Box 888
Syracuse, NY 13210
800-448-8878, fax 315-422-5561

The Peoples Publishing Group
P.O. Box 513
Saddle Brook, NJ 07663
800-822-1080, fax 201-712-0045

Peppercorn Books & Press
P.O. Box 693
Snow Camp, NC 27349
877-574-1634, fax 336-376-9099

Rand McNally Educational Publishing
8255 North Central Park
Skokie, IL 60076-2970
800-678-7263, fax 800-934-3479

Resource Center of the Americas
3019 Minnehaha Avenue
South Minneapolis, MN 55406
800-452-8382, fax 612-276-0898

Rethinking Schools
1001 E. Keefe Ave.
Milwaukee, WI 53212
Fax: 414-964-7220

Scholastic, Inc.
P.O. Box 7502
Jefferson City, MO 65102
800-724-6527, fax 800-223-4011

Steck-Vaughn
P.O. Box 690789
Orlando, FL 32819
800-531-5015, fax 800-699-9459

Teachers & Writers Collaborative
5 Union Square West
New York, NY 10003
888-266-5789, fax 212-675-0171

Teachers College Press
525 West 120th Street, Box 303
New York, NY 10027
800-575-6566, fax 802-864-7626

Teaching for Change
P.O. Box 73038
Washington, D.C. 20056
800-763-9131, fax 202-238-0109

Teaching Tolerance
400 Washington Avenue
Montgomery, AL 36104
334-956-8200, fax 334-956-8488

References

Alamprese, J. (2001). Teaching reading to first level adults. *Focus on Basics*, 5(A), 1–7.

Allington, R. (1977). If they don't read much, how they ever gonna get good? *Journal of Adolescent and Adult Literacy*, 21, 57–61.

Allington, R. (2002). *Big Brother and the National Reading Panel: How ideology trumped evidence*. Portsmouth, NH: Heinemann.

Allington, R. (2004). Setting the record straight. *Educational Leadership*, 61(6), 22–25.

Allington, R. (2007). Intervention all day long: New hope for struggling readers. *Voices from the Middle*, 14(4), 7–14.

Allington, R. & Johnston, P. (2001). *Reading to learn: Lessons from exemplary 4th grade classrooms*. NY: Guilford Press.

Amos, W. (1994). *Man with no name*. Fairfield, CT: Aslan.

Angelou, M. (1983). *I know why the caged bird sings*. New York: Bantam.

Auerbach, A. (1989). Toward a socio-contextual approach to family literacy. *Harvard Educational Review*, 59, 165–181.

Auerbach, E. (1992b). *Making meaning making change: Participatory curriculum development for adult ESL literacy*. McHenry, IL: Center for Applied Linguistics and Delta Systems.

Auerbach, E. (1996). *Adult ESL/Literacy for the community to the community: A guidebook for participatory literacy training*. Mahwah, NJ: Lawrence Erlbaum Associates.

Auerbach, E. (2001). "Yes, but …": Problematizing participatory ESL pedagogy. In P. Campbell & B. Burnaby (Eds.), *Participatory practices in adult education* (pp. 267–306). Mahwah, NJ: Lawrence Erlbaum Associates.

Ayres-Salamon, M. (2006). *A recipe for failure: A year of reform and chaos in the St. Louis Public Schools*. Victoria, BC: Trafford.

Bailey, K. (2006). Issues in teaching speaking skills to adult ESOL learners. *Review of Adult Learning and Literacy*, 6(5), 113–164.

Baker, J. (2002). Trilingualism. In L. Delpit & J. K. Dowdy (Eds.), *The skin that we speak: Thoughts on language and culture in the classroom* (pp. 51–61). New York: New Press.

Baptiste, I. (2001). Educating lone wolves: Pedagogical implications of human capital theory. *Adult Education Quarterly*, 51(3), 184–201.

Barndt, D. (2001). Naming, making, and connecting—reclaiming lost arts: The pedagogical possibilities of photo-story production. In P. Campbell & B. Burnaby (Eds.), *Participatory practices in adult education* (pp. 31–54). Mahwah, NJ: Lawrence Erlbaum Associates.

Barton, D., & Hamilton, M. (1998). *Local literacies: Reading and writing in one community*. London: Routledge.

Barton, D.E. & Tusting, K. (2005). Eds., *Beyond communities of practice: Language, power and social context*. Cambridge: Cambridge University Press.

Baugh, J. (2000). *Beyond Ebonics: Linguistic pride and racial prejudice in the US*. Oxford: Oxford University Press.

Baym, N. (1990). The feminist teacher of literature: Feminist or teacher? In S. Gabriel & I. Smithson (Eds.), *Gender in the classroom: Power and pedagogy* (pp. 60–77). Urbana: University of Illinois Press.

Beggs, J. (1995). The institutional environment: Implications for race and gender inequality in the U.S. market. *American Sociological Review, 60,* 65–68.

Belenky, M., Clinchy, B. M., Goldberger, N., & Tarule, J. (1986). *Women's ways of knowing: The development of self, voice, and mind*. New York: Basic Books.

Bickel, R., & Papagiannis, G. (1988). Post-high school prospects and district level drop-out rates. *Youth and Society, 20*(2), 123–147.

Boal, A. (1985). *Theatre of the oppressed* (C. A. McBridge & M-O. L. McBridge, Trans.). New York: Theatre Community Group.

Boal, A. (2002). *Games for actors and non-actors* (2nd ed.). New York: Routledge.

Boesel, D. (1998). The street value of the GED diploma. *Phi Delta Kappan, 80*(1), 65–68.

Bomer, R., & Bomer, K. (2003). *For a better world: Reading and writing for social action*. Portsmouth, NH: Heinemann.

Bowers, C., & Flinders, D. (1990). *Responsive teaching: An ecological approach to classroom patterns of language, culture and thought*. New York: Teachers College Press.

Boyle-Baise, M. (2005). Preparing community-oriented teachers: Reflections from a multicultural service-learning project. *Journal of Teacher Education, 56*(5), 446–458.

Brice Heath, S. (1983). *Ways with words: Language, life, and work in communities and classrooms*. New York: McGraw-Hill.

Brookfield, S. (2005). *The power of critical theory: Liberating adult learning and teaching*. San Francisco: Jossey-Bass.

Cambourne, B. (1995). Toward an educationally relevant theory of literacy learning: Twenty years of inquiry. *Reading Teacher, 49*(3), 182–190.

Campbell, P. (2001). Participatory literacy practices: Exploring pedagogy. In P. Campbell & B. Burnaby (Eds.), *Participatory practices in adult education* (pp. 55–75). Mahwah, NJ: Lawrence Erlbaum Associates.

Campbell, P., & Burnaby, B. (Eds.). (2001). *Participatory practices in adult education*. Mahwah, NJ: Lawrence Erlbaum Associates.

Cantor, J. (2001). *Delivering instruction to adult learners* (Rev. ed.). Toronto: Wall & Emerson.

Carmack, N. (1992). Women and illiteracy: The need for gender specific programming in literacy education. *Adult Basic Education, 2,* 176–194.

Cervero, R., & Wilson, A. (1999). Beyond learner-centered practice: Adult education, power, and society. *Canadian Journal for the Study of Adult Education, 13*(2), 27–38.

Christie, F. (2003). *Classroom discourse analysis: A functional perspective.* London: Continuum.

Clark, R., & Ivanic, R. (1997). *The politics of writing.* New York: Routledge.

Clark, S., & Brown, C. S. (1990). *Ready from within: A first person narrative.* Trenton, NJ: Africa World Press.

Clay, M. (1990). *Becoming literate: The development of inner control.* Portsmouth, NH: Heinemann.

Clay, M. (1991). Introducing a new storybook to young readers. *Reading Teacher, 54*(4), 264–273.

Clay, M. (1993). *An observation survey of early literacy achievement.* Portsmouth, NH: Heinemann.

Coles, G. (2000). *Misreading reading: The bad science that hurts children.* Portsmouth, NH: Heinemann.

Collins, P. (1998). *Fighting words: Black women and the search for justice.* Minneapolis: University of Minnesota Press.

Collins, P. (2000). *Black feminist thought: Knowledge, consciousness, and the politics of empowerment* (2nd ed.). New York: Routledge.

Collins, J. & Blot, R. (2003). *Literacy and literacies: Texts, power and identity.* Cambridge, MA: Cambridge University Press.

Columbus, G. (2004). Exploring the African American oral tradition: Instructional implications for literacy learning. *Language Arts, 81*(6), 481–490.

Comber, B., & Simpson, A. (Eds.). (2001). *Negotiating critical literacies in classrooms.* Mahwah, NJ: Lawrence Erlbaum Associates.

Cope, B., & Kalantzis, M. (2000a). Designs for social futures. In B. Cope & M. Kalantzis (Eds.), *Multiliteracies: Literacy learning and the design of social futures* (pp. 203–234). New York: Routledge.

Cope, B., & Kalantzis, M. (2000b). (Eds.). *Multiliteracies: Literacy learning and the design of social futures.* New York: Routledge.

Cowan, M. (2006). Beyond single interests: Broad-based organizing as a vehicle for promoting adult literacy. In J. Comings, B. Garner, & C. Smith (Eds.), *Review of adult learning and literacy: Connecting research, policy and practice* (Vol. 6, pp. 241–264). Mahwah, NJ: Lawrence Erlbaum Associates.

Critzer, J. (1998). Racial and gender income inequality in the American states. *Race & Society, 1*(2), 159–176.

Darling-Hammond, L. (2000). Teacher quality and student achievement: A review of state policy evidence. Retrieved December 1, 2006, from http://depts.washington.edu/ctpmail/Reports.html#TeacherQuality.

Dauksza-Cook, W. (1977). *Adult literacy education in the United States.* Newark, DE: International Reading Association.

Deelen, G. (1980). The church on its way to the people: Basic Christian communities in Brazil. *CrossCurrents, 30,* 385–408.

Degener, S. (2001). Making sense of critical pedagogy in adult literacy education. In J. Comings, B. Garner, & C. Smith (Eds.), *Annual review of adult learning and literacy* (pp. 26–62). San Francisco: Jossey-Bass.

Delany, S. L., Delany, A. E., & Hearth, A. H. (1994). *Having our say: The Delaney sisters' first 100 years.* New York: Dell.

Delpit, L. (1995). *Other people's children: Cultural conflict in the classroom.* New York: New Press.

Demetrion, G. (2005). *Conflicting paradigms in adult literacy education: In quest of a US democratic politics of literacy.* Mahwah, NJ: Lawrence Erlbaum Associates.

Denton, V. (1993). *Booker T. Washington and the adult education movement.* Gainesville: University of Florida Press.

Dozier, C., Johnston, P., & Rogers, R. (2005). *Critical literacy/critical teaching: Tools for preparing responsive teachers.* New York: Teachers College Press.

Dozier, C., & Rutten, I. (2006). Responsive teaching toward responsive teachers: Mediating transfer through intentionality, enactment, and articulation. *Journal of Literacy Research, 37*(4), 459–492.

Edwards, P. (1996). Creating sharing time conversations: Parents and teachers work together. *Language Arts, 73*(5), 344–349.

Edwards, P. (1999). *A path to follow: Learning to listen to parents.* Portsmouth, NH: Heinemann.

Elbow, P. (1981). *Writing with power: Techniques for mastering the writing process.* New York: Oxford University Press.

Eldredge, J., Reutzel, D., & Hollingsworth, P. (1996). Comparing the effectiveness of two oral reading practices: Round-robin reading and the shared book experience. *Journal of Literacy Research, 28*(2), 201–225.

Ellner, S., & Hellinger, D. (Eds.). (2003). *Venezuelan politics in the Chavez era: Class, polarization and conflict.* London: Lynne Rienner.

Ellsworth, E. (1989). Why doesn't this feel empowering? Working through the myths of critical pedagogy. *Harvard Educational Review, 59*(3), 297–324.

Fairclough, N. (2003). *Analysing discourse: Textual analysis for social research.* New York: Routledge.

Fine, M. (1991). *Framing dropouts: Notes on the politics of an urban high school.* Albany: State University of New York Press.

Fingeret, A., & Drennon, C. (1997). *Literacy for life: Adult learners, new practices.* New York: Teachers College Press.

Fitzgerald, N. (1995). *ESL instruction in adult education: Findings from a national evaluation.* (ERIC Document Reproduction Services No. ED385171). Washington, DC: ERIC Clearinghouse for ESL Literacy Education.

Fleischer, C. (2000). *Teachers organizing for change: Making literacy everybody's business.* Urbana, IL: National Council of Teachers of English.

Folse, K. (1996). *Discussion starters: Speaking fluency activities for advanced ESL/EFL students.* Ann Arbor: University of Michigan Press.

Foster, M. (1997). *Black teachers on teaching.* New York: New Press.

Fountas, I., & Pinnell, G. (2001). *Guiding readers and writers (grades 3–6): Teaching comprehension, genre, and content literacy.* Portsmouth, NH: Heinemann.

Freire, P. (1973). *Education for critical consciousness.* New York: Seabury.

Freire, P. (1985). *The politics of education: Culture, power and liberation.* Westport, CT: Bergin & Garvey.

Freire, P. (1992). *Pedagogy of hope.* New York: Continuum.

Freire, P. (1993). *Pedagogy of the oppressed.* New York: Continuum.

Freire, P., & Macedo, D. (1987). *Literacy: Reading the word and the world.* Westport, CT: Bergin & Garvey.

Galbraith, M., & Gilley, J. (1985). An examination of professional certification. *Lifelong Learning: An Omnibus of Practice and Research, 9*(2), 12–15.

Gee, J. (1996). *Social linguistics and literacies: Ideology in discourses.* London: Falmer.

Gee, J. (1999/2005). *An introduction to discourse analysis: Theory and method.* New York: Routledge.

Gilyard, K. (1991). *Voices of the self: A study of language competence.* Detroit, MI: Wayne State University Press.

Giroux, H. (1987). Introduction: Literacy and the pedagogy of political empowerment. In P. Freure & D. Macedo. *Literacy: Reading the word and the world*, Westport, CT: Bergin & Garvey. pp. 1–27.

Giroux, H. (1988). Literacy and the pedagogy of voice and political empowerment. *Educational Theory, 38*(1), 61–75.

Glaser, B., & Strauss, A. (1967). *The discovery of grounded theory: Strategies for qualitative research.* Chicago: Aldine.

Goldstein, T. (1997). *Two languages at work: Bilingual life on the production floor.* New York: Mouton de Gruyter.

Gonzalez, N., Moll, L., & Amanti, C. (Eds.). (2005). *Funds of knowledge: Theorizing practices in households, communities, and classrooms.* Mahwah, NJ: Lawrence Erlbaum Associates.

Gore, J. (1993). *The struggle for pedagogies: Critical and feminist discourses as regimes of truth.* New York: Routledge.

Gott, R. (2005). *Hugo Chavez: The Bolivarian revolution in Venezuela.* New York: Verso.

Gottesman, R., Bennett, R., Nathan, R., & Kelly, M. (1996). Inner-city adults with severe reading difficulties: A closer look. *Journal of Reading Disabilities, 29*(6), 589–597.

Gramsci, A. (1971). *Selections from* The Prison Notebook (Q. Hoare and G. N. Smith, Eds.). London: Lawrence and Wishart.

Greenberg, D. (2004). Women and literacy. *Change Agent, 19,* 1, 3.

Greenberg, D., Ehri, L., & Perin, D. (1997). Are word reading processes the same or different in adult literacy students and third-fifth graders matched for reading level? *Journal of Educational Psychology, 89*(2), 262–275.

Greenwood Gowen, S. (1992). *The politics of workplace literacy.* New York: Teachers College Press.

Guerra, J. (1998). *Close to home: Oral and literal practices in a transnational community.* NY: Teachers College Press.

Guthrie, J., & Wigfield, A. (1998). Engaged reading: Processes of motivated strategic, knowledgeable, social readers. In J. T. Guthrie & D. E. Alvermann (Eds.), *Engaged reading: Processes, practice, and policy implications* (pp. 17–45). New York: Teachers College Press.

Guthrie, J., Wigfield, A., Metsala, J., & Cox, K. (1999). Motivational and cognitive predictors of text comprehension and reading amount. *Scientific Studies of Reading, 3*(3), 231–256.

Guy, T. C. (1999). Culture as context for adult education: The need for culturally relevant adult education. In T. C. Guy (Ed.), *Providing relevant adult education: A challenge for the twenty-first century* (pp. 5–18). San Francisco: Jossey-Bass.

Hafernik, J., Messerschmitt, D., & Vandrick, S. (2002). *Ethical issues for ESL faculty: Social justice in practice.* Mahwah, NJ: Lawrence Erlbaum Associates.

Halliday, M. (1978). *Language as social semiotic: The social interpretation of language and meaning.* London: Edward Arnold.

Hammond, J., & Macken-Horarik, M. (1999). Critical literacy: Challenges and questions for ESL Classrooms. *TESOL Quarterly, 33*(3), 528–543.

Hanisch, C. (1969, March). The personal is political. *Feminist Revolution,* 204–205.

Hawisher, G., & Selfe, C. (2000). *Global literacies and the World-Wide Web.* London: Routledge.

Heaney, G., & Uchitelle, S. (2004). *Unending struggle: The long road to an equal education in St. Louis.* St. Louis, MO: Reedy.

Heaney, T. (1992). When adult education stood for democracy. *Adult Education Quarterly, 43*(1), 51–59.

Heffernan, L., & Lewison, M. (2003). Social narrative writing: (Re) constructing kid culture in the writer's workshop. *Language Arts, 80*(6), 435–443.

Henning, P. (1998). Ways of learning: An ethnographic study of the work and situated learning of a group of refrigeration service technicians. *Journal of Contemporary Ethnography, 27*(1), 85–136.

Hickey, D. (1997). Motivation and contemporary socio-constructivist instructional perspectives. *Educational Psychologist, 32*(3), 175–193.

Hidi, S., & Harackiewicz, J. (2000). Motivating the academically unmotivated: A critical issue for the 21st century. *Review of Educational Research, 70*(2), 151–179.

Hirshon, S., & Butler, J. (1983). *And also teach them to read: The National Literacy Crusade of Nicaragua.* Westport, CT: Lawrence Hill.

hooks, bell. (1994). *Teaching to transgress: Education as the practice of freedom.* New York: Routledge.

hooks, bell. (2000). *Where we stand: Class matters.* New York: Routledge.

hooks, bell. (2003). *Rock my soul: Black people and self-esteem.* New York: Washington Square.

Horsman, J. (2000). *Too scared to learn: Women, violence and education.* Mahwah, NJ: Lawrence Erlbaum Associates.

Horton, A. (1989). *The Highlander Folk School: A history of its major programs, 1932–1961.* New York: Carlson.

Hull, G. (1993). Critical literacy and beyond: Lessons learned from students and workers in a vocational program and on the job. *Anthropology & Education Quarterly, 24*(4), 373–396.

Hull, G. (Ed). (1997). *Changing work, changing workers: Critical perspectives on language, literacy and skills.* Albany: State University of New York Press.

Illich, I. (1971). *Deschooling society.* New York: Harper & Row. Retrieved April 24, 2007, from http://www.preservenet.com/theory/Illich/Deschooling/intro.html.

Janks, H. (2002). Critical literacy: Beyond reason. *Australian Educational Researcher, 29*(1), 7–26.

Johnson, D. (1998). Adult educators do need to have enthusiasm. *Adult Learning, 9*(4), 11–14.

Johnston, P. (1997). *Knowing literacy: Constructive literacy assessment.* York, ME: Stenhouse.

Johnston, P. (2002). Commentary on "the interactive strategies approach to reading intervention." *Contemporary Educational Psychology, 27,* 636–647.

Johnston, P. (2004). *Choice words: How our language affects children's learning.* York, ME: Stenhouse.

Jones, K. (2000). Becoming just another alphanumeric code: Farmers' encounters with the literacy and discourse practices of agricultural bureaucracy at the livestock auction. In D. Barton, M. Hamilton, & R. Ivanic (Eds.), *Situated literacies: Reading and writing in context* (pp. 70–90). London: Routledge.

Kazemek, F. E., & Rigg, P. (1986). Four poets: Modern poetry in the adult literacy classroom. *Journal of Reading, 30*(3), 218–225.

Kist, W. (2005). *New literacies in action: Teaching and learning in multiple media.* New York: Teachers College Press.

Knowles, M., Holton, E., & Swanson, R. (1998). *The adult learner: The definitive classic in adult education and human resource development.* Woburn, MA: Butterworth-Heinemann.

Knowles, M. S. (1989). *The making of an adult educator: An autobiographical journey.* San Francisco: Jossey-Bass.

Kramer, M. & Jones, R. (in progress). Designing a cortical literacy lab in an adult education center. In R. Rogers (Ed.). *Designing socially just learning communities: A lifespan perspective.*

Kremer, G. (1991). *James Milton Turner and the promise of America: The public life of a post–Civil War black leader.* Columbia: University of Missouri Press.

Kress, G. (2003). *Literacy in the new media age.* London: Routledge.

Kruidenier, J. (2002a). Literacy assessment in adult basic education. In J. Comings, B. Garner, & C. Smith (Eds.), *Annual review of adult learning and literacy* (Vol. 3, pp. 84–151). San Francisco: Jossey-Bass.

Kruidenier, J. (2002b). Research-based principles for adult basic education reading instruction. Washington, DC: National Institute for Literacy.

Ladson-Billings, G. (1994). *The dreamkeepers: Successful teachers of African American children.* San Francisco: Jossey-Bass.

Ladson-Billings, G. (1995). Toward a critical race theory of education. *Teachers College Record, 97,* 47–68.

Ladson-Billings, G. (2001). *Crossing over to Canaan: The journey of new teachers in diverse classrooms.* San Francisco: Jossey-Bass.

Lankshear, C., & Knobel, M. (2003). *New literacies: Changing knowledge and classroom learning.* New York: Open University Press.

Lave, J., & Wenger, E. (1991). *Situated learning: Legitimate peripheral partici-pation.* Cambridge: Cambridge University Press.

Lee, A. (2001). *Composing critical pedagogies: Teaching writing as revision.* Urbana, IL: National Council of Teachers of English.

Lensmire, T. (2000). *Powerful writing, responsible teaching.* New York: Teachers College Press.

Lewis, C. (2001). Limits of identification: The personal, pleasurable, and criti-cal in reader response. *Journal of Literacy Research, 32*(2), 253–266.

Li, G. (2006). *Culturally contested pedagogy: Battles of literacy and school-ing between mainstream teachers and Asian immigrant parents.* Albany: State University of New York Press.

Lin, Angel M. Y. (1999). Doing-English-lessons in the reproduction or trans-formation of social worlds? *TESOL Quarterly, 33*(3), 393–412.

Lindeman, E. C. (1926). *The meaning of adult education.* New York: New Republic.

Lindeman Center. (N.d.). Lindeman Center introductory brochure. Chicago, IL.

Lorde, A. (1984). The master's tools will never dismantle the master's house. In A. Lorde, *Sister outsider: Essays & speeches.* Trumansburg, NY: Cross-ing Press.

Luke, A. (2000). Critical literacy in Australia: A matter of context and stand-point. *Journal of Adolescent and Adult Literacy, 43*(5), 448–461.

Luke, A., & Freebody, P. (1997). Shaping the social practices of reading. In S. Muspratt, A. Luke, & P. Freebody (Eds.), *Constructing critical literacies* (pp. 185–225). Cresskill, NJ: Hampton.

Luke, A., & Freebody, P. (1999). A map of possible practices: Further notes on the four resources model. *Practically Primary, 4*(2), 5–8.

Luke, A., O'Brien, J., & Comber, B. (1994). Making community texts objects of study. *Australian Journal of Language and Literacy, 17*(2), 139–149.

Luttrell, W. (1997). *School-smart and mother-wise: Working-class women's identity and schooling.* New York: Routledge.

Lyons, C., Pinnell, G., & Deford, D. (1993). *Partners in learning: Teachers and children in reading recovery.* New York: Teachers College Press.

Macedo, D. (1994). *Literacies of power: What Americans are not allowed to know.* Boulder, CO: Westview.

Mackie, R. (Ed.). (1981). *Literacy and revolution: The pedagogy of Paulo Freire.* New York: Continuum.

Maher, F., & Thompson Tetreault, M. K. (1994). *The feminist classroom: An inside look at how professors and students are transforming higher edu-cation for a diverse society.* New York: Basic Books.

Martin, J. (1991). Critical literacy: The role of a functional model of language. *Australian Journal of Reading, 14*(2), 117–132.

Massengill, D. (2003). Guided reading: An instructional framework for adults. *Adult Basic Education, 13*(3), 168–188.

Mayo, P. (1994). Synthesizing Freire and Gramsci: Possibilities for a theory of radical adult education. *International Journal of Lifelong Education, 13*(2), 125–148.

McCall, N. (1995). *Makes me wanna holler.* New York: Vintage.

McMahon, S. I., & Raphael, T. E., with Goatley, V. J., & Pardo, L. S. (1997). *The book club connection: Literacy learning and classroom talk.* New York: Teachers College Press.

Merriweather Hunn, L. (2004). Africentric philosophy: A remedy for Eurocentric dominance. *Promoting Critical Practices in Adult Education, 102,* 65–74.

Merriam, S. (1998). *Qualitative research and case study applications in education.* San Francisco: Jossey-Bass.

Merrifield, J. (2000). *Equipped for the future research report: Building the framework, 1993–1997.* Washington, DC: National Institute for Literacy.

Mikulecky, L. (2000). What will be the demands of literacy in the workplace in the next millennium? *Reading Research Quarterly, 35*(3), 378–384.

Mikulecky, L., & Lloyd, P. (1997). Evaluation of workplace literacy programs: A profile of effective instructional practices. *Journal of Literacy Research, 29*(4), 555–585.

Miles, M., & Huberman, M. (1994). *Qualitative data analysis: An expanded sourcebook.* Thousand Oaks, CA: Sage.

Mills, C. (1954). *Mass society and liberal education.* Chicago: Center for the Study of Liberal Education for Adults.

Moll, L., & Gonzalez, N. (1994). Lessons from research with language minority children. *Journal of Reading Behavior: A Journal of Literacy, 26,* 439–456.

Monaghan, E. (1991). Family literacy in early 18th century Boston: Cotton Mather and his children. *Reading Research Quarterly, 26,* 342–370.

Moore, D., Monaghan, E., & Hartman, D. (1997). Values of literacy history. *Reading Research Quarterly, 32,* 90–102.

Moore, W. (1973). John Berry Meachum (1789–1854): St. Louis pioneer, black abolitionist, educator, and preacher. *Bulletin of the Missouri Historical Society, 29,* 96–103.

Morgan, M. (2002). *Language, discourse, and power in African American culture.* Cambridge: Cambridge University Press.

Morris, J. (2001). Forgotten voices of black educators: Critical race perspectives on the implementation of a desegregation program. *Educational Policy, 15,* 575–600.

Moses, R., Cobb, C., & Cobb, C., Jr. (2002). *Radical equations: Math literacy and civil rights.* New York: Beacon.

Murrell, P. (2001). *The community teacher*. New York: Teachers College Press.

Murrell, P. C., Jr. (2002). *African-centered pedagogy: Developing schools of achievement for African American children*. Albany: State University of New York Press.

National Center for Education Statistics. (N.d.). National Assessment of Adult Literacy (NAAL). Retrieved April 24, 2007, from http://nces.ed.gov/naal/.

National Center for Education Statistics. (n.d.). Literacy in everyday life: Results from the 2003 National Assessment of Adult Literacy. Retrieved June 8, 2007, from http://nces.ed.gov/naal.

Naylor, G. (1982). *The women of Brewster Place*. New York: Penguin.

Nelms, W. (1997). *Cora Wilson Stewart: Crusader against illiteracy*. Jefferson, NC: McFarland.

New London Group. (1996). A pedagogy of multiliteracies: Designing social futures. *Harvard Educational Review, 66*(1), 60–92.

New Readers Press. (1991). *Working experience* (3 vols. and teacher's manual). New York: Author.

Nunez, R., & Fox, C. (1999). A snapshot of family homelessness across America. *Political Science Quarterly, 114*(2), 289–307.

Padak, N., & Bardine, B. (2004). Engaging readers and writers in adult education contexts. *Journal of Adolescent and Adult Literacy, 48*, 126–137.

Pahl, K., & Rowsell, J. (2005). *Literacy and education: Understanding the new literacy studies in the classroom*. London: Paul Chapman.

Pahl, K., & Rowsell, J. (2006). *Travel notes from the new literacy studies*. Clevedon, UK: Multilingual Matters.

Paratore, J., Melzi, G., & Krol-Sinclair, B. (1999). *What should we expect of family literacy? Experiences of Latino children whose parents participate in an intergenerational literacy project*. Newark, DE: International Reading Association.

Patton, M. (1990). *Qualitative evaluation and research methods*. Beverly Hills, CA: Sage

Pennycook, A. (1994). *The cultural politics of English as an international language*. London: Longman.

Perry, T., Steele, C., & Hilliard, A. (2003). *Young, gifted and black: Promoting high achievement among African-American students*. New York: Beacon.

Pitt, K. (2000). Family literacy: A pedagogy for the future? In D. Barton, M. Hamilton, & R. Ivanic (Eds.), *Situated literacies: Reading and writing in context* (pp. 108–124). London: Routledge.

Portz, J., Stein, L., & Jones, R. (1999). *City schools & city politics: Institutions and leadership in Pittsburgh, Boston, and St. Louis*. Lawrence: University of Kansas Press.

Purcell-Gates, V. (1995). *Other people's words: The cycle of low literacy*. Cambridge, MA: Harvard University Press.

Purcell-Gates, V. (2002). "... As soon as she opened her mouth!" Issues of language, literacy and power. In L. Delpit & J. K. Dowdy (Eds.), *The skin that we speak: Thoughts on language and culture in the classroom* (pp. 121–144). New York: New Press.

Purcell-Gates, V., Degener, S., & Jacobson, E. (2001). Adult literacy instruction: Degrees of authenticity and collaboration as described by practitioners. *Journal of Literacy Research, 22*(4), 571–593.

Purcell-Gates, V., & Waterman, R. (2000). *Now we read, we see, we speak: Portrait of literacy development in an Adult Freiran-based class.* Mahwah, NJ: Lawrence Erlbaum Associates.

Quigley, A. B. (1997). *Rethinking literacy education: The critical need for practice based change.* San Francisco: Jossey-Bass.

Quigley, A. B. (2005). "First we must dream. Nothing is harder": Toward a discourse on literacy across the lifespan. In J. Anderson, M. Kendrick, T. Rogers, & S. Smythe (Eds.), *Portraits of literacy across families, communities and schools* (pp. 321–337). Mahwah, NJ: Lawrence Erlbaum Associates.

Quigley, A. B. (2006). *Building professional pride in literacy: A dialogical guide to professional development.* San Francisco: Jossey-Bass.

Quigley, A. B., & Kuhne, G. (Eds.). (1997). *Creating practical knowledge through action research: Posing problems, solving problems, and improving daily practice.* San Francisco: Jossey-Bass.

Richards, J., & McKenna, M. (2003). *Integrating multiple literacies in K–8 classrooms: Cases, commentaries and practical applications.* Mahwah, NJ: Lawrence Erlbaum Associates.

Richardson, E. (2003). *African American literacies.* London: Routledge.

Robertson, D. (1996). Facilitating transformative learning: Attending to the dynamics of the educational helping relationship. *Adult Education Quarterly, 47,* 41–53.

Rockhill, K. (1995). Gender, language and the politics of literacy. In B. Street (Ed.). *Cross cultural approaches to literacy.* Cambridge, U.K.: Cambridge University Press. pp. 156–175.

Rogers, R. (2003). *A critical discourse analysis of family literacy practices: Power in and out of print.* Mahwah, NJ: Lawrence Erlbaum Associates.

Rogers, R. (2004). Storied selves: A critical discourse analysis of adult learners' literate lives. *Reading Research Quarterly, 39*(3), 272–305.

Rogers, R. (2007). Reconstructing pedagogical frameworks: Teaching for literacy acceleration within critical frameworks. *Pedagogies: An International Journal, 2*(4)

Rogers, R., & Fuller, C. (2007). As if you heard it from your mother: Reconstructing histories of participation in an adult education classroom. In C. Lewis, P. Enciso, & E. Moje (Eds.), *Identity, agency, and power: Reframing sociocultural research on literacy* pp. 75–114. Mahwah, NJ: Lawrence Erlbaum Associates.

Rogers, R., Light, R., & Curtis, L. (2004). "Anyone can be an expert in something": Exploring the complexity of discourse conflict and alignment in a 5th grade classroom. *Journal of Literacy Research, 36*(2), 177–210.

Sabatini, J., Ginsburg, L., & Russell, M. (2002). Professionalization and certification for teachers in adult basic education. In *Review of Adult Learning and Literacy* (Vol. 3, Chap. 6). San Francisco: Jossey-Bass. Retrieved April 25, 2007, from http://www.ncsall.net/?id=572.

Schaafsma, D. (1994). *Eating on the streets: Teaching literacy in a multicultural society*. Pittsburgh, PA: University of Pittsburgh Press.

Schon, D. (1983). *The reflective practitioner: How professionals think in action*. New York: Basic Books.

Scott, S., & Schmitt-Boshnick, M. (2001). Power and program planning in a community-based context. In P. Campbell & B. Burnaby (Eds.), *Participatory practices in adult education* (pp. 123–142). Mahwah, NJ: Lawrence Erlbaum Associates.

Shamash, Y. (1990). Learning in translation: Beyond language experience in ESL. *Voices, 2*(2), 71–75.

Shanahan, T., Meehan, M., & Mogge, S. (1994). *The professionalization of the teacher in adult literacy education*. (Technical Report TR94-11). Philadelphia: National Center on Adult Literacy.

Shanahan, T., & Rodriguez-Brown F. (1995). Project FLAME: Lessons learned from a family literacy program for linguistic minority families. *Reading Teacher, 48*, 586–593.

Shannon, P. (1998). *Reading poverty*. Westport, CT: Heinemann.

Shor, I. (1980). *Critical teaching and everyday life*. Chicago: University of Chicago Press.

Shor, I. (1992). *Empowering education: Critical teaching for social change*. Chicago: University of Chicago Press.

Shor, I. (1996). *When students have power*. Chicago: University of Chicago Press.

Shor, I., & Freire, P. (1987). *Pedagogy for liberation: Dialogues on transforming education*. Westport, CT: Bergin & Garvey.

Shulman, L. (1987). Knowledge and teaching: Foundations of the new reform. *Harvard Educational Review, 57*(1), 1–22.

Smith, C. (2006). The preparation and stability of the ABE teaching workforce: Current conditions and future prospects. In J. Comings, B. Garner, & C. Smith (Eds.), *Connecting research, policy, and practice* (pp. 165–195), vol. 6 of *Review of adult learning and literacy*. Mahwah, NJ: Lawrence Erlbaum Associates.

Smith, C., Hofer, J., & Gillespie, M. (2001). The working conditions of adult literacy teachers: Preliminary findings from the NCSALL staff development study. *Focus on Basics*, 4(D). Retrieved April 12, 2007, from http://www.ncsall.net/?id=146.

Smitherman, G. (1977). *Talkin' and testifyin': The language of black America.* Boston: Houghton Mifflin.

Smitherman, G. (2000). *Talkin that talk: Language, culture, and education in African America.* London: Routledge.

Souljah, S. (1996). *No disrespect.* New York: Vintage.

Souljah, S. (2000). *The coldest winter ever.* New York: Pocket.

Spolin, V. (1986). *Theatre games for the classroom: A teacher's handbook.* Evanston, IL: Northwestern University Press.

Spring, J. (1994/2007). *Deculturalization and the struggle for equality: A brief history of the education of dominated cultures in the United States.* New York: McGraw-Hill.

Stahl, S. (1999). Why innovations come and go (and mostly go): The case of whole language. *Educational Researcher, 28*(8), 13–22.

St. Clair, R., & Sandlin, J. (Eds.). (2004). *Promoting critical practice in adult education* (New Directions for Adult and Continuing Education, No. 102). San Francisco: Jossey-Bass.

Stein, P., & Slonimsky, L. (2006). An eye on the text and an eye on the future: Multimodal literacy in three Johannesburg families. In K. Pahl & J. Rowsell (Eds.), *Travel notes from the new literacy studies* (pp. 118–146). Clevedon, UK: Multilingual Matters.

Stein, S. (2000). *Equipped for the future content standards: What adults need to know and be able to do in the 21st century.* Washington, DC: National Institute for Literacy.

Sticht, T. (1989). Adult literacy education. In E. Z. Rothkopf (Ed.), *Review of research in education* (Vol. 15, pp. 59–96). Washington, DC: American Educational Research Association.

Sticht, T. (1997). *Functional context education: Making knowledge relevant.* San Diego, CA: Consortium for Workforce Education and Lifelong Learning.

Street, B. (1985). *Literacy in theory and in practice.* Cambridge: Cambridge University Press.

Stuart-Wells, A., & Crain, R. (1999). *Stepping over the color line: African American students in white, suburban schools.* New Haven, CT: Yale University Press.

Swanson, G. (1989). On the motives and motivations of selves. In T. Hood (Ed.), *The sociology of emotions: Original essays and research papers* (pp. 3–32). Greenwich, CT: JAI.

Taylor, D. (1983). *Family literacy: Young children learning to read and write.* Portsmouth, NH: Heinemann.

Tomlinson, C. (2000). Reconcilable differences? Standards-based teaching and differentiation. *Educational Leadership, 58*(4), 6–11.

Trumpener, B. (1997). *Gimme shelter! A resource for literacy and homelessness.* Toronto: St. Christopher House Adult Literacy Program. Retrieved April 25, 2007, from http://www.nald.ca/library/learning/homeless/lithome.htm.

Tyler, J., Murnane, R., & Willett, J. (2000). Estimating the labor market signaling value of the GED. *Quarterly Journal of Economics, 115*(2), 431–468.

Vasquez, V. (2003). *Getting beyond "I like the book": Creating space for critical literacy in K–6 classrooms.* Newark, DE: International Reading Association.

Venezky, R., Oney, B., Sabatini, J., & Richa, J. (1998). *Teaching adults to read and write: A research synthesis.* Bethesda, MD: Abt. Associates.

Vygotsky, L. (1978). *Mind in society: The development of higher psychological processes.* Cambridge, MA: Harvard University Press.

Walker, A. (1983). *In search of our mother's gardens: Womanist prose.* NY: Harcourt Brace.

Weber, R. (1993). Even in the midst of work: Reading among turn-of-the-century farmers' wives. *Reading Research Quarterly, 28*(4), 292–302.

Weiler, K. (1988). *Women teaching for change: Gender, class and power.* Westport, CT: Bergin & Garvey.

Weiner, E. (2005/2006). Keeping adults behind: Adult literacy education in the age of official reading regimes. *Journal of Adolescent and Adult Literacy, 49*(4), 286–301.

Weis, L., Farrar, E., & Petrie, H. (Eds.). (1989). *Drop outs from school: Issues, dilemmas and solutions.* Albany: State University of New York Press.

Wenger, E. (1998). *Communities of practice: Learning, meaning, and identity.* Cambridge: Cambridge University Press.

West, C. (1982). *Prophesy deliverance: An Afro-American revolutionary Christianity.* Philadelphia: Westminster Press.

Wilson, A. (1993). The common concern: Controlling the professionalization of adult education. *Adult Education Quarterly, 44,* 1–16.

Wood Ray, K. (2002). *What we know by heart: How to develop curriculum for your writing workshop.* Portsmouth, NH: Heinemann.

Wright, R. (1995). *Rites of passage.* New York: HarperCollins.

Young, M. B., Morgan, M., Fitzgerald, N., & Fleishman, H. (1994). *National evaluation of adult education programs* (Draft final report). Arlington, VA: Development Associates.

Youngman, F. (1986). *Adult education and socialist pedagogy.* Cover, NH: Croom Helm.

Index

adult education in St. Louis, 43–50
adult education students, 55–57
case study chapters, 58–59
current organizing for adult literacy education, 57–58
tutors, 54–55
Contrastive language analysis mini-lesson, 170
Controversial issue, student debate on, 72
Cooperative learning, 153
Critical frameworks, *see also* Literacy acceleration within critical frameworks
Critical literacy, *see also* Literacy definition of, 221
emergence of, 244
frameworks for, 21
lab (CLL), 135, 137
meaning of, 262
model of, 124
questions, 126
social justice approach to, 32
struggle for, 221–231
definition of critical literacy, 231
development of critical frame, 231–232
personal development, 223
questions, 225, 227
rethinking practice, 230–231
risk taking, 226
social justice, 222, 228
writing, 224
Cueing systems, reading, 24
Cultural knowledge, literacy learning and, 3
Culturally contested pedagogy, 166
Culturally relevant instruction, 30, 107, 185
Culturally relevant materials, complexity of, 81
Culturally relevant practice, boundaries of, 110
Culturally responsive teaching, 106
Cultural models of education, disruption of, 189–201
andragogy, 198
authenticity, 191

classroom retention rates, 192
community, 200
group instruction, 191
histories of participation, 193
Laubach method, 194–195, 198
multiple literacies, 195
one-on-one reading, 196
Southside Women's Center, 190
strategy for teaching literacy, 197
student progress, 199
tutors, 194, 199
writing, 195
Cultural tools, learning spaces designed using, 9
Culture
ethics of, 163
holiday approach to, 97
Current events time, 75
Curriculum
design of, 94
flexibility of, 79

D

Daily Prescription Sheets (DPS), 149
DEAR, *see* Drop Everything and Read
Decoding activity, 194
Deeply literature based program, 81
Democracy, commitment to, 222
Department of Elementary and Secondary Education (DESE), 47
Dependence, fine line between support and, 86
Description of teachers, 10, 11–13
DESE, *see* Department of Elementary and Secondary Education
Desegregation program, court-ordered, 91
Dialogue partners, 182, 183
Differentiated instruction, 115
Discrimination
hometown, 132
racial, 139
DPS, *see* Daily Prescription Sheets

Drop Everything and Read (DEAR), 99
Dropouts, 64, 93, 85, 95
Dynamics of position, 215

E

Ebonics, 165
Educating for Change Curriculum Fair, 188
Education, *see also* Adult education; Adult literacy education
  consciousness-raising education, 167, 168
  core purposes of, 137
  credentials, lack of, 6
  goal of, 39
  humanistic form of, 217
  K–12, 246, 253
  limits of, 254
  as means of socialization, 18–19
  model, problem-posing/problem-solving, 37, 58
  noncritical, 40
  as opening doors, 96
  philosophy of, 136
  purpose of, 65
  socially transforming, 86
  transmission model of, 193
  value free, 49
Educational rights, struggle for, 43
EFF initiative, *see* Equipped for the Future initiative
Emergent critical frameworks, 33
Emergent framework, 42
Employment vulnerability, African-American, 96
Empowerment, 137, 207, 224
English
  as means of inclusion, 150
  -only legislation, resistance to, 152
  teaching, 224, *see also* Ethics and English teaching
English as a Second Language (ESL), 148

English for Speakers of Other Languages (ESOL), 10, 49, 147, 175, *see also* Ethics and English teaching
  classroom(s)
    in college setting, 147
    picture stories in, 178
    teaching for social justice in, 185
    ethics and, 151
    family literacy center, 148
    family literacy coordinator, 136
    learners, academic characteristics of, 56
    participatory, 186
    students, denial of cultural identities, 164
    teacher(s), 235
      complexity of stances as, 151
      ethical roles of, 152
      speech used by, 72
    teaching, participatory, 150
Equal Rights Amendment (ERA), 158
Equipped for the Future (EFF) initiative, 166
ERA, *see* Equal Rights Amendment
ESL, *see* English as a Second Language
ESOL, *see* English for Speakers of Other Languages
Essence, 121
Ethical dilemma, 151
Ethics and English teaching, 147–158
  case study, 148
  classroom hopes, 149
  cooperative learning, 153
  debate, 150
  ethical dilemma, 151
  instruction models, 154
  justice, 152
  racial issues, 156
  reflective teachers, 157
  social justice, 158
  writing instruction, 155
Ethnographies of communication, 31
Even Start, 11, 16, 77, 148

National Reading Panel (NRP), 22
National Reporting System (NRS),
51
NCSALL, *see* National Center
for the Study of Adult
Learning and Literacy
Neighborhood Associations, 46
New Literacy Studies (NLS), 7–8
News junkies, 176
Newsletters, 291
Newspaper(s), 291
articles, 209
use as resource, 111
Newsweek, 121
NLS, *see* New Literacy Studies
No Disrespect, 68, 69, 70, 78, 79,
81, 108, 109
Nomination letter, 256, 267–269
Noncritical education, 40
Novels, hi-lo, 111
NPR, *see* National Public Radio
NRP, *see* National Reading Panel
NRS, *see* National Reporting
System

O

Obituaries, 210
One-on-one reading, 196
Online instructional resources,
285–287
Open-ended inquiry, 105
Opening doors, education as, 96
Oppositional knowledge, 163
Oppressed groups, building
alliances between, 227
Oppression, language and literacy
as tools of, 224
Oral reading, assessment of, 26
Oral tradition, 163, 164
Organic intellectuals, 10
Out-of-class leadership, 144
Outreach into the society, 151
Out-of-school life experiences, 132

P

PACT, *see* Parent and Child
Together
Pan Africanism, 263

Parent activist group, 46
Parent and Child Together Time
(PACT), 17, 92
Parent stories, 128
Participatory approach, functional
approach vs., 23
Participatory literacy education,
21, 31, 265
Partnership for Reading (PFR), 22
PCW, *see* Pre-Certification
Workshop
Pedagogical project, 33
Performance-based practices, 244
Personal development
opportunities, 225
Personal interests, turning
situational interests into,
108
Personal is political, 141
Personhood, verbal assaults on,
152
PFR, *see* Partnership for Reading
Phonemic awareness, 140
Phonics
importance of, 208
overreliance on, 199
rules, words vs., 155
sight approaches and, 194
Photographs, dialogue started
using, 154
Photo-stories, 178
Picture stories, 178, 179, 180
Poetry, 87, 142
Political campaigns, 201
Political process, student
disconnection from, 74
Political project, English teaching
as, 150
Politics, discussion around, 230
Power, *see* Codes of power
PowerPoint presentation, 180, 181
Practices, designing communities
of, 63–75
activism, 75
AEL classroom, 63–64
authority, 70–71
classroom structure, 65, 68
critical literacy practices, 69
goals for students, 64
historical role models, 72

styles, connections between, 236
value laden, 222
Teaching English for Speakers of Other Languages (TESOL), 16, 175
Technology, integration into teaching, 179
TESOL, *see* Teaching English for Speakers of Other Languages
Test of Adult Basic Education (TABE), 52, 78, 126, 161, 189, 205, 238
Test of English as a Foreign Language (TOEFL), 49
Text(s)
  community, 123
  critical interrogation of, 124
  debugging of, 138
  instructional-level, 25
  material consequences, 32
  readability, 26
  types of, 86
Think It, Speak It, Write It, Read It, Live It, 138
Third way, 23, 38
Time, 121
TOEFL, *see* Test of English as a Foreign Language
Top-down approaches, bottom-up vs., 23
Transitional housing, 92
Trust, 122
Tutor(s)
  function of, 54–55
  myth dispelled with, 200
  reliance on phonics, 199
  training, 18, 55, 194
Tutoring
  method, summary of, 49
  programs, 46

U

Union activist, 175
Union bands, 44
United States
  literacy campaigns in, 32
  powerful educator-activists of, 4

Queen Mother of civil rights movement, 277
United Way funding, 50
Urban League
  adult education class at, 16
  Community Outreach, 11

V

VALUE, *see* Voices of Adult Literacy United for Education
Value free education, 40
Venn diagrams, 260
Violence, rejection of, 216
Visionary pragmatism, 68, 258
Vocation, adult education as, 190
Voice, social justice and, 228
Voice cultivation, 91–103
  academics, 103
  authority, 95
  education as opening doors, 96
  expectations for students, 94
  family literacy program, 93
  GED materials, 99
  homeless women, 92
  idea development, 100
  literacy materials, 98
  literacy practices, 97
  student codes of power, 101
  student success, 102
  volunteerism, 91
  writing instruction, 99
Voices of Adult Literacy United for Education (VALUE), 57, 58, 75
Volunteer Improvement Program tutoring program, 46
Volunteerism, 91
Voter
  registration test, 36
  rights, 74

W

Want-hate relationship, with U.S. citizenship, 152
Whisper reading, 205
Whole language, importance of, 208